Strategies for the Electronic Futures Trader

Strategies for the Electronic Futures Trader

Jake Bernstein

McGraw-Hill, Inc.

New York   San Francisco   Washington, D.C.   Auckland   Bogotá
Caracas   Lisbon   London   Madrid   Mexico City   Milan
Montreal   New Delhi   San Juan   Singapore
Sydney   Tokyo   Toronto

Library of Congress Cataloging-in-Publication Data

Bernstein, Jacob
    Strategies for the electronic futures trader / by Jake Bernstein.
      p. cm.
    Includes bibliographical references.
    ISBN 0-07-135232-5
    1. Electronic trading of securities.   2. Futures.
  3. Commodity futures.   4. Financial futures.   5. Stocks—Data
  processing.   I. Title.
HG4515.95.B47   2000
332.64'5—dc21   99-053047

McGraw-Hill

A Division of The McGraw·Hill Companies

  2 3 4 5 6 7 8 9 0   QWM / QWM 0 9 8 7 6 5 4 3 2 1 0

ISBN 0-07-135232-5

The sponsoring editor for this book was Stephen Isaacs, the editing supervisor was John M. Morriss, and the production supervisor was Tina Cameron. It was set in Palatino.

Printed and bound by R. R. Donnelley & Sons Company.

McGraw-Hill books are available at special quality discounts to use
as premiums and sales promotions, or for use in corporate training
programs. For more information, please write to the Director of
Special Sales, McGraw-Hill, Professional Publishing, Two Penn
Plaza, New York, NY 10121-2298. Or contact your local bookstore.

 This book is printed on recycled, acid-free paper contain-
ing a minimum of 50% recycled, de-inked fiber.

Contents

Preface

This is my third book on short-term trading and day trading since 1996. As you are well aware, the market for books on short-term trading and day trading in commodities and stocks has mushroomed since the mid-1990s. With so many books to choose from, the average reader is often confused as to a good starting point. There are those who claim that my books are designed to capitalize on the recent trend toward short-term trading; that my goal is to reap the rewards of a public hungry for information on short-term trading; and that my books are devoid of meaning and substance. In fact, nothing could be further from the truth. My books are designed with one primary purpose in mind—to help traders travel safely on the rocky road to success.

My motivation for writing this book—or, for that matter, my last two books on short-term trading and day trading—does not come from the expectation of public approval. Nor does it come from the primary perspective of financial rewards. Writing books is a difficult undertaking. Literally hundreds of hours are spent in research, organization, production of visuals, and in the actual writing. In the long run, the hourly rate is about the same as I'd get by working the counter of a fast-food restaurant.

Unless this book becomes a runaway success, selling more than 50,000 copies in a relatively short period of time, it is unlikely that my financial benefits will be particularly impressive. What, then, motivates me? What is it that satisfies me in writing books? This I can tell you with total honesty and candor. These books are written from my heart, motivated by a sincere lifelong need to educate and a desire to see traders succeed. For all too long, the average trader, the newcomer and the tyro, have been grist for the mill. They have fed the pocketbooks of professional traders for many decades. They have been the small fish upon which the big fish have fed, and they have been the lowest form of life in the markets.

There are many professional traders within the futures industry who take issue with my desire to educate the public. They would rather see an ignorant public that continues to lose money than an educated public that stands a chance of making money. My efforts to bring solid information to the public has made me the target of such professionals, who have sought to discredit me and will continue in their efforts as long I persist in my goals. But this is no surprise to me. The futures industry is highly competitive and it's all about money. More specifically, it's about the big traders taking money legally from the small traders. Further, it is my belief that efforts to keep the small trader uninformed reach into the highest levels of the industry, even into the ranks of those who purport to protect the public.

The impressionable new trader with $5000 in risk capital approaches the markets with the innocence of a lamb entering a den of wolves. Soon the innocence is gone, and so is the money. Yet, there are also those new traders who come to the markets from a scientific or professional background and who feel that, by virtue of their education and profession, they are somehow immune to losing money. They approach trading from a methodical perspective and learn all they can about the game before they play it. They begin confidently, and yet they, too, lose money, although perhaps more slowly than the uneducated.

The waters of commodity trading are deep and treacherous. The waters of day trading and short-term trading are even more dangerous. And the waters of electronic trading are still more difficult to navigate inasmuch as they move more quickly. In the time it takes to press a button on your computer, you can lose or make a vast sum of money. Mistakes are frequent. Errors in judgment abound, and ignorance leads to emotional reactions which, in turn, lead to impulsive decisions and more losses.

One of my goals in writing this book is to help stem or, more ambitiously, to reverse the losing ways of traders. Some of my contemporaries claim to have the all the answers. Their advertising reads like a list of riches left by the genie in the bottle. One claim outdoes the other. Promises are plentiful, and yet results are rarely even close to what has been promised. At times this is due to the inability of the trader as opposed to the speciousness of the system—but all too often, the combination is poor and the results are, therefore, abysmal.

A recent reading of advertising in various trade publications as well as direct mail and Internet advertising yields the following assortment of claims:

Unlimited Income—Goal: $500–$1000 a Day! . . . a Highly Accurate Low-Risk/High-Reward S&P Day Trading Methodology . . .

How to Easily Amass a Mega-Fortune Trading Options! . . . Guarantees You'll Win on Better than 9 Out of Every 10 Trades!

The best money-maker in the world . . .

You can begin earning triple-digit returns almost immediately . . .

Now it's your turn to cash in on the big winners. If you want to win—and win consistently—this new book is must reading . . . "the most significant money-making breakthrough since the invention of the personal computer" . . .

Discover how you can rapidly and easily make more profits . . . Learn how to Double or even Triple Your Profits trading the S&P's . . .

While this book cannot single-handedly refute these claims, I believe that my common-sense approach to electronic trading (e-trading) can help point you in the right direction, and keep you from becoming a food fish in the sea of sharks. I cannot protect you, but I can give you tools for self-defense and profits, as well as tips and strategies that can help you on the path to success.

My reward will come from your success and from knowing that perhaps in my small way I have helped you keep a clear head and an objective direction in your trading. My reward comes from the many letters of praise and appreciation I get from readers and students of my methods. Perhaps one day you will write me too, telling me of your success. And if you do, this will, in part, be one of my rewards. Let me know. I can be reached at the following address: jake@trade-futures.com.

Acknowledgments

I extend my thanks to the following individuals and/or firms for their assistance in making this book possible.

To my right hand and long-time business manager, Marilyn Kinney, for her always valuable help in completing this labor-intensive project; Patricia Lomax, my administrative assistant, for organizing me and screening out those annoying phone calls from insurance salespeople and toner-cartridge peddlers; Mary Kinney, administrative assistant, for her help in keeping me on schedule and prompting me for the numerous reports I produce daily; Pauline Green, also at my office, for her assistance in keeping the newsletters and mail flowing smoothly; and Nan Martin Barnum, for her expert work in editing and preparing this manuscript prior to its editing at McGraw-Hill, I owe many thanks.

I thank Commodity Quote Graphics™ (CQG), Inc., for permission to reproduce charts and graphs from their excellent market analysis software.

I also thank Omega Research, Inc., for permission to use their market analysis software products, TradeStation™ and TradeStation 2000i™.

To Danielle Bourbeau, Paul Kavanaugh, and Kevin Riordan, my brokers at Fox Investments, I give a special word of thanks for their skill and expertise in understanding my systems and methods better than I do.

Finally, to my clients, students, and business associates too numerous to mention individually by name, I offer my thanks for helping me learn by teaching you.

Strategies for the Electronic Futures Trader

Introduction

What was once the domain of the pit broker in commodities is now open and available to all traders. Affordable high-powered computers, advanced analytical software, instant access to order entry, and high levels of market volatility have all combined to produce a market environment that is ideal for the electronic day trader. Whether in stocks, futures, or foreign currencies (FOREX), the times are right and ripe for the day trader.

Since access to immediate order execution and instant knowledge of price fluctuations was open only to those on the trading floor, day trading and its even speedier cousin, known as *scalping*, were the vehicles to riches for many floor traders. The old boys' club fiercely protected its treasure chest, resisting attempts by the public to encroach on its sacred realm. As long as the public was unable to take advantage of intraday price swings, floor brokers could reap the rewards of quick price fluctuations. But all good games eventually come to an end. The 1990s witnessed a variety of factors, as noted here, that combined to open this long-protected area of market speculation to the general public.

It should be noted that the availability of day trading and short-term trading as vehicles open to the trading public is not in any way synonymous with profits. The trader who lacks discipline, who does not employ a sound trading methodology, who seeks to trade with insufficient capital, or who is unable to effectively manage risk will be a net loser no matter how expensive or sophisticated his or her computer system may be. In this respect the journeyman trader will still emerge as the victor more often than not.

My observation of traders and their behavior in the markets spans 30 years. During this time I have seen traders fall victim to a plethora of errors, the vast majority of which are senseless and essentially due to either a lack of discipline or a lack of knowledge. The opportunity to turn a relatively small amount of capital into a relatively large amount of capital in the markets is overshadowed by the fact that futures trading is a difficult game to play. Paradoxically, however, it is not a difficult game to understand. The rules are clear. The methods are available, and the process by which one can win is neither enigmatic nor closely guarded.

In 1995, my book *The Compleat Day Trader* (McGraw-Hill) set forth a variety of methods by which one could take advantage of the numerous and large market moves within the day time frame. Public interest in day trading was still relatively limited when the book was published. Yet, several years later, when my book *The Compleat Day Trader II* (McGraw-Hill, 1998) was published, the markets had become even more volatile, traders were just beginning to day trade stocks, and electronic order entry was in its infancy.

Now, five years later, the stock and commodity markets are more volatile than ever before. Intraday moves in stocks are fast and furious. Intraday moves in Treasury bond, stock index, and currency futures are also substantial. Some of the reasons for present-day volatility are discussed later in this book; however, for now, suffice it to say that *change equals opportunity*. The larger the change, the greater the opportunity. But where there exists the opportunity for great profit, there also exists the opportunity for considerable loss. One of my goals in this book is to provide you with tools that will help facilitate the opportunity for great profit while minimizing the risk of severe loss.

Trading in the futures markets cannot be viewed either as a hobby or as something that one should "take a shot at." Day trading is a serious business. It can lead you to a treasure or it can take you on the path to emotional and financial ruin. These are the extremes that await you as possibilities on your trip into the realm of electronic day trading.

The disciplined trader who follows a slow and steady course, managing risk, implementing rules, evaluating situations, and controlling emotions will be rewarded with an opportunity to remove wealth from the treasure chest of the market. Sadly, however, the vast majority of my readers will fail at this venture because they are either undisciplined, incapable of following a methodology, emotionally unable to cope with the challenges of the markets, or unwilling to learn the proper techniques for success. But hope springs eternal in the soul of the risk taker.

Although the odds are clearly against winning, the game of electronic futures trading will continue to attract an army of lemmings waiting to step off the cliff into the frigid waters of the futures market. Among the minions there will be those few superlemmings who can rise above the masses by virtue of their energy, drive, stamina, willingness to learn, self-discipline and passion to succeed. To those few individuals I offer my kudos. And to those who are grist for the mill I offer my heartfelt condolences and the advice to try again, but with more knowledge from the lessons learned.

Yes, the floor broker is no longer king of the commodity pits. Within several years most floor brokers will vanish, as did the dinosaurs. Their absence will create opportunities for traders like us. But we will need to be astute, informed, highly disciplined, perspicacious, and passionate to succeed. The game of electronic day trading is a big game with potentially big rewards. Looking at the game head on we see a large front view. But the back view is also important. Remember always that in futures trading and in life, the bigger the front, the bigger the back.

The Changing Landscape of Stock and Commodity Trading

Short-term trading and day trading have grown in popularity as a result of several factors. Among these are the following:

- Increased price volatility in virtually all stock and commodity markets the world over has created intraday trading ranges that make day trading worthwhile for the average trader.
- Brokerage commissions have declined to very affordable levels. With the right commission and the right market, a day trader can make money on a one-tick price move (provided that timing is correct).
- Reasonably priced trading software, hardware, and live price quotations have all brought down the cost of day trading to its lowest level ever.
- Live price quotations via Internet delivery have further lowered the cost of data delivery, thereby increasing the attractiveness of day trading.
- The very high price level of stock index futures has, in spite of a smaller contract size (i.e., Standard & Poor's [S&P]), has caused many traders to avoid carrying positions overnight, forcing them into the day time frame instead.
- The speed of order execution in various markets is now faster than ever before. This has given day traders confidence that they will be able to move into and out of markets quickly with virtually immediate information about their price fills. And this has increased their confidence in short-term and day trading as a viable vehicle to profits.

- Trading by electronic order entry has become very popular and continues to grow rapidly.

- Large overnight price movements have frightened many traders, thereby causing them to be less interested in carrying positions overnight for fear of a large market move against them. This has forced many traders to carry out their activities within the day time frame.

- New systems, methods, and timing indicators designed specifically for day trading have increased the probability of success, thereby attracting more traders to the markets.

As you can see, many aspects of futures trading have changed since the mid-1990s. The sum total of these changes has been to significantly increase short-term and day-trading activities by speculators of all types. Some of the factors that have been listed here are discussed in greater detail in the following sections. Whereas short-term and day trading were once seen as methods practiced by professional traders and floor traders, the field has opened to all traders who can afford the necessary equipment and who can develop the requisite skills for success.

Affordable Computers and Data and the Revolution in Day Trading

For many years the cost of computer systems was very high. The revolution in personal computers and its attendant competition have resulted in steadily declining costs. At this writing it is possible to purchase a new computer with considerable memory and storage for about $1000. In some cases you can acquire used systems for under $1000. Hence, computer power is not a limiting factor for the electronic futures trader.

In addition to the low price of computer power, the cost of trading software has declined substantially. High-powered system development and real-time trading software is available at reasonable prices. For as little as $400 in software costs you can go on line in real time and begin to trade. Should you wish to back-test indicators, systems, and/or a method, the cost of a lengthy historical database is only a few hundred dollars.

Combining the hardware, system-testing software, and historical data, you can develop and test an unlimited number of systems in order to determine which have profit potential. As you can see, advances in technology as well as decreased costs in hardware and data have contributed to the short-term and day-trading revolution.

The Declining Role of the Pit Broker

For many decades the *open outcry* system was the method by which business was conducted on the trading floor. With only minor variations in methodology, the procedure is essentially similar on most world exchanges where open outcry is still used. The customer calls an order in to the brokers. The broker writes the customer order on an order ticket and time stamps it. The broker calls the order in to the trading floor or places it on an electronic order entry system.

On the trading floor, the order is received by a clerk who transcribes it and hands it to a runner. The runner carries the order ticket into the trading pit and hands it to the appropriate floor broker. When the order is filled the floor broker endorses it, writes down the price at which the transaction took place, hands the ticket to the runner (or places it on the floor in a specified location), and the runner brings the filled ticket back to the order desk. The order desk calls the order up to the broker, and the broker reports the fill back to the customer.

In some cases, an order is sent to the trading pit from the floor order desk by hand signal, thereby speeding up the process and eliminating the runner. In so doing, a quick fill, called a *flash fill*, can be reported back to the customer, often while he or she is still waiting on the telephone. The runner is eliminated from the equation.

The purpose of having a floor broker act as an intermediary between buyer and seller was purportedly to facilitate trade. In other words, floor brokers would buffer wide swings in the market by either buying or selling for their own accounts when other traders were not willing to do so. The open outcry system served its purpose for many years. In spite of the effective functioning of the system, many traders felt that floor brokers at times took advantage of them by executing orders at unfair prices and pocketing the difference to pad their own wallets.

It is likely that this was (and still is) true to a certain extent. Some futures markets are notorious for poor price executions by floor brokers. It is typical for market orders to be executed at a higher price than expected when the customer is buying and at a lower price than expected when the customer is selling. While a tick here or a tick there may not be important for the position trader, it is of the utmost importance to short-term and day traders.

Over the years, resentment about poor price executions has fostered in the trading public a sense of being victimized by the floor broker. And I must say that from what I've seen in my own trading over 30 years, the public is justified in its anger and frustration. To a certain extent these feelings have prompted the development of fully electronic trading in which the floor broker is eliminated from the equation. Price orders of buyers and sellers are matched and executed by computer. Hence, the floor broker is bypassed, and in the process the additional point "shaving" is also eliminated, much to the satisfaction of the trader.

Naturally, floor brokers and their representatives have resisted this change as long as possible, since it sounds the death knell for their game. However, as the London International Financial Futures and Options Exchange (LIFFE) increased its competitive edge, attracting considerable business to some of its fully electronic trading facilities, other exchanges felt the need to compete. Competition on other exchanges such as the French *Marché à Terme des Instruments Financiers* (MATIF) eventually forced a change in the U.S. exchanges. Although the U.S. exchanges have introduced a few fully electronic trading vehicles (such as S&P E-Mini), they are still sadly behind the times in this respect. Within the next few years, the open outcry system may be a thing of the past. This will result in even more short-term and day trading, as the general public will begin to feel more fairly treated.

Opportunities in Increased International Market Volatility

International price volatility has increased substantially. A number of factors and forces have contributed to the situation. Among them are the following:

- Growing industrialization in third-world countries has created more demand for raw commodities.
- Growing industrialization in third-world countries has created demand for money and thereby for hedges in currency and interest-rate futures.
- Large fluctuations in currency relationships have forced many businesses and banks into the futures markets in order to avoid the potentially serious losses as a result of these large changes in cross-currency rates.
- Large fluctuations in world stock markets have created more opportunities for substantial profits in stock index futures.
- Worldwide extremes in weather have created short-term and day-trading opportunities in grain and soybean futures, as well as in a variety of other agricultural markets (although these markets are not generally suitable for day trading).

All of these international factors have resulted in increased futures trading activity and, with it, increased short-term and day-trading opportunities. It is highly likely that the revolution in computerized position trading as well as computerized day trading will bring even more participants into the markets. This will create more liquidity—the end result of which will be to increase even further the number of market participants. Yet it must be remembered that in order to take advantage of these opportunities, the trader will need to act promptly and efficiently. And this can best be done via the medium of electronic trading.

The Risks and Rewards of Short-Term and Day Trading

Although it is true that change equals opportunity, the mere existence of day-trading opportunities does not guarantee the success of a futures trader or of any given futures trade. The fact remains that futures trading has its attendant risks as well as its promise of reward. The trader who can harness the potential of short-term and day trading can, with proper risk management, do very well in the long run.

However, the sad fact remains that a very small percentage of traders will be able to capitalize on these opportunities given their lack of methodology, self-discipline, experience, and sufficient trading capital. It is hoped that this book will increase the odds of success for those who find themselves in the category of day-trade losers. While the rewards of short-term and day trading are clearly there, they are not there merely for the taking. Work, experience, persistence, and good trading techniques are necessary if one wants to reap the rewards.

Decisions, Decisions, Decisions

In the hope of facilitating a decision for the new trader, or perhaps of changing some ideas in an experienced trader, here are some suggestions. Perhaps they will help you find your place as a trader.

1. *Risk.* How much risk capital do you have? This is an important first decision since it will help you decide whether you want to trade futures, options, futures spreads, or all of the above. As a rule, if you have less than $5000 your chances of making money in futures are slim to none (no matter what you've been told to the contrary). Although I think your odds of success are much better with spreads and/or futures, you *can* do well with futures options *if* you avoid deep, out-of-the-money options.
2. *Technical or fundamental method?* Learn the differences between the fundamental approach and the technical approach to trading. Make a decision.

Try to be in one camp or the other, but *not* in both at the same time. To do both at first will confuse you. For most traders, technical methods are better since they require less work, less attention, and fewer decisions.

3. *Short-term, day trade, or position trade?* Take the time to get in touch with your temperament as a trader. If you have a natural tendency toward good self-control, discipline, patience, and organization, then you may do well as a position trader. But if you're generally impatient, if you can't wait a long time for market moves to occur, or if you thrive on action, then short-term trading and/or day trading might be best for you.

4. *How much time do you have?* No matter how you look at it, trading *does* take time. It's a business that requires study, evaluation, preparation, homework, some thought, and some degree of organization. You can do your work while the markets are closed, or you can follow the markets all day. You just make the choice.

    There are pros and cons to each approach but only *you* can decide on the amount of time you can give to the business. This will be an integral decision for you. It will likely precede all other decisions, with the possible exception of how much starting capital you have.

5. *Do you need a computer and tick-by-tick data?* For most traders the answer to both questions is clearly *no*. There is *no need* for the additional expense. Those who sell data and computerized systems would have you believe otherwise, but believe me, there is *no guarantee* that you'll make money trading futures if you have live quotes, a computer, and a computerized trading system.

6. *Do you need a chart service or newsletters?* In most cases traders get too much information. And too much information confuses. *Be selective.* Allow only a small amount of information to affect your decision-making process. Once you have learned the basics, try to go with your own analyses and methods. If you've found a trading advisor, newsletter, or hotline that works for you, then trade with it and don't second-guess it.

7. *Find a broker you trust and who will work with you.* The relationship between client and broker has not been given enough attention or consideration over the years. If you have an antagonistic or otherwise negative relationship with your broker, then your chances of success will be minimized. You may also want to seriously consider whether a discount broker or a full-service broker is best for you. Generally, full-service brokers tend to be better for new traders or for those who rely on their brokers for implementing trades consistently and/or according to a certain methodology.

8. *Learn the vocabulary and the definitions.* The law says that you can't drive without a license. You might hurt yourself or other people—you might even kill or get killed. But the law *doesn't* mandate against ignorance and stupidity in trading. There's no law that says you can't lose money trading because you choose to be an idiot or an ignoramus. Take my advice. *Learn the rules of the markets* before you risk a single dollar. Learn the vocabulary, the jargon, the meanings and uses of different types of orders. In short, learn before you try to earn.

Once you've made the decisions just discussed, and once you've learned what you need to know, you'll be in a much better place. You'll see new avenues for yourself and certain types of trading will appeal to you naturally, given your personality. Only then will you find your niche as a trader. Before you jump into the saddle and follow the cowboy trader into the dollar-sign sunset, make sure you want to ride that horse. Before you send money to the honest-looking man standing in front of his large yacht, make certain you need that type of psychological compensation.

When you think, learn, and plan ahead, you'll find that you're quite capable of making your own decisions with only a small amount of input from others. But, if you *do* decide to align yourself with any professional in the advisory business (even yours truly), take the time to evaluate, to ask questions, to try it on for fit, to take a test drive, to kick some tires, and to assess the honesty and longevity of the person or persons whose information and advice you buy. If the fit isn't right then you need to find a new home or you need to find a new place for yourself as a trader.

Factors Affecting Success or Failure as an E-Trader

There are many factors that can affect your odds of success as an electronic trader (e-trader). Here are the major ones, not necessarily in order of importance. Many of these are discussed in greater detail later in this book.

- *Trading capital.* Unless you begin your trading with sufficient capital, you will find yourself unable to play the game effectively. Should you suffer more than several successive losses, you will be out of the game and unable to take advantage of the big winner when it comes. Hence, you need enough money to play the game effectively while allowing yourself sufficient room for the losses that are part of all trading plans or programs.

- *Persistence is important.* You cannot achieve success immediately. Yes, there will be those rare individuals who through good fortune or amazing skill will find success quickly, but this is atypical. You will need to be persistent in your efforts at success. You will need to learn how to take your losses and how to get back into the game again in spite of repeated losses.

And well before you even begin your e-trading activities, you will need to be persistent in learning the rules and procedures of the game. This book will not teach you how to be persistent, but it will give you many ideas of how to improve your persistence as a trader.

- *Self-discipline is one of the key ingredients of the e-trading game.* But it is not unique to this game alone. Success in virtually any endeavor is a direct function of the discipline you have in learning and applying skills. Furthermore, it takes considerable self-discipline to thwart the emotions that are a constant part of the trading game. Although this book cannot give you the self-discipline you need as a trader, it will give you some valid and cogent suggestions along these lines.

- *Trading methodology.* It is very important to have an effective, well-researched, and objective trading methodology. I believe that the vast majority of e-traders make their decisions on the fly. They decide whether to buy or sell based on intuition or seat-of-the-pants decisions. In the short run such practices may be effective, but they will almost always lose money in the long run. What traders need is a defined set of rules and procedures. This book will help you find some of these methods.

- *Computerized trading systems and electronic order entry.* While these are both important, they do not guarantee success. Although e-trading and day trading may be in vogue, they are not necessarily the right things for all investors or traders. What separates the winners from the losers in the game of e-trading is the ability to fulfill the important requirements and prerequisites for success. While it is clear that there are various factors that affect success (as noted in the preceding section) there are various prerequisites above and beyond those noted.

  The mere availability of a computerized trading system or online access to a trading account is not all that is necessary. A computerized trading system in the hands of an undisciplined trader can often prove more destructive than can trading without the assistance of a computer. In short, a computer will not and cannot guarantee that success will follow.

  Furthermore, electronic order entry is not a panacea. Although it can make for fast order execution and facilitate active trading, it can also be abused or misused by those who are either inexperienced or uninformed. On the other hand, a computerized approach to day trading, either in stocks or commodities, combined with electronic order entry, can be highly successful if the operator (trader) has developed (or, in rare cases, is innately equipped with) the necessary qualities for success. Later chapters elaborate on this list.

- *Organization.* While it is important for the position trader to be organized, it is even more important for the e-trader to have consistent methods and procedures. The purpose of such procedures is to avoid errors that can prove costly. Errors fall into two categories: *errors of omission* and *errors in judgment.*

  An error of omission, such as forgetting to put in an order or neglecting to cancel an order, can lead to serious problems. And an error of judgment, such as intentionally ignoring your trading system or method, can also prove costly. Although all traders can make these errors, they are more likely to occur when there is a lack of organization. Organization is one of the prerequisites to success as a day trader. Having your trading programs on a computer can be a great help in keeping you organized, and organization will be your ally, just as disorganization will be your enemy. More about this later.

- *Sufficient computer power and storage.* This subject also receives considerable attention later on. Given the advances in computer technology and software as well as the declining prices of both, there is no excuse for a trader to be without the most up-to-date equipment. While it is not necessary to have a computer in order to day trade, it can help you considerably.

- *Accurate data feed.* For the active day trader, another important prerequisite is an accurate data feed. There are numerous choices and varying levels of quality in data service. These are also discussed in the chapters that follow.

Is Electronic Futures Trading Right for All Futures Traders?

The simple answer *no* is insufficient and unacceptable to most would-be traders unless a more detailed explanation is offered. With the day-trading craze sweeping the financial markets, there are many who stand to profit from the end result. Yet, the last to profit will be the day trader. On the other hand, the big winners in this game will be brokers, brokerage houses, data vendors, software sellers, seminar givers, and, of course, booksellers and authors. The bottom line, however, is that short-term and day trading have never been and never will be appropriate for all futures or stock traders. Although these approaches pose a significant challenge and offer vast potential rewards, the fact is that most people have neither the discipline nor the ability to succeed as day traders.

The mere fact that you have been a successful investor, or that you have run a profitable business, does not necessarily assure your success as a day trader or short-term trader, even with the power of e-trading on your side. Of all the things a trader can do, short-term and day trading are the most challenging and offer the lowest probability of success. The rewards are there for those who can meet the challenge. Perhaps you will not read or hear anywhere else a caveat as candid as what I offer herein. Perhaps you do not want to know.

But consider yourself as having been told by one who knows whereof he speaks. Am I concerned that these honest words will dissuade my readers from going on, or that my words will have a negative impact on book sales? No! I'd rather have fewer books sold than deal with e-mail from an army of losers bemoaning their misfortunes. No doubt, these words will anger my competitors. They will feel as if I have spoiled the waters for them, alerting the weaklings to what awaits them, but this does not concern me either.

Before you take the plunge and enter the e-trading arena, make certain that this is what you really want to do. Make certain that you have the capital, the time, the skills, and above all, the persistence to take on this major task. Remember that short-term trading is not a hobby, it is not something in which to dabble, and it is not something that you "take a shot at." Day trading or short-term trading via the electronic medium is a serious business that can bring you great rewards, cause you severe losses, and tax your emotions as they have rarely (if ever) been taxed. So think about it at length, and step slowly, carefully, and well protected into the arena.

Do You Have What It Takes to Succeed as an E-Trader?

It is not possible a priori to know whether you have the skills and potential to succeed as an e-trader. Since trading by computer (or otherwise) requires both knowledge and experience, it is impossible to determine in advance whether you have the necessary abilities to learn the techniques.

Yet, there are certain basic personality traits that correlate highly with success as a short-term e-trader. Some of these have been discussed in this introduction. Other, less obvious traits and skills are discussed in the chapters that follow.

1

Short-Term Futures Trading

An Overview

The Traditional View of the Short-Term Futures Trader

Until the early 1990s, those who traded futures for the short term or within the day time frame were considered risk takers and perhaps fools. Since floor brokers often retained the competitive edge, the average short-term trader or day trader had a difficult time extracting a profit from his or her trades. The day trader was, in fact, considered to be the ultimate risk taker because of the limited time frame during which trades could be made. But technology and progress have changed everything. Just as the long-standing Berlin Wall came tumbling down in a matter of days, the floor broker monopoly on short-term trading and day trading crumbled under the weight of new technology and competition.

Since the mid-1980s stock prices have risen dramatically, thereby expanding daily trading ranges. The Small Order Execution System (SOES) was introduced to give the small trader as much of an edge in getting prices filled as was enjoyed by professional money managers who often moved large blocks of shares. And commissions came tumbling down. Day trading in stocks became a viable undertaking. Within months there were more day traders in stocks than there were in commodities.

Notwithstanding the fact that there are more stock day traders than commodity day traders, the fact remains that the traditional view of the day trader has changed. What was once considered on the fringe, off the beaten track, and the ultimate gamble is now relatively common and sought after. Thousands of would-be day traders are willing to take their turn at the plate in hopes that they can hit a few home runs.

The day trader is now a fairly common participant in the trading game. Stock brokerage firms that specialize exclusively in day trading have mushroomed all over the world. Whether it is a fad, a losing proposition, or a fast way to profits remains to be seen. The simple fact is, however, that the traditional view of day trading and of the day trader has changed dramatically since the early 1990s.

Electronic order entry has further facilitated the task of the short-term and day trader. Orders can be executed online, promptly, efficiently, and often at considerably lower commissions that can be obtained by using a live broker. Traders can buy and sell stocks and commodities many times daily, placing their orders via the Internet and having their price fills reported back to them promptly. The process is now a highly impersonal one, mimicking many of the characteristics of a video game. Yet the risks involved are real and not imaginary. The profits are real and not imaginary. Furthermore, the emotions are also real because they reflect real concerns.

Economic Importance and Significance of the Pit Broker

The long-standing role of the pit broker has been to buffer the market and help smooth out erratic moves by providing liquidity. In order to fulfill their role, pit brokers were granted certain broad privileges. The system was an effective one for many years. The profit margins that characterize floor broker operations are small, but their trading takes place on a larger scale. Hence, a two-tick profit shaved off orders numerous times daily adds up to a fairly good income. The buffer once provided by the pit broker is now, in many ways, provided by the day trader, although not in a formalized fashion.

When important market-related news affects prices, the day trader is willing to take the risk of entering a market. While this is still true of the pit broker, the day trader has taken on a significant amount of the buffering function, although this was not intended as the role of the day trader. As more futures markets become electronically traded and the open outcry system is slowly but surely replaced by computer-matched orders, the role of the pit broker will decline even further. The result will be better order executions and, therefore, more profits for the day trader who is experienced and who employs a valid methodology.

Advantages of Contemporary Short-Term Trading

When I entered my first day-trade order in the early 1970s, I updated my intraday charts manually. I did not have access to live tick-by-tick quotations. My prices were obtained by numerous calls to the broker, which did not please him. Oftentimes I'd call 20 times daily, making a trade perhaps once or twice weekly. As you can imagine, my frequent calls angered him.

The playing field among off-the-floor day traders was level. There were all of us, and then there were the floor traders. Today, however, the playing field is diverse. The floor trader now has less of an advantage and off-the-floor day traders vary considerably in their skills, experience, hardware, software, trading systems, data feeds, and available capital.

The day trader nowadays has numerous advantages over the day trader of several decades ago. Not only are data delivery systems lower priced and faster, but prices are also considerably lower. With prices down, speed up, and computers more powerful, the contemporary day trader is clearly at a distinct advantage over the trader of the past. Yet, as I have warned many times earlier in this book (and as I will warn you again in future chapters), these advantages do not necessarily correspond with a concomitant increase in trader success or profitability.

The Pros and Cons of Day Trading

The inevitable passage of time often renders old rules obsolete, replacing them with new rules and new points of view. For many years, day trading was not something that was either advisable or easily implemented by the vast majority of traders.

Day trading was the sole domain of the floor trader, the scalper, and those who were very close to the market. By *close* I mean able to afford and obtain live quotes and immediate access to the trading floor. But things have changed dramatically, particularly in the last 10 years. Among the factors which have made day trading a reality for all traders are the following:

1. *Price volatility has increased substantially,* and with it, daily price ranges have become extremely large in some cases. The currencies, Treasury

bonds, S&P futures, coffee, and the energies have all shown large trading ranges. Such large ranges provide numerous opportunities within the day to enter and exit trades with considerable profit potential.

2. *International political and economic events* are also volatile. At one and the same time the world is in crisis on many fronts. From the currency crisis in Mexico and its deleterious effect on the U.S. dollar to the saber-rattling in the Middle East, and from the violence in Japan to the numerous ethnic and religious wars throughout the world, hardly a day goes by without news that moves markets. Hence, the opportunities for day trading are further enhanced.

3. *The speed of information dissemination* has made the financial world a very small place in comparison to what it was even 10 years ago. The collapse of a bank in London becomes worldwide news within minutes, if not seconds, of its becoming public information at home. Traders jump on the bandwagon and express their opinions in the markets. This creates movement and the day-trading game is afoot!

4. *The affordability and availability of high-powered computers, data, and programs* has allowed all traders access to information and analysis which puts them on the same level as most floor brokers. This is why so many floor traders have left the floor in recent years. They no longer have the edge that helped them reap large profits in the past.

5. *Speed of order execution* has reduced the possibility of poor price fills. While it's true that the floor trader can get consistently better fills than the off-floor trader can, the advantage is slowly disappearing. Within seconds you can have your order executed at the market as a flash fill. And knowing where you've been filled is *vital* if you want to day trade effectively.

6. *Discount commissions* have substantially reduced the cost of doing business. At low rates it's possible to trade for smaller moves. Even at rates of $40 to $60 per trade, a day trader can do well using a disciplined methodology.

These are some of the reasons why day trading is a more viable approach today than it has ever been. But there are two sides to every coin.

What are the pros and cons of day trading? Here are some points to consider before you plunge. I present each argument along with my analysis and commentary. Remember that these are my opinions. You may disagree. The whole world may disagree. But I won't change my mind because I have learned what I know from experience and not theory.

The Pros of Day Trading

1. *Day trading, if done correctly, will* force *you to take your losses quickly.* As you know, the undoing of many a trader is the fatal flaw of riding losses. If you're truly day trading then you are *forced* to exit at the end of the day, win, lose; or break even. This can be *very* helpful to traders who tend to ride losses. There are few traders who could find fault with this point.

   It might be argued that exiting a trade prematurely would force you to take a loss that might turn into a profit if carried long enough. There may be some validity to this objection, yet I've noticed that unless trades become profitable very soon after they are entered, the odds of their ever showing a profit are low.

2. *A good day trader can maximize results with very little initial margin.* But good traders are generally experienced traders who have more than enough capital. The newcomer who wants to day trade will usually lose all of his or her capital very quickly, not necessarily due to day trading but rather due to lack of discipline and methodology.

3. *Feedback as to whether you are right or wrong comes quickly, often within minutes.* Feedback is important not only in the development and refinement of trading methods, but also in the process of learning how to be a successful trader. There are few valid objections to this point.

4. *Overnight news won't affect your positions since you won't be carrying any positions beyond the day session close.* This will eliminate unexpected and unwelcome surprises, and it will also increase the quality of your nightly sleep. Opponents might reasonably argue that if your position trading system was good you would be on the right side of the market when news breaks.

   In other words, a good system should be able to anticipate bullish or bearish news. And I can't disagree with this point. There are good points as well as bad points to riding positions.

5. *It is easier to accurately predict very short-term price swings than it is to predict longer-term moves.* Hence, one should be able to day trade with a higher degree of accuracy than one can achieve in position trading. This is, of course, my opinion. I have no solid evidence to support my case, with the exception of day-trading systems I've developed and tested that appear to favor day trading in terms of overall accuracy.

6. *Certain indicators, such as daily market sentiment, lend themselves readily to use by day traders.* They are also prone to be more accurate for such very

short-term use than they are for position trading. Yet, there are also indicators for position trading, which can be used effectively.

7. *Due to the volatile nature of markets, there are more day-trading opportunities than there are position-trading opportunities.* This point may be valid, yet opponents would argue that although there are more opportunities, they are generally smaller in terms of dollar potential. The day trader would retort by saying that trading larger positions can compensate for the smaller profit per trade.

The Cons of Day Trading

As in all things, there's a negative side to day trading. Here are the negatives to consider, along with my commentary.

1. *For the most part, day trading requires full attention.* Some traders feel that in order to be successful at day trading they need to sit by a screen all day and watch prices. This is not, however, always the case. There are numerous day-trading methods that don't require you to sit and watch the markets.

2. *Some traders claim that day-trading profits tend to be smaller on a per-trade basis.* After slippage and commission costs, the average trade may be so small as to not make day trading worthwhile. This is also not the case. If you're selective in trading only the markets that have the highest daily price ranges, you can show good average profits per trade.

3. *Day traders trade more frequently and therefore generate higher overall cost for a smaller return.* This is a valid point, but it can be countered with the argument that if reliability is high, then the small size of the move can be overcome by trading larger positions.

4. *Day trading isn't for everyone.* This is essentially correct. Day trading is a very specific form of speculation, which cannot be used effectively by all traders due to limitations of time, discipline, and system. But for those who *are* willing to make the commitment the results *can be* very positive. The fact that day trading isn't right for everyone doesn't mean that it's not right for some of us. The fact is that futures trading isn't right for everyone. Stock trading isn't right for everyone, either.

5. *A bad position trader will also be a bad day trader.* I agree with this for the most part. Yet, consider this: a position trader whose main fault is riding losses can benefit substantially from being *forced* to take a loss at the end of each day.

6. *Intraday moves are too much a function of news and emotion and are, therefore, unpredictable.* I agree and I disagree. It's the emotion that the day trader seeks to capitalize upon. Emotion makes markets move. A good day-trading system can *capitalize* on emotions.

7. *Floor traders have the advantage over the public.* Indeed, this is partially true. Floor traders pay very low commissions and they also get their price fills very quickly. Yet, many floor traders are scalpers. They trade for only a few ticks at a time. The methods, orientation, and goals of the off-the-floor day trader are considerably different from those of the typical floor trader who trades only for that one- or two-tick edge.

These, then, are some of the arguments presented in opposition to day trading. As you can see, there are some valid points; however, logical, cogent points in favor of day trading can counter virtually all of them. Of all the points raised, both pro and con, I think that these are the salient issues:

1. *Day trading* can *be very profitable,* provided you have the emotional make-up, discipline, and methodology to do it consistently.

2. *Day trading is a much more viable approach today than ever before,* given not only the large and frequent moves, but also the technology which allows for quick order execution and market analysis.

In addition, there are many different technical approaches that may be used by day traders. What follows is my evaluation of a few methods. Note that these opinions are based on my experiences. I'm certain that I'll ruffle the feathers of those who have their own pet methods. For this I apologize in advance. The exclusion of any approach is not intended to cast doubt on its efficacy. I can only comment upon the day-trading methods with which I've had experience.

Day Trading, Discipline, and Persistence

The single most important aspect of any trading methodology, whether for the long-term, intermediate-term, short-term, or day trade, is the psychology of the trader. My work with trader psychology dates back to 1968. Having been educated in clinical psychology, I am well familiar with the limitations of the trader and with the psychological roadblocks which traders constantly throw in their own paths.

While many of you may choose either to ignore what I have said or to skip it entirely, I do sincerely believe that to do so would be the worst mistake you could make. Although it is impossible to completely discuss in several paragraphs what would take several books to explain thoroughly, I will do my best to acquaint you with the pitfalls which plague all futures traders, limiting their success.

Advantages of Day Trading

For many years, day trading has been considered to be the most speculative of speculative trading activities. I believe that this is a market myth that has been perpetuated by those who are unable to day trade or who are afraid to do so.

The fact of the matter is that the day trader is in an advantageous position. The true day trader understands the limitations of what can be achieved within the day time frame. The day trader is, therefore, the sharpshooter of speculation.

The day trader is interested in finding the correct target, taking aim at it, pulling the trigger, and bagging the prey. *As mercenary as this may sound, that's what all futures trading is about.* The effective futures trader will keep his or her powder dry, will aim only at the most promising targets, and will aim only at targets that are likely to be hit.

Ingredients for Success

All futures traders must be consistent, efficient, adaptable and persistent. These are the most important qualities that a futures trader can develop. But because day trading is unique among the many different avenues that are open to traders, day trading has its special brand of psychology.

The following sections will attempt to acquaint you with the major issues that face the day trader and, moreover, to suggest to you methods which may be used to overcome your limitations, and to maximize your strong points as a day trader.

Qualities of a Successful Futures Trader

Before we examine the psychological and behavioral issues that limit success in futures trading, let's examine the qualities that facilitate or enhance futures trading results. The first among these is *discipline*.

Certainly by now you've heard the word discipline hundreds, if not thousands, of times. It is probably one of the most effete terms in all of futures trading. The problem is that merely saying the word is one thing, but understanding its true definition operationally, or on a behavioral level, is a far more important thing.

Discipline Defined

- *Discipline* is not merely the ability to develop a trading plan and to stay with it—it is also the ability to know when your trading plan is not working and, therefore, to know when to abandon it.
- *Discipline* is the ability to give your futures trading positions sufficient time to work in your favor—or, for that matter, sufficient time to work against you.
- *Discipline* is the ability to trade again once you've taken a loss or a series of losses.
- *Discipline* is the ability to ignore extraneous information and to avoid inputs that are not related to the system you are using.
- *Discipline* is the ability to maintain a reasonable position size and to avoid the emotion that leads to overtrading.
- *Discipline* is the persistence required to maintain your trading systems and to calculate the necessary timing indicators consistently, either manually or by computer.
- Above all, however, *discipline* is the ability to come back to the trading arena every day, regardless of whether you have won, lost, or broken even the day before.

You can see, therefore, that discipline consists of many different things. Discipline is not any one particular skill but many. Perhaps the best way to understand trading discipline is to examine some of its component behaviors. Let's look at a couple of these, *persistence* and *the willingness to accept losses.*

Persistence. This is, perhaps, the single most important of all qualities that a trader can possess. Futures trading is an endeavor which requires the ability to continue trading even when results have not been good. Due to the nature of markets and trading systems, bad times are frequently followed by good times, and good times are frequently followed by bad.

Some of a trader's greatest successes will occur following a string of losses. This is why it is extremely important for traders to be persistent in applying their trading methods, and to continue using them for a reasonable period of time.

Those who quit too soon will not be in the markets when their systems begin to work; those who quit too late will run out of trading capital. Therefore, while persistence is important, it is also important to know when you have been too patient—when it is time to quit and not play any longer using the system that you have been using.

If persistence is so important, then how does the trader develop it? While the answer is simple, the implementation is not. Being persistent develops persistence. While this may sound like a circular answer, it is truly not. *The only way to be persistent is to force yourself initially to do everything that must be done according to the dictates of your systems or method.*

Try this, if you're having difficulty. Make a commitment to a trading system or method. Follow through with that approach for a specific amount of time, taking every trade according to the rules, or, if the system is subjective, attempting to trade the system with as much consistency as possible. *If you are consistent in applying your rules, then you will find that, in most cases, your consistency will pay off and you will have profits to show for your efforts.*

Even if your trading is not successful, you will have learned a great deal. You will have learned that you can follow a system or method, that you can trade in a disciplined fashion, and, moreover, that the only way to do so is to be persistent by following as many of the trading rules as possible.

Compare this to the ignorance and confusion that come from haphazard trading or from applying trading rules inconsistently. Think back to your experiences as a trader. Remember your worst losing trades. You will find that *those losses which occur as a result of following a system or method are easier to accept psychologically than are those that result from breaking the rules.*

Losses due to lack of discipline often turn into terrible monsters, ultimately costing you much, much more than they should, financially as well as psychologically. If you would like to master the skill of persistence, then you will need to practice it. Make the commitment and I think you will see some wonderful results, even over the short term.

Willingness to Accept Losses. Here is yet another important quality that the effective futures trader must either possess, acquire, or develop. Perhaps the single greatest downfall of all traders is the inability to take a loss when it should be taken.

Losses have a nasty habit of becoming worse rather than better. Unless they are taken when they should be, the results will not be to your liking.

Although it is easier on one hand for the futures trader to take a loss than it is for the position trader (since a loss must be accepted by the end of the trading day), it is still the downfall of many a futures trader who is unwilling to accept a loss when it is a reasonable one. The good futures trader must have the ability to take a loss when the time to take that loss is right.

What's right is dictated by the particular trading system or risk management technique being used. I would venture to say from my experience and observations that *perhaps 75 percent or more* of all large losses are due to the fact that losses were not taken when they were small, relatively small, or when they should have been taken.

These are just a few of my random thoughts on the topic of day trading and discipline. More will follow in the discussion of future issues. Remember that in the day time frame, events, prices, and trends move quickly. Decisions must be made almost instantly. Hence, your discipline and persistence are of paramount importance. There are many wrong things you can do and only a few right things. Know the right ones and *do* them.

The Electronic Short-Term and Day Trader

Few contemporary short-term and day traders operate without computers. As the use of computers for trading becomes more prevalent, virtually all traders will eventually be dependent upon their machines. There are literally hundreds of indicators, systems, methods, and programs that short-term and day traders can use. All too many are worthless and will not lead to anything of substance. Hence, rather than being limited in the number of available choices, the electronic trader has far too many choices. Knowing what to trade, the methods by which to trade it, and the rules for managing risk are the critical issues for the computerized trader.

While the computer has made the trader's job easier in many respects, it has paradoxically complicated it in other ways. The computerized trader must be careful to avoid using technology in a way that will minimize results as opposed to maximizing them. One purpose of this book is to help you avoid the pitfalls that are part and parcel of a computerized approach to short-term and day trading while at the same time maximizing the potential results that are attainable when using this powerful technology. In order to achieve this end I must first introduce you to the electronic trading game, its rules, purpose, and players.

The Game Called E-Trading

Ladies and gentlemen, we are about to learn the rules of a high-risk, high-reward game. Like all games, this game has its rules, tools, and procedures. Please allow me to introduce you to the goal of the game. The name of this game is *electronic trading* (ET). Some players prefer to call this game *the ultimate gamble*. Yet, however you choose to name it, your goal is to make money. And the goal never changes. Every player begins with a given amount of money.

By using a variety of strategies you must take as much money from your opponents as quickly as possible. The game is played on a large playing field with tens of thousands of opponents. You may play the game only within specified hours. Once the game is over for the day, your score will be measured in dollars. For those who wish to play the game at night, a playing field is available, yet this is not advisable. This is a zero-sum game. For every dollar you make, a dollar is lost by another player.

Although your opponent is invisible, he or she is always there, seeking to take as much of your bankroll as possible. Therefore, your goal is actually twofold. First, you must protect your bankroll from attack by money-hungry predators. And second, you must move ahead and attempt to take as much money from your opponents as possible. Once you have taken money from your opponents by following a given set of rules, your goal is then yet again twofold. First, you must keep as much of the money as possible, and second, you must seek to multiply your money using your expanded base of capital.

Your game is not too different from Parker Brothers' Monopoly. Yet there is a distinct difference. In the game of ET there is no bank and no banker. You will never collect $200 for passing Go, and there is no particular use for the "Get Out of Jail Free" card. Yet your goal is still to accumulate as much money as possible, beginning with an amount you can afford to lose.

The ET game is also not too different from the game of poker. The maximum amount of money you can win at poker is determined by the size of the pot. The maximum amount of money you can win at ET is similarly determined by the size of the pot. The good news is that the pot is exceptionally large and that it is always restocked. The bad news is that you are unlikely to win the entire pot. You must share it with other players. You must be content to settle for a piece of the pot rather than the entire pot.

Yet another aspect of the ET game is its anonymity. You will never need to look your opponent eye to eye as you take his or her money. The process buffers you from knowing who has been hurt by your gain. Yet you must know that for every dollar you win, there has been a dollar lost by a less fortunate player.

The rules of the game are generally as follows:

- Take as much money as possible from your opponent.
- Have no mercy on your adversary since he or she will show you no mercy.
- Play often, play for keeps, and play consistently.
- Always follow the rules.
- Protect your stake fiercely.
- Attack your opponent mercilessly.

- You have a limited amount of ammunition—use it wisely.
- Do not shoot at any target unless you have a good chance of hitting it.

The game has good news and bad news in addition to rules. The good news is that there is considerable money to be made. The bad news is that your odds of making it are exceptionally low unless you are educated, experienced in the game, and well capitalized. But the game is, in spite of its relatively low odds of success, still attractive and growing more attractive by the day. The reasons for this growing appeal are discussed and analyzed later. Now, let us return to the game itself.

The Equipment

In order to play ET successfully you'll need some equipment. In this modern age of game playing, the equipment will consist of computer hardware and software rather than a helmet, shin guards, or special shoes. The cost of all necessary equipment can be as low as $1500 or as much as $10,000 (or more), depending on how sophisticated you want to be.

Naturally, the question arises as to whether more expensive equipment will yield either greater potential for success or greater profits. This issue is discussed in Chapter 2. At this time, however, know that there will most definitely be an investment in equipment if you wish to play the game from your home or office.

The ET game in stocks can be played away from your home or office at specially designed and designated locations that are frequently run by brokerage firms that stand to profit from your playing the game at their locations. This is because the money you pay them in commissions will defray the cost of the equipment they provide you. In futures trading, the availability of such game locations is still limited. In time, however, futures-trading rooms will be more plentiful. Such facilities will be provided by brokerage houses whose goal is not benevolence or the desire to see traders succeed, but rather who are motivated by their desire to make commission dollars and interest income on the trades of ET players.

The necessary equipment required to play ET consists not only of a computer with an Internet connection, but also of software designed to analyze the playing field, data input that provides information about the game, and sufficient capital to compete effectively. The range of choices in all three areas of necessary equipment is quite diverse, ranging from the basic to the advanced. Here is a general description of the different levels of equipment. Each area is described in considerable detail in later chapters.

Computer Hardware

Computer hardware is changing rapidly, both in its degree of sophistication and in its cost. There are essentially four factors to consider in buying a computer for the purpose of ET. They are as follows:

Memory. Computer memory is no longer a high-priced item. For a few hundred dollars you can outfit your computer with its maximum possible memory. The maximum available memory for computers continues to grow almost daily with the introduction of new computer models.

The computer you select for ET should ideally have the maximum amount of memory that can be placed into the box. Your computer will need to process many calculations and track a voluminous amount of inputs. You will, therefore, want to make certain that your computer is operating as its maximum potential if you plan to compete effectively with other players whose goal it is to take your money.

Data. Success at the ET game depends to a large extent on the availability of reliable data that is delivered to your computer as quickly as possible. You will need a data feed for your computer that is reasonably priced, quick, reliable, and above all, accurate. Incorrect data can cause you to make an incorrect decision in the game. And making an incorrect decision can prove very costly. Due to the speed with which the ET game is played, you may not have time to realize that a data error has occurred.

And, you may therefore take action that is totally unwarranted on the basis of the actual facts. I compare this error to that of the duck hunter who erroneously takes aim and shoots at a decoy rather than at a real duck. Of course, things could be worse. The errant duck hunter could shoot at another duck hunter rather than at the real target. The ET player, acting on incorrect information, could shoot himself or herself in the foot.

As another consideration, the data you will need in order to make profitable ET decisions must be delivered to your computer promptly. The ET player who gets his or her data more slowly than other competitors will be at a distinct disadvantage. It therefore behooves the ET player to obtain the services of a reliable data vendor who can deliver the necessary information quickly, reliably (i.e., free of errors or with prompt error correction), and at a reasonable price. There are various options. These are discussed in a later chapter.

Software. The analytical software to profitably play ET is a critical variable in the game. Many roads lead to Rome. Some roads lead nowhere. Still other roads lead to destruction. Analytical software that is often required in the ET game can indeed make the difference between success and failure. Since this topic is so very important, all of Chapter 3 is devoted to discussing it.

Capital. ET is a money game. Success at ET is closely related to the amount of money you bring into the game. The more you start with, the better are your chances of winning the game. There is a low cutoff point, but there is no high cutoff. Either extreme is a function of how much you can risk.

- Never take risks you cannot afford.
- Never play the game with borrowed or "scared" money.
- Never play the game with insufficient funds.
- Always play only when you can afford the potential loss.
- Make certain you're willing to lose at least 10 times in a row.
- Be certain that your capital is risk capital—money you can afford to lose.

Your capital will need a home, called a *trading account.* You will need to establish an account with a brokerage firm. There are pros and cons to the various firms that are available. The speed, accuracy, and efficiency with which a firm processes and executes your instructions can also be a critically important variable in your success; take the time to research and find a good broker.

These, then, are the general aspects of the equipment necessary to play ET successfully. Having the necessary equipment is not a guarantee of success. Perhaps I should have added the presence of a brain to this equipment list. However, I hold this need to be self-evident. Yet I'd like to stress my belief that the brain necessary to win at ET should not be one that is too sophisticated or prone to excessive analysis. Before taking a few steps into how the game is played, I must familiarize you with a few important facts of life about this high-stakes game of day trading.

Sad Fact of the Game: Your Chances of Success in Trading

After more than 30 years as a trader, writer, and market analyst, I find that traders and their orientation to the markets have changed very little. In spite of major advances in systems research, timing methods, computer hardware, and computer software, the average trader is still, in my opinion, an overall loser in the markets. This is particularly true in the day-trading game. Here are a few cogent questions and their answers:

- Why do so many players lose and so few win?
- Why hasn't the lot of the average trader improved?
- Is success in short-term and day trading so elusive and difficult to achieve that it will forever be unattainable?
- What skills, tools, or materials are necessary in order to succeed at this ultimate game of risk and reward?
- What can the average short-term and day trader do in order to improve his or her chances of success?
- Can courses, computer programs, and/or personal training be worthwhile?

These are only a few of the many questions that players of the ET game should ask and have answered. I will attempt to provide the answers. Know that my replies are based on a considerable amount of experience. Hence, do not take my suggestions lightly. While there are varying opinions on these vital issues, I have every confidence that what you will read here is correct, complete, and important.

Q: Why is the average e-trader an overall loser in the futures markets?

A: This question is fuel enough for several volumes. A brief reply, however, is that the average trader is a loser in the markets because of the following reasons (not necessarily in order of importance):

- Insufficient starting capital
- Lack of discipline
- Inability to follow a systematic trading approach
- Information overload
- Inability to control emotional reactions to trading
- Use of stop losses that are too small
- Focus on taking small profits while riding losses
- Inconsistency
- Disorganization

While one could amplify on this list, I believe that the major issues and aspects have been covered.

Q: Why hasn't the lot of the average trader improved, even with significant advances in computer technology and trading systems?

A: I believe that the average trader has been unable to overcome the limitations and difficulties already cited since there is a general lack of knowledge as to what is necessary for success as a trader. I believe that the entire futures industry is to blame for this deplorable state of affairs. Futures trading is essentially a zero-sum game.

In other words, the pool of available money that can be made is determined by the amount of money in the game. The size of the pot minus commission dollars is equal to the amount of money that is put into the pot. This means that for every dollar won, a dollar is lost (minus commission).

Ignorance, Fish, and Losers

The game of futures trading (and in particular, the e-trading game) thrives on the misfortune and ignorance of the loser. For all intents and purposes, the game of futures trading is like the food chain. The big fish at the top eat the smaller fish, and the smaller fish eat the smallest fish. The smallest fish in this case is the trader with a small amount of capital.

Is it in the best interest of larger traders to educate new traders? Is the money spent by the Commodity Futures Trading Commission and the National Futures Association best used to investigate and punish supposed wrongdoers, or should some of the millions be used to give new traders a solid education? Perhaps the futures exchanges might spend a little of their vast profits on educating the public. Might there be a reason why professionals have no interest in an informed public?

Education: The Key

I sincerely believe that traders *can* be educated and trained in methods that will facilitate their success, or, at the very minimum, decrease their tendency to lose in the markets. I further believe that it is in the best interest of all professionals in the futures industry to provide a formalized means of educating newcomers to the markets. As it now stands, this education has been left to individuals such as myself who hold seminars and provide instructional materials, tapes, and books.

The *good* news is that there *are* many sources of information available to the new trader. The *bad* news is that the lack of available education has created an opportunity for many unethical and unscrupulous operators. Isn't it ironic: by not educating the public in the basics of trading, the regulatory agencies and exchanges have created an opportunity for unethical operators who sell everything from newsletters to courses and software. The regulatory agencies then spend millions of dollars trying to stop these individuals and firms. Having an educated public would help avoid many problems.

Q: Is success in trading so elusive and difficult to achieve that it will forever be unattainable?

A: *No.* I believe that there are steps a trader can take in order to facilitate success or, at the very minimum, to make losing less likely. As in all businesses, there is a learning curve. Tuition must be paid. The proper sequence of steps must be taken. There will be failures along the way. However, in following an organized and logical series of steps, success will not be elusive or unattainable.

I must add here that there are some individuals who, by their very nature and personality, may never be successful *unless* they are able to effect major changes in their behavior and personality. Success in trading is, in many ways, unattainable unless one has been able to achieve success in one's personal and/or professional life. Trading futures is, in many ways, a reflection of real life. It must be approached from that perspective.

Q: What skills, tools, or materials are necessary and/or prerequisite in order to succeed at this ultimate game of risk and reward?

A: The skills that are necessary for success fall into the following general categories. Some have been discussed earlier and will be discussed in detail later in this book.

- Self-discipline
- The ability to follow a plan or trading program
- Consistency in doing one's market research or analyses
- Organization and good record-keeping
- Sufficient starting capital (must be pure risk capital)
- The ability to control emotions and not be swayed by fear, news, greed, or the opinions of others
- The ability to take losses when necessary
- Knowledge of correct and effective order placement
- A thorough understanding of trading systems, risk management, and timing indicators
- An understanding of trends and their importance

- The ability to ride profits until the system or methods signal exit or reversal of position
- A realistic attitude in terms of expectations

Q: What can the average short-term and day trader do in order to improve his or her chances of success?

A: Study, read, get organized, focus, eliminate distractions, don't listen to too many opinions, begin with sufficient capital, know yourself, trade only within your financial capabilities, use iron discipline, and don't get out of your winning trades quickly. This is a very brief synopsis of what you can do. All of these areas should be explored in considerable detail.

Q: Can trading courses, computer programs, and/or personal training help?

A: Yes, they can help, but you must be *very selective* in what you decide to do. Price is not necessarily equivalent to quality. Some courses are not worthwhile at all. Some courses promise much but deliver very little. Before you spend any money on a trading course or training course, ask for a synopsis of topics (i.e., an outline) and/or a sample.

Defining the Food Chain

In nature, big fish get bigger by feeding on small fish. Small fish feed on smaller fish. And the smallest fish feed on plants and other organisms known as filter feeders that in turn feed on microscopic organisms, which they filter through their rudimentary digestive systems. The largest fish are the most aggressive fish. They are often highly skilled at hunting and bagging their prey. And they often have special biological weapons that help them kill smaller, weaker fish.

A sardine will never defeat a shark. In fact, the shark will swallow hundreds of sardines in one fell swoop! A shark might have trouble killing a barracuda; however, either of the two will easily defeat a shrimp or a lobster. The rules of the food chain are clear. Darwin's law applies. The strongest and fittest will survive, while the weakest and least fit will die.

Natural selection is the order of the biological world. And natural selection is the law that rules the markets. You might call this interpretation a variation on the theme of economic Darwinism. Regardless of the name we attach to it, the fact remains that life and death in the futures markets closely parallel life and death in the biological food chain. Simply stated, strong traders survive while weak traders perish.

Strong Versus Weak, Brains Versus Brawn

But what exactly do the terms *strong* and *weak* mean? In the animal kingdom, strong and weak are defined on several levels. The first level is physical stature. The larger the animal, the more difficult it is to kill and eat. Smaller animals cannot easily kill a larger animal. Hence, a large animal has a distinct advantage over a smaller one. Yet size is not always a determinant of survival.

As an example, consider the dinosaurs. These largest of all land animals were driven to extinction by a combination of environmental factors that resulted in a shortage of food (as well as other factors, such as those proposed by the Alvarez theory, not directly the result of death by predators). In this case the large size of the dinosaurs was a detriment to their survival since they required massive amounts of food to thrive and multiply.

Does Size Count?

Now consider the floor trader or pit broker in terms of the physical size issue. If you've been on the floor of a futures exchange you will see that the larger traders have a distinct advantage. They stand above the crowd, yell louder, attract more attention, and often intimidate smaller traders. Yet the physical size of a pit broker is rapidly becoming a nonissue, inasmuch as electronic trading will soon replace most if not all floor traders. Floor traders who, for many years, won at the game by their sheer size and by bullying smaller traders will no longer be able to use these assets. Lacking other skills, they will vanish. In this case, size no longer counts.

Consider the trader with the large trading account. This is clearly an element of size. And in this case, size *does* count. The larger your account, the longer you can stay in the game. The longer you can stay in the game, the more likely you are to hit the big winners. Hence, the trader with a bigger account has a clear and undeniable advantage. The trader who has funded his or her account with a few thousand dollars will be the sardine of the markets. Commissions and losses will quickly gobble up the account. Staying power is important!

Furthermore, size also counts when it comes to *stop losses*. Traders with larger accounts can use larger stop losses. We know that, up to a point, larger stop losses result in better performance. The trader with a small account will often be forced to use a small stop loss. And a stop loss that is too small will virtually guarantee a loss. The day trader who wishes to succeed at the game must be willing to risk a larger amount on each trade in order to increase his or her odds of success.

Skills

A second aspect of the strong versus the weak is skill. In studying the animal kingdom, we know that some species have been provided with more functional protective skills than others have. The area of innate intelligence is one that has been hotly debated for many years. Whether intelligence is a function of environment or heredity is a controversy I refuse to get involved in publicly. However, one thing we know about the markets is that informed and educated traders can make more profitable decisions. Hence, the special skills that we bring to the markets can also make a difference in our ability to survive and prosper.

Some traders seem to have acquired these skills at an early age, either from their parents, who may have been in the futures-trading business, or via another method of training, such as competitive sports. These skills can assist a trader immeasurably. Consider an example taken from the animal kingdom. A hawk raised in captivity without parents will likely not learn the skills necessary for survival in the wild. Hence, the hawk must be taught various skills before being released into the cold, cruel world.

Survival of the fittest in the markets may also be a function of acquired knowledge. While the dominant dinosaurs were big and brawny, they are also purported to have had small brains. This was yet another cause of the dinosaurs' demise. There have been many physically large and imposing traders who, nonetheless, suffered from a lack of intelligence. In the old days, such human dinosaurs were often successful. In recent years, however, many of these Goliaths have been felled by quick-thinking, agile Davids equipped with computerized slingshots. The Bible states that "the meek shall inherit the earth." Scientists tell us that in the event of a nuclear holocaust the only creatures to survive may be insects.

Enter the Electronic Age of Trading

In the modern world of futures trading, the days of brawn and size are gone. The electronic age has taken over futures trading. The game is now one of brains, knowledge, and sufficient trading capital. Those who are lacking in these abilities and skills will continue to be the lowest form of life in the food chain. As the new age of trading expands to encompass virtually all areas of finance, investment, and speculation, the big fish will not necessarily be those that have the largest physical stature.

But the law of the jungle will still apply. The big fish will eat the small fish. Approximately 10 percent of the big fish will make their fortunes on the misfortunes of the lower 90 percent. This is how it has always been, and this is how it will always remain, unless the game becomes so predictable, so efficient, so taxed, or so severely regulated that there is no advantage in taking risk.

What Can We Learn from This?

What we can learn from the preceding discussion can be summarized in a few cogent and concise points. In effect, we can learn nothing new. But we can restate clearly what all traders should know about their chances of survival and profit in the futures markets.

- The less money a trader puts into the markets, the lower his or her chances of survival and/or profit. To be successful, the day trader must begin with sufficient capital. If starting capital is too limited, then a few losses in succession will force you out of the game. And if you can't play the game, then your chances of winning will be nonexistent.

- There is no one-to-one correlation between starting capital and success. Traders who begin with a large amount of money can also be losers. However they may not lose as quickly, and, provided they have some discipline, they will have more of a chance to win if they can stay in the game longer

- Savvy traders will continue to be winners. Uninformed traders will continue to be losers no matter how much money they start with.

- Starting with a very small amount of money, regardless of how much knowledge and training you have, will still work against you. Perhaps you will lose your money at a slower pace. Since day trading is by definition a fast game, a small amount of starting capital can disappear in a matter of days (or even less).

- The ideal combination is to begin with sufficient capital as well as sufficient knowledge.

- Too much knowledge can be detrimental, since it can be confusing. Therefore, don't try to learn everything about trading, since much of what's available to be learned is essentially useless.

- Try to be a perspicacious little David rather than an awkward and dull Goliath. In other words, don't be a market bully. Let the market tell you what to do. Don't try to impose your will on the market. It won't work. It never does. I've tried it. So have many others. The dollars we lost in that game of futility now line the pockets of other traders.

Advantages and Disadvantages of E-Trading

As in the case of all trading systems and methods, there is good news and bad news for the e-trader. The good news is that the computerized trader will have speed, technology, and sophisticated systems (in most cases) at his or her disposal. He or she will be able to analyze markets on a tick-by-tick basis and enter buy and sell orders instantly (depending on the software that is being used).

If your computer is functioning properly, and if your systems are working, and if your data is correct, and if market volatility is conducive to profitable trading, then you will have better overall odds of making money, provided you have the discipline to follow your systems and/or signals.

The bad news is that a computerized approach to short-term and day trading can give you too many systems, too many signals, and too many trades. You will be tempted to use too many indicators, and you may be tempted to follow the markets too closely. The result will be that you are trading too often, taking trades that are low in quality in order to trade more often. In the case of all day trading, whether by computer or not, quality is much better than quantity.

Another drawback to the computerized trading approach is that you will become dependent on the computer. Computers can crash, leaving you without new signals. Therefore, you must be certain to have your systems backed up regularly, and you must have standby power in the event that the electricity fails while the markets are open. Far too many traders are left in the lurch during a failure because they have neglected to institute adequate backup systems.

Why Play the Game?

Before you play ET, or any game, you must ask yourself a few probing questions, the first of which is "Why play the game?" There can be only one acceptable answer to this question. Any answer other than "For the money!" is unacceptable. But what other answers could there possibly be? Strangely enough, one of the most frequent responses I get to this question is "I play the game because I love the challenge."

In my estimation, this is a poor response, one which suggests strongly to me that this individual will not likely succeed at the game. Yes, there is clearly a challenge in the game of ET; however, the challenge alone should *not* be one's primary response to the question of "Why play the game?" I respectfully suggest that the only acceptable response is the response that is directed at the sole purpose of the game. And that sole purpose is, as stated earlier, to take money from your opponents.

Let us examine the question of why to play the game in somewhat greater detail. I suggest you read this chapter carefully, perhaps even several times, so that you may assess and evaluate the motivation that prompted you to buy this book and the motivation that pushes you to play the game. While my in-depth psychological look at the "why" question may not please you (and may, in fact, cause me to make some enemies), I will proceed regardless. After more than 30 years in the markets, I am far too entrenched in my views to sugarcoat anything for my readers. And I believe that my readers, if given the choice, will opt for no placebos in the pursuit of their goal which is, of course, to be a winner at ET.

The Compensation

ET, and futures trading in general, attracts a wide variety of individuals. I have had the good fortune to meet aspiring ET players from all walks of life, from all social strata, and from virtually all mindsets. In conducting well over 600 seminars throughout the world, I have seen it all. I've met frustrated surgeons who, dissatisfied with the cost of their malpractice insurance and disenchanted with the routine of their work, are willing to give it all up in order to pursue a career in ET or in position trading in futures.

These cases make me sad. What gives me sorrow is that a doctor who may be very talented in his or her work is willing to give up a skill that helps humankind in order to pursue a game that can ultimately contribute very little, if anything, to the common good. Mind you, I am not passing a value judgment in making this statement. I am merely stating my view.

The odds of a surgeon (or for that matter, any doctor, lawyer, engineer, or professional) becoming an overnight success at ET are slim indeed. What would my surgeon say to me if I showed up in his office and asked him to teach me how to be a surgeon? While I am not comparing the job of a short-term or day trader with that of a surgeon, there is still a period during which learning must take place. Successful ET cannot be learned in a matter of hours, or even weeks. There is considerable trial and error that is part and parcel of the learning process.

What, then, is it that motivates or inspires individuals to abandon their existing professions in favor of ET? Certainly there can be many explanations; however, there are a few that appear to be rather common, based on my observations. I find that the most frequent is compensation. "Compensation for what?" you ask. "For a substantial void in one's life," I reply. You ask how that could be. Why would successful physicians, architects, or engineers seek to compensate for possible deficits in their lives?

All too many individuals are lulled into a life of routine and boredom in their professional lives. Their skills have been honed to a fine degree. They have often reached the height of their profession. They are often successful at their work. And they are often looking for the next goal. Few individuals can rest on their laurels. Fewer individuals can accept a life that offers nothing but sameness. Sadly, this is the disease that afflicts far too many professionals.

Is Technological Progress Illusory?

If the game of futures trading is built upon the backs of losers, and if advanced technology is now available to virtually all traders who are willing to spend a few thousand dollars, then most traders should ideally be able to advance together. And if they advance together, who benefits in the long run? How does the lot of the individual trader improve if he or she still competes with professionals who also have access to the same (or even better) technology?

In this respect, technology may be nothing more than an illusion. And this may well be one of the reasons that the lot of the average trader has not significantly improved in spite of the major advances in software, hardware, and the speed of data delivery. In a sense, therefore, advances in trading technology may mean little in the long run. On the other hand, if you have the creativity and intelligence to harness the power of new technology and to avoid some of the pitfalls previously cited, you may have a distinct advantage over your fellow ET competitors.

The Scope and Limits of Computerized Trading

As pointed out in previous pages, the use of a computerized trading approach does not guarantee success. Such an approach is limited by a number of factors, not the least of which is market volatility. Unless markets are volatile or have sufficient daily ranges, the amount of money you can make is limited. The markets you choose to trade also limit your potential profits. Some markets are more volatile than others are. Trading less volatile markets means you will have less potential for profits.

2
Mechanical Requirements

How Much Computer Power Will You Need?

There are many different programs for market analysis. And there is no doubt that there will be many more in the months and years ahead. Each has its own requirements in terms of memory and space on your hard drive. Naturally, this should be your first consideration in selecting a computer for e-trading. But there are considerations well above and beyond the minimum requirements stated by the trading program developers. While the minimum requirements will satisfy the basic program needs, they may not necessarily be sufficient for the speedy operation of your e-trading activities.

Remember that if you trade actively and want to monitor many different stocks and/or futures contracts, you will need substantial memory and disk space in order to accommodate these operations. Furthermore, if you're tracking markets in small time frames (i.e., one-minute charts), you will need even more memory in order to handle all the graphics and ongoing calculations. Add to this the incoming Internet data, as well as your outgoing electronic orders, and you have a system that eats considerable memory and disk space.

Given all this, I urge you to make your choice of a computer system based on how actively you want to trade, how much data you want to store and retrieve, and how many different systems and/or timing indicators you plan to have running at the same time.

To a given extent, these considerations are academic if you decide to buy the biggest, the fastest, and the best computer that's available. In today's highly competitive market, $5000 will buy you such a system. And with a little shopping around you can get what you want for as little as $3000 (or even less).

I would suggest that you begin with a computer system whose memory is expandable should you find that you need additional power. Furthermore, select a high-speed state-of-the-art machine with a large amount of storage space. I strongly recommend a built-in CD-ROM writer so that you may store historical data on CD once your hard drive has reached more than 75 percent of its capacity. In fact, you may wish to have several hard drives in your machine.

Finally, I recommend that your machine have high-end graphics capability, as well as a video board with sufficient memory. Much of your work as an e-trader will depend on visuals, in the form of charts and graphs. Having fast, high-quality graphics as well as high resolution will help you considerably.

The Pace of Progress: How Requirements Will Change

Technology moves very quickly in the computer field. What is state-of-the-art today will be outdated in several months and will be archaic in a few years. The system you buy today will likely outlive its usefulness in several years. You should, therefore, do your best to buy a system that is capable of being upgraded. Note that some manufacturers now offer computer systems on a monthly charge basis that are continually upgradable as new features and major advances are introduced.

Remember that in developing your trading methods you will likely create many files, charts, systems, methods, and indicators. These should be stored in an organized fashion, and backed up accordingly, so that when you upgrade to a more advanced computer hardware configuration your job will not be difficult or even impossible.

Coming Advances in Computer Hardware

As noted, computer hardware is becoming more advanced and sophisticated daily. In fact, the progress is so rapid that it can often be frustrating. Prices are coming down as quality and processing speeds are going up. A computer system bought today may be cheaper in several months and may, in fact, then no longer be state-of-the-art. And there are even more changes coming. By the year 2005 the progress is likely to be astounding, making the most advanced machines today totally archaic.

Computing speeds will increase well beyond those of today's fastest machines as data storage may no longer be maintained on a hard drive. Rather, I suspect that data will be stored on chips rather than on mechanical media such as CD-ROM, disk drives, or hard drives. This will markedly increase data access and processing speeds. And this will allow the e-trader to trade many more markets and to enter orders more quickly, have them filled more quickly, and thereby trade more often. How fast can things get? Clearly there is a limit to how fast data can be processed and orders can be entered and executed. We may soon reach the point of diminishing returns until a new level of technological sophistication takes us over the next barrier.

What this all means for the e-trader is simple enough to figure out. Clearly, it means that e-trading is here to stay; that e-trading will spread dramatically over the next few years; that e-trading will become more efficient, sophisticated and pervasive; and that this will create many more opportunities for those who know how to play the game.

Data Storage and Retrieval

The importance of data storage and retrieval has already been noted. It should be noted that both of these are vital issues for the e-trader. You will want to have sufficient storage space as well as methods for retrieving the data promptly when it is needed.

The Dos and Don'ts of Data

In order to compete effectively in the game, the electronic trader must not only have sufficient trading capital and effective systems or methods, but must also have a reliable stream of live data. There are a variety of considerations that must be taken into account in selecting a data vendor. While cost may be an important factor to some traders, the fact is that the most reliable data feeds tend to be the more expensive ones. But before going into the details of cost, let's examine the major categories that should be evaluated in making your decision. Here are the major categories to consider.

End-of-Day, Delayed, or Live Data

While some people believe that the e-trader can only conduct trading on live or tick-by-tick data, I do not agree. It is entirely possible to enter orders electronically using end-of-day data. There are numerous methods that can be used to determine trades using end-of-day data. However, the active e-trader will want to use live data. By *live data* I mean data that comes into the trader's computer on a trade-by-trade basis while the markets are open.

To the active e-trader, such live data is vital to the timely execution of trades. The trader who has a live data feed can execute orders promptly, thereby entering and exiting the markets quickly when a trade has been signaled. In terms of costs, live data is considerably more expensive than is end-of-day data. Depending on the type of live data feed you use, the cost can be as much as 20 times the cost of end-of-day data. Yet those who trade using real-time data often feel that they would not be able to do their trading without live data.

Some trading methods, however, are not as time sensitive as are others. They can do their work well enough with data that is slightly delayed. Delayed data is often available at no charge or at significantly reduced charge at various Internet sites or through various brokerage firms that provide it as a service to their more active trader clients. Some data delays are 10 minutes, whereas others run delays as late as 20 minutes. There are even some traders who use the various television business shows as their data source.

I make no value judgment as to which type of data feed is best for the individual trader. Since traders vary not only in their personalities but also in the types of systems they trade, the type of data used must be suited to its application. If you plan to trade numerous times daily, then your best choice will be an efficient and accurate data feed that is not delayed. In fact, you will want a data stream that is quick and relatively error-free. This aspect of data is discussed in a later section.

Delivery Mode

Market data, whether in stocks or commodities, can be delivered in either of several ways. As already noted, there are those traders who obtain their data free of charge, either via television business news or in delayed form via Internet. Yet tick-by-tick data is also available via Internet delivery. As the speed of data transmission via Internet improves over time, the preferred method of delivery will be the Internet. And it will also be the most cost-efficient method.

Data can also be delivered via dish antenna by satellite. This delivery mode is highly reliable, as well as fast and reasonably priced. For those who cannot receive their live data in this form, a dedicated telephone line can be used for modem delivery. As noted earlier, the delivery of data via Internet will gradually replace telephone delivery. Furthermore, the delivery of price data via cable-television lines is rapidly becoming a method choice inasmuch as it is cost-efficient and high-speed.

Inasmuch as the active e-trader becomes highly dependent on reliable and fast data delivery, the method of delivery must be relatively free of errors and service interruptions. If a trader has taken a position in the market and then suffers a disruption in data delivery, the result could be an unnecessary loss; or, if there is no position when the data is disrupted, a trade could be missed.

In either case, the result is not good. It is important, therefore, that you always consider the reliability of the data service before you pay good money for it. To find out which data service meets the necessary requirements, ask questions not only of the providers but also of other e-traders. Find out what they're using and how they like it. Before you sign up with a data service, ask questions or see if they'll let you have a trial period.

And, above all, be careful of long-term contracts. Many data providers no longer require a long-term contract; be careful before you sign anything. Some data vendors require a lengthy commitment. You will want to avoid this type of arrangement.

Error Correction

Many e-traders do not realize that errors in data transmission can prove very costly. What exactly do I mean by an error? A data transmission error can be either obvious or subtle. As an example, consider the following string of prices as they come across the data line:

$$22.50 \ldots 22.51 \ldots 22.50 \ldots 22.51 \ldots 22.52A \ldots 22.52 \ldots 29.70 \ldots$$

(Note that *A* indicates an *asked* or offered price.)

Clearly, the last number in the series is incorrect. It shows a price that is considerably different than the price at which the given market is trading. In such a case, the error is obvious to the trader and will show on a chart as clearly outside the current range of trading. Having knowledge of such an error, the trader can repair it manually (as is required in most cases), or the computer program will find the error and correct it automatically (the preferred method).

More often than not, such errors are obvious and can be corrected promptly. However, there are some errors that are not obvious to the trader and can, therefore, affect the timing methods, indicators, or trading systems that are being used. A subtle error might appear as follows in a stream of data:

$$22.50 \ldots 22.51 \ldots 22.50 \ldots 22.51 \ldots 22.52A \ldots$$
$$22.52 \ldots 22.53 \ldots 22.59 \ldots 22.53 \ldots 22.52 \ldots$$

The 22.59 price is an incorrect price or tick that may later be changed, but the trader will not know for certain whether this is a bad tick or not. The trader is left in the lurch. He or she knows not whether the price is correct. In most cases, however, the trader will not notice this at all. Yet this one price, depending on the trader's system, could generate a signal to buy or to sell. In the event of several incorrect prices, the trader could very well enter a position that would not have been otherwise indicated by the system.

As you can see, correct data is vital to the effective functioning of the e-trader. Some data feeds are notorious for numerous errors, while others are relatively free of errors. And there is at least one data feed that corrects its errors automatically once it has found them. Therefore, if your trading approach is dependent upon the availability of correct data, then you are advised to ask your prospective or current data vendor how often errors occur and whether they must be repaired manually.

Cost

Cost is an important consideration. The more data you get, the more expensive will be the price. Therefore, I urge you not to get more data than you can use. Futures traders can sign on to get live data on virtually all the major exchanges in the world, yet in practice, this is not needed unless you are a professional money manager who trades an international portfolio of commodities and/or stocks. While it's a good idea to trade a diversified group of stocks or commodities, there are only so many markets that a trader can realistically handle effectively. Furthermore, there is no need to clutter your computer with vast amounts of data that will not be used. You are better off trading fewer markets well than many markets poorly.

Another consideration in the cost of data, as previously noted, is that there are various forms in which data can be delivered to the trader. Costs range from free of charge to as much as $1000 monthly, depending on the amount of data you need. Some delivery methods are cheaper than others are. Furthermore, the data-vending business has become highly competitive. Active traders who wish to trade from their broker's office can, in many cases, have free access to live data and to data analyses software as long as they conduct their activities from the brokerage office. This is much more common in stocks than it is in futures. Be sure to evaluate all of your choices.

The Cost of Privacy

While the cost of data, a computer, software, and telephones is significant, the value of privacy is also important. Some traders are lured into trading from their brokerage firms in order to take advantage of the many perks offered to clients who actively day trade or short-term trade. Yet there are many traders who are either unduly influenced by the activity in such trading rooms or who prefer to trade from the peace and quiet of their own home or office.

My preference is for solitude and quiet. Regardless of what you decide, make certain you are in touch with your needs as a trader before you sacrifice your privacy and solitude for the din of a trading room, even if it means free data and more.

Historical Data: Access, Storage, and Retrieval

Historical market analysis is built upon research. And research depends on the availability of data. With so many markets and so much data to evaluate, traders can find themselves inundated with huge data files that cannot all be handled at one time on even the largest of disk drives. Therefore, I urge you to prepare in advance for data storage, preferably on CD-ROM. If you have a CD writer, you can store your data to the CD and remove it regularly from your hard drive. This will not only free up space on your computer, but it will also allow your computer to run faster. When you need the data for research you can retrieve it and use it as needed.

Historical research also depends on accurate data. In the same way that live e-trading can be thrown off course by incorrect data, so can historical market research. Hence, you would do well to check your historical data for errors and to fix them as soon as possible. And this brings me to the point of historical data as a means of beginning your research. Just as there are numerous live data vendors, there are also vendors who sell historical data on stocks and futures. You can buy end-of-day data dating back many years, and you can buy tick-by-tick data dating back many years, as well.

Costs can vary considerably. In some cases the data is free, whereas in other cases it can be quite costly. You would do well to evaluate your many options here, as well. Unless you plan to trade or need to trade all of the markets, you won't have to buy data on everything. Remember, however, that in order to develop your own trading style you will need to do some studying and research. And this will require historical data. The amount of the data you'll need is a function of how far back you plan to carry out your research.

Selecting a Historical Database

A historical database is necessary for research on trading systems, methods, and signals. The longer your historical database, the more valid will be your research. Unfortunately, there is a general lack of lengthy historical testing in the stock and commodity fields. This detracts from the accuracy of trading methods and could well limit profits while increasing trading losses. There are several important considerations you must take into account when selecting a historical database for your market research.

Of course, this assumes that you want to do your own historical research. And perhaps I may be presumptuous in assuming that you want to have a solid research basis for your trading. In fact, I believe that the vast majority of stock and commodity traders, whether trading online or not, do not have a valid historical research basis for their work. Their historical analyses are severely limited or based on only a relatively small history base.

Here are the general factors to consider in buying a historical database:

Length of History. How far back in time do you want your data files to go? I suggest an absolute minimum of 10 years, although I prefer 25 years for most markets. Of course, many stocks and commodity markets have not been trading for many years. In such cases I recommend going back to the first trading day.

Types of Files. I recommend daily open, high-low, and close data, or at least high, low, and close. Trading volume and open interest for commodities can be helpful. For stocks, split-adjusted data is important so that the continuous file will not have gaps and major price changes due to splits.

For commodity markets it's a good idea to also have a cash file in the event you need to check these. And finally, for commodity prices continuous data files of various kinds (to be discussed) are extremely helpful when conducting research.

Tick Data. Commodity and stock traders who wish to trade on the very short term, either over the course of several days or intraday, are advised to have a database of accurate tick data for their work. The amount of data can be voluminous. So you'll need to make sure you have the computer storage capabilities to save the data.

Accuracy.   This is a very important issue when conducting research. Ask questions and determine which vendors have the most accurate data.

Ease of Access.   Some data files are not readable by certain software programs. Before buying a historical database make sure it is compatible with your software. In fact, it would be better if the data files are readable by various software programs in the event you make a change.

Ease of Distribution.   Make certain that the data, once updated, automatically distributes to the various files. This will save you time and difficulty.

Updating.   For active e-traders, it is best to have a data file that can be updated via daily download, whether over the Internet or by modem. This will allow you to keep your files up to date.

Record-Keeping Methods and Procedures

Many traders underestimate the importance of good record-keeping. The active e-trader may trade many times daily. Those who trade stocks and commodities at the same time will have even more transactions to track. At times errors can be costly, particularly if you forget about a trade. I urge you to develop an accurate and efficient record-keeping method, preferably on computer.

There are various spreadsheet programs available for this purpose. The most effective are those that track positions live, updating your equity with each change in your individual positions. Many of the higher-end trading software programs have built in position-trading software. If you have it, use it! It will save you many problems, it will give you active tracing of your profits and losses, and it will keep you apprised of all your positions.

Brokerage Accounts

Yes, this is a mechanical requirement, inasmuch as you can't trade without one. As you know, the stock and commodity brokerage businesses have become highly competitive in recent years. Different firms offer various incentives to their clients. Some firms specialize in discount commissions, while others have higher commissions but provide individualized service. There are other considerations in opening a trading account. They are as follows:

Minimum Starting Capital. Some trading firms have high minimum amounts for starting an account. In some cases the starting amount is prohibitive to most traders. While it is reasonable to begin only with an amount you can comfortably afford, it is also important to begin with sufficient capital. If you start with a very small amount you will likely be knocked out of the game quickly, and you won't be able to participate in the game when the big moves finally come.

Commissions. While discount commissions are important, it is also important for the new trader to get his or her questions answered. I recommend that new traders work with a broker at first in order to become familiar with terminology, procedures, and so on. Once you have become familiar with the markets you can shop around for commission savings, provided you feel comfortable with your ability to enter orders electronically.

Service. If you deal with a broker, then you'll want to make certain that the service is prompt and efficient, that the broker truly has your best interests at heart, and that you learn from the broker. If you use an online brokerage firm it is important to have orders executed quickly, with order fills reported back promptly.

3
Software Requirements

A Multiplicity of Choices

One of the first major decisions that a trader must make is that concerning trading software. There are many different types of trading software, some cheap and some very expensive. Some software delivers excellent value for the money, while some software is absurdly overpriced. Naturally, beauty will be in the eye of the buyer. Some traders are perfectly happy with low-end, low-priced software, while others crave the costly and seemingly sophisticated. Yet, you should know that, as is true in many cases, price is not necessarily a measure of value and efficacy.

Clearly, your choice of trading software will be a function of what you plan to do with it and the type of trading you plan to do. This chapter evaluates the various categories of trading software, explaining what's available so that you may determine what's right for you. It should be noted that many e-trading firms provide clients with their own custom trading software at their websites. For some traders this may be sufficient if they do not have a specific system or method they have developed using other programs. I highly recommend getting your own analytical and testing software.

Categories of Trading Software

There are generally four categories of trading software. They are as follows:

- *Market-tracking software.* This type of software merely tracks prices and has limited charting capabilities. It can help you display prices in a quote-board format, and it can display charts. However, it has limited ability to display market indicators and it cannot back-test systems or methods.

- *Market-tracking and indicator software.* This type of software is more advanced than market-tracking software. This category of software can keep track of many different markets in different time frames. It allows you to display numerous timing indicators on your charts. It may also contain position-tracking features that update your portfolio in real time with every change in prices. End-of-day and real-time versions are often available.

- *Market-tracking and analysis software.* This software will perform all functions of the preceding two categories, and it will also allow you to write system codes for custom indicators and systems. These programs often contain options evaluation modules. This software will also allow you to back-test systems that you have developed.

  Some programs contain optimizing programs that will allow you to determine the best combination of timing indicator lengths, variables, stop loss, and other risk management features. There are many different levels of sophistication and a wide range of prices. Some programs are available via monthly lease only, whereas others are available for a one-time charge other than the cost of monthly data.

- *Specialized and add-on programs.* There are literally hundreds of aftermarket or add-on programs that work with some of the programs in the preceding category. These programs are designed to enhance the operation of other software.

  In addition to the add-on programs, there are many stand-alone programs whose functions vary from accounting to artificial intelligence. The majority of these stand-alone or add-on programs offer specific trading systems, some of which reveal their logic and indicators, while others are black-box systems that do not reveal to their buyers what they do or exactly how they work.

Trading-System Software Versus Market-Analysis Software

The big break point in terms of software costs is that between trading-system software and market-analysis software. Trading-system software can either allow you to develop your own system or give you the final product of another's work. Before you spend any money buying the trading system or systems developed by someone else, you must ask certain important questions, not the least of which is whether the program is right for your needs as a trader and for your available capital.

In many cases the claims of the software seller or developer can be exaggerated. You need to do your diligence in validating the claims yourself before you spend a single penny on any program. I believe that you are far better off developing your own program since it will be suited to your particular needs. There are a number of steps to take in developing your own program. These are discussed in Chapter 4.

How to Determine What's Right for You

Given the plethora of programs available, it is often difficult to make a decision. The claims of system promoters can often mislead you. While a given program may make fantastic claims, you may not have the capital, experience, time, or financial ability to follow such programs.

You must, therefore, know how much the trading system requires you to invest, how bad the drawdowns have been, and what will be required from you in time commitment. Systems can be very attractive at first blush; however, after detailed examination they may not be right for you. Always consider your available capital, time, and ability to ride losses before you buy a system. Think seriously about developing your own trading systems and/or methods.

Black-Box Systems

Occasionally, you many find advertising that promises fantastic trading results if you buy a computerized trading system. The price of such systems is usually very high, and in most cases, the results never match the claims made by the promoters. Frequently, these systems are *black-box* systems. By this I mean that their logic, rules, and system codes are not revealed to the buyer. What you buy is a black box whose insides you do not know.

The promoter of the system not only asks you to pay a high price for the system, but also asks you not to question its internal workings. While I can't say that all systems of this nature are worthless, I can warn you that a good majority of them are not worth buying since they will rarely produce consistent profits. While the claims of the black-box peddlers may be attractive, I caution you to spend your money wisely by avoiding such systems. Unless the system seller is willing to reveal, at the very minimum, the basic logic and theory behind the system, your best bet is to be cautious.

Still another problem with the black-box system is that you will not learn a thing about improving the performance of the system when it fails unless you know how and where it went wrong. However, if you know how the system works you can study your losses and perhaps determine what went wrong. In this way your losses will have produced some meaningful results.

When the black-box fails you have learned nothing. You may argue that the developer of the black-box system wants to keep the system confidential in order to prevent too many traders from knowing the "secret." This is pure rubbish and is the tool the black-box promoter uses to pander to the gullible buyer. Note that this does not mean, conversely, that systems which reveal their logic will ipso facto make money. There are bad systems everywhere, and there are no guarantees.

Caveat Emptor

Clearly, it is in your best interest to fully evaluate any program, system, method, piece of trading software, data, order entry system, analysis program, or other product before you spend any money. Follow the dictum of Occam's razor, which says that given the choice between a simple effective solution and a complicated effective solution, the simple solution is best. In your trading experience you have most likely encountered all manner and types of products, each one competing for your dollar.

I sincerely believe that the vast majority of these products are either unnecessary, overrated, or totally useless. I have found that the simple often works the best. A Volkswagen will get you to New York at about the same time as will a Bentley. Your ride may not be as luxurious, your creature comforts will be considerably less, your gas mileage will be better, your challenge may be more exciting, your ride may not be as safe, your insurance costs may be less, your capital outlay will be much smaller, and no one will ask you to pass the Grey Poupon, but you will get to New York.

Lest I begin to sound like a conservative old fuddy-duddy, I hasten to add that I am most certainly in favor of any tool that will help you succeed as a trader, via electronic means or otherwise. However, bigger toys do not necessarily make for bigger bucks in profit.

Where to Begin

The new trader will be confronted by numerous choices that become more plentiful every day. Your trading capital will be limited, and you will need to be frugal and highly selective in your choices. There are a number of worthwhile programs that will cost you less than $500, provided you are satisfied analyzing end-of-day data.

This does not mean that you cannot enter orders electronically via the Internet through your online broker. Nor does it necessarily mean that you cannot trade certain methods within the day time frame. However, it means that your graphs, charts, and trading systems will not update on a tick-by-tick basis. Yet, this is not a limitation, and may in fact prove to be an asset.

For approximately twice the money (or much more), you can get intraday trading software that will update prices live, tick by tick, as they change. The overall cost here jumps several quanta, thereby increasing your initial outlay and reducing your trading capital.

I am not thoroughly convinced that successful electronic trading requires tick-by-tick data or intraday analysis of market trends. In fact, I have presented several approaches to trading that debunk this myth. Yet, for those who insist on tick-by-tick data I have provided numerous systems to satisfy the need. The appendix provides the names of various software suppliers that you may consider in your search. I may be biased in my evaluation, but I share my recommendations with you in the appendix.

4

Systems, Methods, Techniques, or Seat-of-the-Pants

What Is a Trading System?

In order to trade effectively, whether as a short-term trader, position trader, or investor, you will need to follow a specific system or method. Experience teaches that traders who follow a definitive set of rules have a significantly greater chance of making money than do those who do not follow rules. The sad but true fact is that most traders are intuitive traders—they trade whatever "feels" right. They use words like "I think the market is going higher," or "I feel like this is the right time to buy," or "I'm buying stocks because I just know that the market is going higher." On the other hand, systems traders will rarely use terms like that. Rather, they will say "I have a signal to buy S&P futures at 1344 stop with a risk of 475 points."

A trading system has a defined set of rules and procedures. It contains specific entry and exit signals; it tells the trader how much to risk, when to buy, and when to sell. The system can be back-tested and a plethora of relevant performance statistics can be derived regarding its historical performance. In addition, various risk management and money management rules can be applied to improve its performance.

A trading system is, therefore, complete in all aspects. The trader who has confidence in the system's historical ability and who may have seen it work in real time subsequent to its development will likely use it. And if it continues to perform, then the trader will be even more confident. Having a trading system takes a great deal of the burden from the trader, provided the trader is willing and able to follow the system. But this is a tall order for most traders.

Here are the positive aspects of a trading system:

- It provides exact entry and exit prices, points, times and/or dates. As an example, a system may generate the following orders:

BUY MARCH SWISS FRANC 5580 STOP. RISK 53 POINTS STOP
SELL SHORT JUNE TBONDS 116 STOP. STOP LOSS 11624
BUY JUNE GOLD 267 STOP; SELL JUNE GOLD 253 STOP OCO

- It provides complete historical performance statistics, including the following vital information: percentage accuracy, drawdowns, upswing, average profit per trade, average losing trade, cumulative performance, maximum losing trade, maximum winning trade, profit/loss ratio, maximum successive losers, and much more.
- It provides specific levels of risk, either in dollar terms or in an exit price as the stop loss.
- It often provides a trailing stop-loss level once a given profit objective has been hit.
- It can tell you how many contracts to trade each time.
- It can tell you when to avoid trading.

All of these features are a function of the manner in which the system was developed. When correctly researched and developed, a trading system is the pinnacle of what a trader can achieve. Those who attempt to trade without a valid system are unlikely to achieve consistent profits regardless of their good intentions, starting capital, or motivation. A trader without a system is like a pilot without a plan. You can either go for a joy ride without a goal or you can take a serious flight with a plan that will get you where you want to go.

The systems featured in Chapters 7 through 9 were developed on TradeStation 4.0 and TradeStation ProSuite using the PowerEditor and StrategyBuilder features. Although the systems were optimized, such optimization was within reasonable limits. Note, however, that since they are optimized to a certain extent, you will need to update or reoptimize them from time to time following the parameters presented in Chapter 5.

More important than the performance histories are the concepts on which the systems are based. These concepts, along with illustrations and historical summaries, are provided for each of the systems. Note that the systems are all short-term. Inasmuch as they all generate real-time signals on the computer, they can all be used to enter orders electronically via the

Internet. As with all systems, there are limitations on future performance about which you should be aware. Here is what I would like you to learn from this presentation of systems:

- With a little effort and knowledge of systems and methods, anyone can develop systems that show profitable historical testing. *The key is to make them go forward in real time with profitable results.*
- Since I believe that the concepts upon which these systems are based are valid, logical, and testable, I also believe that they are likely to go forward with good results in real time.
- While optimization of systems is reasonable, overly optimizing systems can yield excellent back-tested results, yet *such systems may not prove effective in real time.*
- All the systems presented in this book share several common elements, as discussed in the next section.
- All the systems presented in the chapters that follow use intraday data, but not all of the systems are day-trading systems.
- Suggestions for reoptimizing the systems are provided in each chapter.
- *Do not trade any of these systems until you have had an opportunity to evaluate them in terms of their efficacy, risk, and reward.*

Necessary System Elements

Trading system developers and system traders have various ideas about what elements should be included as part of an effective trading system. My approach uses the same essential model for developing systems. I consider a number of elements necessary for the effective implementation of a system. These elements are as follows:

Concept, Indicator, or Method. I believe that a profitable system or a system that has profit potential should begin with an idea, concept, method, or indicator that has face validity. In other words, the idea must at least have some degree of logic to it. While I would agree that not all logical ideas will ultimately prove profitable in a trading system, I do believe that the odds of such ideas ultimately being profitable are better than they are for trading concepts that do not appear to have any reason or logic to them. This is *not* to say that I reject ideas which do not seem immediately reasonable or valid.

There are many market myths that, although seemingly valid on the surface, prove to be essentially useless when applied in a systematic fashion and tested rigorously. As an example, the simple idea of a key reversal seems worthwhile; yet, in practice, its value is borderline. Therefore, begin with an idea that makes some sense to you. Once you have your idea you can, in most cases, write the system rules or algorithms for your system in the language that is supported by the software you are using.

Vendors such as Omega Research, MetaStock, and CQG provide their own programming languages or features that will allow you to do this. If you are not capable of writing the system rules, you can hire an outside programmer who specializes in writing system code for the software you are using; or, where provided, you can use the built-in system development tools.

Omega Research, for example, has a built-in feature called StrategyBuilder that allows you to build systems easily using strategies, signals, functions, and risk management tools that are part of the software. Most of the systems presented in the chapters that follow were developed using the built-in features of the Omega Research 2000i software. It is no longer necessary to have programming skills or to hire a programmer to do the job of developing a system.

In time, as more advances are made in computer software, it will be possible to develop highly sophisticated systems with a minimum of effort. Progress is being made so quickly in this area that you are well advised to do a little investigating before you buy any trading software program, since some of my comments here may be outdated by the time you read this book. Suffice it to say that you will need to have your market concept or method programmed if you want to test it or trade it using a computer. The essence of e-trading is to be able to generate signals and specific orders promptly.

Risk Management.   An integral aspect of all trading systems is risk management. You will need to deal with losses effectively and efficiently. Your system will need to provide you with an initial stop loss and a trailing stop loss. An *initial stop loss* is the maximum dollar amount you want to risk on the trade. An initial stop loss need not be a specific dollar amount if your position can be closed out or reversed by signals from your trading system.

A *trailing stop loss* is the amount of profit you are willing to give back once you have reached a given profit target (called the *floor level*). Traders like the idea of trailing stops on a system; however, they are rarely willing to give a market enough room. They are bound and determined to use trailing stop losses that are so small, they might as well just exit their positions without using a trailing stop. You will notice that the initial stops and trailing stops used in my systems are large by necessity.

How a Trading System Differs
from a Trading Method

A trading method is the *first step* toward a trading system. A trading method contains many elements of a system, but it fails to include a set of firm rules, and it does not include risk management. A trading method follows given rules but stops short of the organizational aspects that are part of a fully developed system. All too often, a trading method fails to provide the follow-through and risk management that help preserve capital.

Which Approach Is Better for You?

While there are those who argue that a trading method is preferable to a trading system because a trading system is too rigid, I sincerely believe that the vast majority of traders are better off with a *system*, as opposed to a *method*. A trading method leaves too much open to the whims and emotions of the trader.

Whereas a disciplined and experienced trader can follow a valid method profitably, most traders cannot do so and may never be able to do so. They need specific rules and procedures of the type that are provided by a system. Yet, it is also true that many traders cannot follow a system, either. Sooner or later they will either learn to trade by a set or rules, or they will continue to lose money. Every now and then there is a trader who can do consistently well without following a formalized set of rules, but such cases are exceptional and certainly not the norm.

Assets and Liabilities of E-Trading
Without a System

It can be reasonably argued that a trader who is experienced does not need to follow a system. Yet, it can also be argued reasonably that traders who follow specific systems will avoid the problems that emotion can bring to the trading equation. And both arguments would be partially correct. There is yet a third and new difficulty that I have seen only since the popularization of e-trading. It is perhaps incorrect to claim that this is an entirely new problem, inasmuch as it existed well before the advent of e-trading. The problem is specifically *overtrading*, or trading too often.

The ability to enter orders at the push of a button may cater to the trader who is manic or who thrives on the *action* of trading, as opposed to the *profits* of trading. Some traders become seemingly addicted to placing orders, since they crave the virtually immediate feedback in the same way that a player of slot machines will keep feeding money to the mill.

I believe that having a definitive system will help avoid or overcome what, for lack of a better term, I call *e-trade addiction* (ETA). It may not be too long before we begin to hear about e-trade addicts. We have already heard much about the potential problems that those who are addicted to e-trading can experience. We will hear more in time. Yet, I believe that you can avoid becoming an ETA victim if you develop and *follow* a specific trading plan.

When Is a System Not a System?

A system is a system when it's a system. If a system contains the following elements, then it is a bona fide system, as opposed to a method or indicator:

- Specific, objective, clear rules for buying and selling
- A specific stop-loss procedure

In addition, a system must be capable of being back-tested according to its own rules. Any method, indicator, or approach that does not meet these criteria is not a system.

If you told me you had a simple system for trading S&P futures and I asked you what it was, your reply would tell me whether it was a system or not. Here are several possible replies, with my evaluation of whether each reply is a system or not:

- I buy S&P on Monday at 10 A.M. if it looks strong, and if it closes strong I keep it until Tuesday. *This is not a system.*
- I buy T-bonds when the 14-period momentum crosses above the 10-period momentum. I reverse when the two values cross the other way. I use a $2500 money management stop loss. *This is a system.*
- I watch the business news, and when the experts agree that the market is going up, I buy Internet stocks. When they say it's going down, I sell. *This is not a system.*
- I watch prices for the first few hours of the day. If the market makes a new high after the first two hours I buy stocks, and I get out when they go up, but in any event I'm out at the end of the day. *This is not a system.*

I think you get the idea of what I mean. While I do not wish to insult your intelligence, there are many traders who believe that all of the preceding examples are systems.

The Lure of E-Trading Methods and Techniques

Many people believe that an e-trader must necessarily be a day trader. This is not the case. Short-term traders and investors as well as day traders can do trading online. There are three main elements of attraction to e-trading. They are as follows:

- Brokerage commissions on trades entered via Internet are considerably lower than those requiring a broker as the intermediary.
- Orders are typically filled and reported back more quickly since several steps are removed from the trading sequence.
- As a consequence of the two preceding aspects, the trader may trade more frequently in the hope and expectation of making more money.

Do not jump to the erroneous conclusion that these three elements must necessarily translate into higher profits. All too often, they translate into larger losses. One purpose of this book is to help you implement strategies, systems, and methods to help you take advantage of e-trading technology. Do not make the mistake of concluding that technological advances guarantee profits. The lure of e-trading can only be translated into profitable reality by the application of worthwhile methods and systems in a disciplined and consistent approach.

The Reality of E-Trading

I have briefly noted that e-trading does not necessarily lead to greater profits. I have been very clear in my warnings that e-trading can often lead to larger losses. But why and how? First, the average trader, but in particular the new trader, will be prone to overtrade. The mere fact that markets make large moves within the day does not necessarily mean that the trader can capture all of these moves.

Many price movements are random. They are not predictable and therefore not capable of being captured. To believe otherwise is self-deception. There is most likely a point of diminishing returns subsequent to which more trades do not necessarily lead to more profits. The reality may in fact be quite the opposite.

Another reality of e-trading is that it may very well be addictive, as noted earlier. Laugh if you wish, but I envision the day in the not-too-distant future when psychiatrists may have programs to treat the addicted e-trader as they now treat the gambling addict. We live in an age of "instantism." We want everything now. Profits now. Bigger cars now. Instant soup, instant pudding, fast delivery, fast food, faster cars, faster Internet access, faster data, faster results, immediate feedback, daily interest, 60-second micro-wave meals, instant order execution, 24-hour supermarkets, drive-through prescriptions, and more.

All of this focus on speed and immediacy creates in the mind of the trader a frenzy and a competitive urgency. In some individuals this need translates into excessive trading as a means to a lofty goal. We are further prompted by the media's focus on young millionaires. Is it any wonder that the pressure to succeed is being felt at a younger and younger age? And is it therefore any wonder that psychiatric manifestations are becoming more severe and more frequent throughout the world?

A valid question to ask yourself is whether the pressure of the e-trading game is worth the candle. It is said that legendary supertrader Jesse Livermore was once approached by a trader who complained that his position in the stock market was so large that he was losing sleep. He asked how he could reduce his anxiety. Livermore quipped, "Sell down to the sleeping level." The implication for you as an electronic trader is obvious.

Dynamic Systems Versus Static Systems

Another important issue for the e-trader who plans to use a systematic approach to trading relates to the type of system that will be used. There are many different types of trading systems. Different systems use different technical models of the markets upon which to base their buy or sell signals. Most systems are static. In other words, they begin with a given theory or model of the markets and maintain their rigid approach regardless of underlying market conditions.

While such systems have the potential to work well in markets whose underlying fundamentals rarely change, they tend to show poor performance in markets that are frequently affected by significant changes in underlying fundamentals. Markets such as the grains or meats tend to be fairly stable and work well with static systems, whereas markets such as the currencies, stock index futures, and energy futures are more responsive to dynamic systems.

A dynamic system is one that adjusts to changes in underlying market conditions using a filtered approach. As an example consider the following comparison:

Seasonal Trading Approach—Static Model. Many markets have shown a tendency to move in a given direction at certain times of the year. By knowing in advance the direction of these moves, as well as the approximate starting and ending date of the moves, one should be able to achieve high accuracy by trading with the seasonal patterns (assuming, of course, that they exist).

A trader might therefore buy on a given date and sell out on a given date using appropriate risk management. The same procedure would be carried out each year regardless of any other factors, fundamental or technical. The approach is rigid and does not change as a function of any external variables other than the supposed seasonal pattern. Imposing such a framework on the market produces trading signals or strategies.

Seasonal Trading Approach—Dynamic Model. Now consider an alternative approach to the seasonal method. The same procedure would apply, as would the same basic theory. There would, however, be one significant difference. Rather than take a static approach to the seasonal trade, you would approach the trade using a filter or several filters that would either negate the trade or confirm it. These filters could be timing, current trend, or a variety of indicators.

Hence, the seasonal trade would be adjusted to reflect current market conditions. Therefore, the trade would be dynamic, or changeable depending on current market conditions. Figure 4-1 shows is an example of what might have happened historically to the seasonal trade using a filtered approach. A positive signal indicates years in which timing confirmed a buy trade. As you can see, the back-tested results using a dynamic approach are quite favorable. Note, however, even the dynamic system does not guarantee profits or success.

Do Markets Have Personalities?

After trading the futures markets for more than 30 years, it is clear to me that markets appear to have their own personalities. Systems that work well in soybeans do not necessarily work well in S&P or T-bond futures. Different individuals and institutions trade different markets. The trading style of an agricultural firm that hedges soybeans is not the same as the trading style of a financial institution that needs to hedge currencies on a very short term basis.

And, the trading style of a short-term corn trader is likely to be very different from that of the short-term S&P trader. Given not only the differences in

ContractYr	Date In	Price In	Date Out	Price Out	Prof/Loss	Total	Signal
— OCT GOLD LONG Enter: 9/4 Exit: 9/24 Stop: 4 P/L Ratio: 3.46							
75	9/4/75	152.9	9/16/75	145.9	−7.0	−7.0	−
76	9/7/76	111.3	9/24/76	118.5	7.2	0.2	+
77	9/6/77	147.9	9/26/77	154.0	6.1	6.3	+
78	9/5/78	214.5	9/25/78	218.3	3.8	10.1	+
79	9/4/79	323.9	9/24/79	374.6	50.7	60.8	+
80	9/4/80	657.5	9/24/80	710.0	52.5	113.3	+
81	9/4/81	442.0	9/24/81	447.5	5.5	118.8	+
82	9/7/82	473.3	9/10/82	444.0	−29.3	89.5	+
83	9/6/83	415.3	9/26/83	415.5	0.2	89.7	−
84	9/4/84	340.6	9/24/84	345.8	5.2	94.9	−
85	9/4/85	326.7	9/24/85	330.5	3.8	98.7	+
86	9/4/86	411.6	9/24/86	431.9	20.3	119.0	+
87	9/4/87	465.1	9/24/87	462.4	−2.7	116.3	−
88	9/6/88	429.2	9/19/88	410.2	−19.0	97.3	−
89	9/5/89	361.4	9/25/89	370.3	8.9	106.2	−
90	9/4/90	386.0	9/24/90	403.5	17.5	123.7	+
91	9/4/91	349.8	9/24/91	354.0	4.2	127.9	−
92	9/4/92	342.2	9/24/92	349.4	7.2	135.1	+
93	9/7/93	350.8	9/24/93	357.5	6.7	141.8	+
94	9/6/94	389.2	9/26/94	394.5	5.3	147.1	+
95	9/5/95	381.5	9/25/95	383.7	2.2	149.3	+
96	9/4/96	386.9	9/24/96	382.8	−4.1	145.2	−
97	9/4/97	322.6	9/24/97	324.0	1.4	146.6	+
98	9/4/98	287.8	9/24/98	293.9	6.1	152.7	+
Trades: 24		Winners: 19		Losers: 5		%Winners: 79.17	
Avg Prof: 11.31		Avg Loss: -12.42		%Avg Prof: 3.24		%Avg Loss: -3.37	

Figure 4-1. Key date seasonal listing for gold. Signal column shows years in which timing confirmed (+) or negated (–) a buy.

underlying fundamentals for each market but also the differences in the market participants who trade in these markets, it is only logical and reasonable that trading systems would differ from one market to another. It might be helpful for you to understand the personality traits of each market before you trade it and certainly before you develop a system for a given market.

Personality Characteristics of the Futures Markets

The study and delineation of differences in market personality have not received sufficient attention over the years. Since every futures market is affected by numerous and diverse fundamentals—fundamentals that are at times radically different from one another—markets behave differently when evaluated technically.

As previously explained, this is due to a variety of factors, some fundamental and others based on market participants. My choice of the term *personality* to describe the markets may cause psychologists and psychiatrists to bristle, but I am convinced, based on my length of experience, that the term is appropriate since it describes a given set of characteristics.

In the clinical evaluation of human personality traits, the psychologist can choose from numerous assessment tools in order to gain a glimpse into given aspects of human personality. The psychology of tests and measurements provides mental health practitioners with a variety of tools, ranging from the purely technical to the intuitive and interpretive. While most lay people are familiar with the Rorschach ink-blot test, they are unfamiliar with the many other tools that are used.

In studying market behavior, the trader who evaluates systems is doing essentially the same thing as the clinical psychologist or psychiatrist. The trader who follows a technical approach to the market evaluates market personality by imposing a set of standards on the market (i.e., timing indicators or a trading system), and by determining how well the indicators evaluate the personality of the market.

A system that has tested well in hypothetical back-testing is assumed (right or wrong) to be a system that is likely to continue to work (i.e., produce profits) in the future. The system test will give you insight into the personality of the given market. Different markets require different stop losses, different input variables, and even different systems. Testing various systems and input variables on a given market can help you find the best method—one that is suitable to the underlying personality of the market.

The Intuitive Approach to Market Evaluation

Another way of evaluating market behavior is more intuitive, although with intensive study and examination the intuitive process could be quantified. An intuitive approach to evaluating the futures markets could consider a variety of variables, some of which have already been mentioned. Using such an approach prior to testing a system might save considerable time and effort. Here are some questions and issues to consider in the intuitive evaluation of market personality.

Who Are the Major Players?

Large producers and grain companies, for example, dominate the grain- and soybean-complex markets. All grain-complex markets are affected by weather, which has always played a dominant role in determining price trends. Knowing this about the personality of grain and soybean futures, a trader would be more inclined to use seasonally based indicators and/or systems, since they would most likely produce the best results.

If the key players in these markets are larger (i.e., highly capitalized) traders, then the market might be in a reasonably good state of balance most of the time (i.e., supply and demand are in balance), and prices might, therefore, be at a fair value most of the time. Hence, the grain and soybean markets might not be a good vehicle for short-term speculators other than at times when weather is a factor.

Soybean oil and soybean meal, on the other hand, are markets that work well on a spread or ratio basis. More demand for soybean oil causes end users to pay higher prices for soybean oil, which in turn causes more beans to be crushed and creates an oversupply of soybean meal. The spreads and ratios between soybeans, soybean oil, and soybean meal are important in understanding these markets. Professional traders heavily trade these spreads, as well as the crush spread. A technical trading system that considers these factors as part of the overall approach might yield excellent results.

An important consideration in trading soybean oil is the supply and demand for competitive oil seeds such as cottonseed oil, palm oil, and canola oil. Problems with these crops will affect the price of soybean oil. And the buying and selling actions of large commercial traders, both producers and end users, will reflect this. A thorough understanding of these factors can be helpful in understanding the personality of the soybean oil market, and in developing a trading system that will be effective in this market.

Stock index futures are among the most active markets. They are traded not only by mutual fund and pension fund managers who use the markets as a vehicle for hedging against their stock portfolios, but also by speculators whose orientation is often ultra-short-term. The vast majority of trading in S&P futures, for example, is purely speculative. The market can gyrate wildly in a matter of minutes as speculators respond to news announcements and/or political events. The personality of stock index futures, both in the United States and abroad, is distinctly different from that of all other markets.

Hence, the systems used in S&P trading must reflect these factors. S&P trading systems must use large stop losses due to high market volatility. Most S&P traders are short-term or day traders. Market volatility makes S&P (and most other stock index) trading conducive to short-term and day trading by electronic order entry. The psychology in this market is to grab the money and run. While there are indeed long-term players, they are in the minority.

As another example, the platinum and palladium markets have had two major players. The markets are significantly affected by fundamental events in Russia, which produces a large amount of the world supply. Japan has been one of the world's largest buyers. The markets tend to be somewhat inflexible and highly sensitive to disruptions in supply and changes in demand.

Threat of a miners' strike in Russia or aggressive buying by Japanese automobile manufacturers (e.g., for catalytic converters) can cause large price swings. This is why the platinum and palladium markets have exhibited extreme volatility in the past. Once these markets begin a major trend, they tend to continue in that trend. Knowing this, the trader could use a volatility breakout system on these markets since it would be imperative to avoid the many small whipsaws that can occur during periods of relative stability.

Palladium futures, although not actively traded, could one day become explosive since more than 95 percent of all world supplies are produced by Russia. A supply cutoff could send the price of palladium into the stratosphere should the Russians ever decide to exercise their power. This is most revealing concerning the personality of palladium as a sleeping giant. Volume is thin, but one day prices may explode again as they have done in the past.

Given the thin volume, this is not a good market for the e-trader; yet, things could change in the future, depending on fundamentals. Short-term traders should avoid palladium most of the time while closely monitoring trading volume. A sudden increase in trading volume and open interest would be prima facie evidence that something major is about to happen. In this case, knowing the personality of the palladium market could prove to be extremely profitable to the speculator.

Political Factors and Forces

Do political factors help shape the personality of a market? Indeed they do. In the current markets, for example, intervention by central banks and governments can and will have a significant impact on currency futures. Since currency exchange rates are closely correlated with interest-rate trends in their respective countries, and by virtue of the interrelationships between interest rates in different countries, currency futures have had a volatile history.

Central banks (i.e., government banks) tend to change their interest-rate policies slowly. Once set into motion, a trend in interest rates tends to continue for a fairly long time, and this, in turn, results in fairly lengthy currency trends. This is an important revelation about market personality since it clearly directs the trader to use trend-following systems in the currencies. And we know from experience that such systems work well in the interest-rate and currency markets.

Within these longer-term trends there have been periods of extreme short-term volatility in the currency futures markets. Such volatility occurs when governments buy or sell their own (or other) currencies in large amounts in order to stabilize their own currencies. This causes large short-term swings within the longer-term trend (also called the *secular* trend). Hence, the currency markets are well suited to short-term as well as long-term trading, and systems used in these markets should ideally reflect these personality traits.

A host of other political factors can have a marked effect on prices. These factors include changes in government, wars, domestic insurrections and violence, domestic economic policies, and more. The politics of petroleum prices, for example, have been a major cause of wild fluctuations in the price of petroleum-complex commodities for many years now.

Weather Markets

Some commodities are primarily weather markets. They make their moves at certain times of the year, based primarily on weather that may affect supplies. Such markets include coffee; orange juice; the grain- and soybean-complex markets during the planting, growing, and harvest seasons; and the energy markets during periods of severe heat or cold. Knowing that certain markets are strongly influenced by weather patterns or other seasonal patterns not primarily a result of weather would lead the astute trader to use seasonally based trading systems and methods.

Does the Market Follow Through or Fizzle?

Some markets tend to continue moves for a long time once they break out in one direction or another. Coffee, Japanese yen and lumber are among the best in this respect. Other markets, such as wheat, corn, and oats, tend to have large moves over relatively brief periods of time, and they can have numerous false starts that create problems for systems traders. Knowing this, the astute futures trader would adjust the type of system and signals used in the different markets to suit their individual propensities for trends or the lack thereof.

Does the Market Exhibit Unique Behavior at Tops and Bottoms?

Some markets tend to form climactic tops and bottoms. Among these are gold, silver, cotton, soybeans, and pork bellies. Some markets tend to establish rounding or base-building bottoms. Among these are sugar, live hogs, corn, wheat, oats, and the Canadian dollar. While these characteristics will not always be constant, there have been enough cases of such formations to make the trader alert to such formations in the future.

Knowing that a market tends to bottom slowly over an extended period of time enables a trader to be patient in awaiting lows. Quick exit of long positions or prompt entry of short positions near tops in markets such as gold, silver, cotton, soybeans, and pork bellies is also advisable, given the nature of these markets to establish climactic tops.

Is the Public More Active in Certain Markets than in Others?

And if so, of what value might this information be? The trading public dominates some markets, while others have more of a professional following. Lumber futures, for example, are not particularly popular with the trading public; however, the market is one of the most seasonally predictable and strongest-trending markets. If we observe that the public has suddenly acquired an active buying interest in lumber futures following a sustained uptrend in price, it is safe to assume that the price move is nearing its end.

Furthermore, the knowledge that professional traders dominate a given market leads one to expect relatively poor liquidity, since the public is not present to buffer large moves. The lumber market is a prime example where such a condition exists. The market is notorious for making numerous limit-up and limit-down moves. This is, in part, a function of the fact that professionals dominate the market. The absence of the trading public results in poor liquidity.

Is the Market Dominated by Day Traders or Position Traders?

As noted earlier, day-time-frame traders, for example, dominate the S&P futures market. In addition to the points cited earlier, there is yet another important consideration. The contract margin in many stock index futures is so high it dissuades many traders both on and off the floor from carrying a large or, at times, even a small position overnight. Hence, considerable intraday activity and volatility dominate S&P futures, making it a prime market for e-trading. Knowing this aspect of the S&P futures market's personality can easily point the futures trader in the direction of short-term trading and day trading, using intraday timing systems to catch the short-term swings.

This introduction only scratches the surface of market personality evaluation. The following pages present my thoughts regarding the personality of each major futures market in greater detail. Knowing these traits may help you considerably in researching trading systems and methods that are effective.

Bear in mind that the personality of a market may change; however, this process usually takes a considerable amount of time, and there is often sufficient warning that things are changing. Those who actively traded shell-egg futures in the late 1960s and early 1970s, for example, will recall that this was the preeminent seasonal market for a number of years. But when egg production facilities were upgraded and temperature-controlled, the market began to fade, and trading volume eventually dwindled to nil. And, of course, there were onion futures in the 1950s and potato futures in the 1970s, each with its unique personality. Just as human personality can change, so can market personalities, but the process usually takes time.

A Brief Overview of Markets by Their Personality Traits

What follows is a brief personality evaluation of the major U.S. markets as I have come to know them during my years as a trader. Remember that these evaluations are subjective, but not entirely so, since they are based on observation, first-hand experience, and technical studies.

I offer you these analyses, however, in the hope that they may lead you to profitable avenues of systems research. In addition, you will see clearly that many markets are not suitable for online or active trading. This does not mean that orders cannot be entered electronically. It merely means that you will not want to focus on these markets for active e-trading.

Live Cattle.   This is a highly seasonal market that can sustain trends for a considerable length of time. Of all the futures markets, live cattle (and feeder cattle) exhibit the most regular and predictable price cycles. These cyclical patterns are a direct result of the production process, gestation, and the time required to bring animals to market readiness. Trading systems should, therefore, be more cyclically and seasonally oriented, attempting to play the numerous uptrends, downtrends, and cycles within the longer-term or secular trend.

Because hedgers and commercial users dominate the cattle market, the downside corrections in a bull market tend to last longer than expected, while the upside corrections in bear markets can be quite strong. In general, cattle producers are slow to admit to errors and are inclined, therefore, to hold on to livestock without hedging them until prices have fallen considerably.

Then, at low ebb they are often pressured by their bankers to sell their animals, often at a loss, which gives the market its tendency toward a final and strong push down. The market produces *holes* of supply caused by such forced liquidation. The holes, both up and down, account for some brief but fairly strong moves both up and down. Timing indicators should focus on cyclical lengths as valuable guidelines.

Generally, the cattle markets are not good markets for short-term trading. Those who want to trade these markets using electronic order entry can do so, but I advise against trading market swings shorter than 3 to 5 days unless you watch the market closely and pay minimal commissions. The intraday swings in price are often insufficient to make quick trading profitable.

Lean Hogs. Since the fundamentals of hog production differ from those of cattle production, the hog market is quite different from the cattle market. The life cycle of hogs is considerably shorter than that of cattle, which makes the hog market more immediately responsive to fundamentals. While the hedging element still accounts for sharp and sudden changes in trend, the market is an excellent trading vehicle, provided the trader approaches prices from a shorter-term perspective.

Technical trading systems that are short-term oriented have good potential. By *short term* I mean an approximate 5- to 15-day perspective. For e-traders who are willing to trade within this time constraint, the hog market might be a good place to get started. In 1998 and 1999 the market has become even more volatile, and therefore conducive to short-term trading.

A combination of short-term timing indicators and seasonal indicators is very effective in hog futures, given this market's well-established personality. And the size of the hog contract in terms of dollars per tick is attractive to new futures traders, who won't need to risk as much as they might in other futures markets.

Pork Bellies. The pork belly market is and almost always since its inception has been a volatile market. The best way to describe this market is "live fast, die young." In the 1970s it was the preeminent market for speculators. Although trading volume has declined significantly as traders have turned their attention to more volatile markets, such as currencies and stock index futures, pork bellies remain high on the list of higher-risk, high-reward markets. Bellies are suitable for day trading, short-term trading, cyclical trading, technical trading, seasonal trading, and spread trading. Hence, the e-trader who is willing to risk the possibility of having a market order filled at considerable slippage could trade bellies.

In addition to the preceding characteristics, the belly market has been the whipping boy of health-conscious consumers and physicians for many years. Everything about eating bacon is unhealthy—it's high in fat and cholesterol, high in salt, and loaded with nitrites that purportedly increase the risk of cancer. Islamic and Judaic religious teachings prohibit the eating of pork. These objections and events relating to them have exacerbated the volatile personality of bellies.

Finally, the pork belly market has for many years been dominated by a handful of aggressive pit readers who frequently drive prices to considerable extremes even on an intraday basis. Tops and bottoms in this market, therefore, do not form slowly. They are often violent and dynamic. It has not been unusual for pork belly prices to move up several hundred percent following an extreme and sustained bear market.

Given the nature of the pork belly market, I advise against using market orders unless absolutely necessary. Stop-limit orders, and stop-limit orders with a few ticks discretion, are recommended alternatives, as are fill-or-kill orders. Be particularly cautious with market-if-touched (MIT) orders since they are frequently filled a distance from the specified price in fast market conditions.

Corn.   This market has been the mainstay of the grain- and soybean-complex commodities. Its futures history is a long and reliable one, based both on seasonal and cyclical patterns. Due to the dependence of corn production on weather factors, the market has often violently responded to such conditions. The rallies have been relatively brief but very dynamic when there has been drought, disease, excessive rainfall, or an early frost. These are, however, the exception rather than the rule.

The overall personality of the corn futures market is relatively mild mannered. The market tends to make slow and steady moves in both directions, interspersed with periods of violent up and down moves due to the previously described factors. As a result, the corn market is not suitable for e-trading other than on a position-trading basis.

Short-term trades are not recommended unless the market is in a period of high volatility. The speculator has two choices: either trade corn futures for the very short term when weather becomes an important consideration, or trade corn from an extremely long-term orientation using wide stop losses to avoid the substantial market corrections that characterize the long-term bull markets in corn.

If you use a short-term system that keys in only on weather-related markets, be prepared to take profits quickly. This is something that e-traders can do very well, provided there is sufficient liquidity and prompt order execution.

Oats.   While there is no doubt that trading activity in oats is very limited, it is also true that the oats market tends to lead the other grain markets. In addition to this tendency, the oats market also exhibits strong seasonal tendencies, as well as strong uptrends and downtrends. Due to the very low volume of trading in oats, this market is not recommended for the short-term trader, or for e-trading. Typically, speed of order entry is not an issue.

There has also been a tendency for oats to react violently to weather developments; however, the bull and bear markets tend to be longer lasting than they do in corn and some other grain-complex markets. Given these characteristics of the oats market, I recommend a trend-following system and advise traders who have not studied or traded in the oats market to do so.

Wheat.   I have found very few systems that produce consistently good results in wheat other than those based on seasonal tendencies. During the early 1900s the market was extremely active, which contributed to liquidity and made wheat futures an excellent trading vehicle. Things have changed, however, and now wheat futures are not the premier grain market.

While there are several periods of highly reliable seasonality during the year, wheat is generally a difficult market to trade from a technical standpoint. This market is not suited for the short-term e-trader.

Soybeans.   Soybean futures have become the preeminent agricultural futures market. The market has both a strong speculative following as well as diverse commercial and hedger components. Trading activity is quite good, and the market tends to establish fairly good trends lasting for longer periods of time. E-trading for short-term and intraday swings is certainly viable, particularly when trading ranges are large and trading volume is high.

In the American and South American growing regions, weather is a primary factor in soybean futures. Bull markets inspired by weather have been very volatile but tend to last for a relatively short time. Traders who are able to withstand considerable price corrections both up and down should participate in the market using a trend-following system. The magnitude of intraday price moves during weather-inspired moves is very often sufficient for short-term trading. The e-trader can consider this market as a viable one for trading some of the weather markets.

Because soybeans are crushed for the production of soybean meal and soybean oil, there are spread relationships between the price of soybeans, soybean oil, and soybean meal that can affect the markets considerably over the short run. Some knowledge of the soybean crush spread would, therefore, be helpful in evaluating the personality of the soybean futures market and determining which type of trading system and signals might work best.

Naturally, soybeans also have a strong seasonal component. For a complete picture of the market, the serious futures trader should be familiar with the soybean seasonals. Since seasonals are primarily a function of weather, most market up moves begin in late October to early November and are frequently over by the middle of July.

As with most of the grain-complex markets, soybean futures are difficult to trade from a purely technical standpoint due to their often erratic nature. Soybeans may be traded on the basis of technical systems; however, many of the traditional approaches are not effective when considered on a longer-term basis.

Soybean Oil.   While soybean oil futures are subject to many of the same influences that affect soybean prices, the market tends to be a better trading vehicle in terms of trends. There is an important relationship among soybeans, soybean oil, and soybean meal. The so-called crush spread can, at times, distort the individual behavior of soybean oil and soybean meal as supply-and-demand factors affect the spreads.

Those who are willing to study the spread and combine it with their technical trading system in soybean oil and soybean meal could greatly improve their results. Yet, the trading activity and intraday trading ranges in soybean oil do not make this market conducive for short-term trading.

Soybean Meal.   Meal has been more of a professional market than a public market. Commercial activity is dominant, and many trading systems will not fare well. However, a system that takes into consideration the activity of large traders can do well in meal. The trading activity and intraday trading ranges in soybean meal do not make this market conducive for short-term trading.

Gold.   Precious metals have been among the most widely followed markets. Given the international interest in gold, it is the premier metals market. But this does not automatically mean that gold is a good trading market or that technical trading systems will work well at all times. The core issues are volatility and trading volume. When trading volume and speculative interest are high, trading systems will do well; when there is little interest in gold, the market will slip into a narrow trading range, rendering most trend-following systems virtually useless.

Gold has other aspects to its personality, as well. It has been regarded as a safe haven during times of crisis, and often responds dramatically to political and financial crises, both domestically and internationally. Such reactions, however, are often short lived if they are not consistent with the existing trend. Hence, one good short-term method for trading gold is to buy on expectation of a crisis and sell on the news that a crisis has actually developed. There are a number of intraday timing tools that can be used effectively in such cases.

There has also been an important seasonal tendency in gold prices. For many years, gold futures have made their low in the late summer and turned higher through year-end. Many of the largest up moves in the history of gold futures have taken place from mid- to late August through mid- to late September.

In recent years the market has been suffering from very narrow trading ranges and a slow but steady deterioration in price. Gold has lost its luster for short-term traders. Unless trading ranges expand significantly, this market will continue to be unsuitable for the e-trader.

Silver. For many years, silver futures traded in a narrow range. But with the assistance of a bull market in gold, inflation, and the Hunt brothers, the market moved sharply higher only to establish a major peak in 1980. Since the dynamic bull market of the late 1970s and early 1980s, silver has become a quiet market, spending more time in long periods of ennui than in volatile bull moves.

Silver is not primarily a precious metal nor an industrial metal—it is both. Hence, silver prices have the dual ability to rise in a demand market based on utilization as well as in an inflationary market in sympathy with gold. Silver futures is a good market technically, provided, of course, that there is sufficient range to allow for speculative activity.

Silver has been an excellent trending market, which is ideal for systems traders using trend-following systems. When silver futures become active, the market can also be an excellent vehicle for day traders. Hence, I recommend watching this market for possible short-term trading if and when daily ranges expand.

Platinum. Just as silver is known as the poor trader's gold, platinum is known as the rich trader's gold. The platinum market is highly specialized, affected strongly by developments in Russia and Africa, its two major producers, and by economic trends in Japan, its largest consumer. Platinum can make very large price moves over relatively short periods of time; however, it is not suitable for day trading since trading volume is often comparatively thin.

Given platinum's roles in industries such as automobile manufacturing and petroleum production, the market has important industrial applications. While one might think that Japan is a large consumer due to its preeminent role in auto production, the fact is that Japanese investors have long favored platinum as an investment vehicle. Hence, Japanese involvement can drive prices sharply lower or higher based on two significant factors.

Trend-following systems work well in platinum provided one is willing to accept rather large risks in initial and trailing stop losses. The market needs plenty of leeway due to its volatility. I recommend platinum trading for experienced traders only. Order placement is very important in this market, given its volatile and relatively thin trading.

The importance of the platinum versus gold ratio or spread in shaping the personality of this market should not be overlooked. Platinum prices spend most of their time at a hefty premium to gold. On occasion, however, platinum prices fall below gold prices. While there is no hard-and-fast rule about the ideal spread relationship, it is generally felt that a spread of more than $75 premium to gold is usually a precursor to platinum lows (i.e., gold $75 higher than platinum). At these levels platinum prices are relatively cheap, and long-term accumulation of platinum is usually a wise investment.

While platinum can often fall below gold for many months, the rise in platinum prices relative to gold from spread lows has frequently been extremely large. Speculatively inclined traders should consider following the spread when it falls below even. Track the spread using trend indicators to detect a turn, and when the turn comes, enter the spread by buying platinum and selling short gold.

Since gold and platinum have a different point value, remember to buy two platinum futures contracts for every gold contract you sell. Since the markets are traded on different exchanges, you'll need to margin both sides, as opposed to being given the advantages of spread margins. In summary, platinum is a higher-risk market recommended for journeymen position traders only. It is not suitable for short-term trading.

Palladium.   Although it is one of the most thinly traded of all markets, all speculators should closely watch this market. The fundamentals of palladium are unique since well over 95 percent of all palladium is produced by Russia. From this important fundamental derives the unique personality of palladium futures, and in spite of it, the strategic value of palladium continues to increase.

As a substitute for platinum in various industrial applications, palladium, which is considerably lower in price than platinum, will continue to grow in popularity and usage. In the event of a production cutoff by Russia, prices will soar virtually uncontrollably, and speculators on the long side of the market will reap tremendous profits as long as the government or the exchange allows trading to continue.

However, palladium spends most of its time as a thinly traded market dominated by professional traders. Given the low volume of activity, there are few trading systems that work well unless they are intermediate- to longer-term in their orientation. Naturally, price fills and position size will be problems unless the market becomes more active.

While I do not recommend trading this market unless you are quite experienced, I do advise watching palladium closely for signs of an impending breakout to the upside. Due to thin volume and low open interest, any attempt by insiders to accumulate a large position will not go undetected, and you may be able to enter the market before a large move.

Copper. Copper futures have a long history. Of all the metals, copper is the most stable and also the most seasonal. The use of copper in housing, automobile production, and many other industries, combined with the instability of mining operations in South America and South Africa, have directly influenced copper price trends. Copper has, therefore, been a relatively good trading market both seasonally and from a long-term position perspective. It has had a generally stable but at times violent personality.

Because some of the highest reliability seasonal trades are found in the copper futures market, I recommend applying a short-term trend-following system to copper during the window of up and down seasonals in order to fine-tune timing. The characteristics of copper futures do not qualify it as a day trader's market; however, there are often good short-term opportunities. While trading volume is rarely very high, it is often extremely stable, with few extreme peaks or troughs. And open interest is often sufficiently high to permit relatively good price fills and sufficiently large positions.

Japanese Yen. Developers of trading systems know that the yen is the one market that has shown the best historical results using virtually any reasonable trading system. The market has a history of strong and lasting trends, up as well as down, and technical indicators are very effective. If a system won't work in the yen, the odds are it won't work in most other markets. The yen is a speculative market, which attracts traders from throughout the world, including banks, individual hedgers, cross-rate traders, and others.

Due to the stable and often heavy trading volume, as well as the high open interest, I recommend that all traders study, follow, and trade yen futures. However, note that the market is volatile and can make large swings overnight. For the e-trader who has nerves of steel, the yen can be a very good market to trade. But if you do trade the yen, either trade within the day time frame only, or be prepared for large opening price gaps.

Swiss Franc and Deutsche Mark.   These markets are not far behind the yen in terms of volume, trend, open interest, and the applicability of technical trading systems. Of the two, I prefer the Swiss franc. The Swiss franc is good day-trading vehicle. As of August 1999, the deutsche mark is no longer traded by open outcry in Chicago, but is, rather, an electronically traded market.

As in the case of the yen, I strongly recommend tracking and trading these markets using a variety of trend-following systems, most of which should produce good results as long as the markets remain relatively active and volatile. Both markets exhibit stable trend personalities due to their broad base of international participation. E-trading the Swiss franc for day trade and position trading is viable and can yield good profits if an effective trading system is employed.

British Pound.   Unless you are interested in position trading, I do not recommend this market for the short term. While you may find some success in day trading the British pound, other currencies previously mentioned are preferable. Technically speaking, the pound is a good market that acts well using trend-following indicators. Due to comparatively thin trading volume, some intraday moves prompted by news can be exaggerated.

Canadian Dollar.   While the Canadian dollar has had some very strong up and down trends, they have not been without significant interruption. Trading volume is very light compared to the other currencies, making this market unsuitable for day traders.

Technically, however, the Canadian dollar is a good market for trend trading and should produce good results using trend-following systems. There are also some good seasonal trends in this market. For the short-term trader, however, the relatively low volume can be a problem. The overall personality of this market is stable, conservative, and quiet—just like Canada itself.

Treasury Bond Futures.   T-bond futures have become one the most active financial markets in a relatively short time. On a very short term and day-trade basis, T-bond futures have performed extremely well and offer numerous opportunities for the e-trader. The market is much more stable than the S&P and is more actively traded than most markets.

Given the heavy participation of banks and other financial institutions, as well as numerous well-capitalized traders and the general public, T-bond futures have been highly liquid, permitting very large positions to be transacted with little or no slippage in price. The personality of the T-bond futures market is stable and ideally suited to systems trading for short-term as well as long-term perspectives, using electronic order entry.

As long as international and domestic economies continue in their erratic and often unstable trends, T-bond futures will continue to provide excellent short-term and day-trading opportunities. A variety of trading systems are, therefore, applicable. Note that whenever there has been a flight to quality due to international events or stock market declines, T-bond futures have moved up quickly and sharply.

Treasury Bill Futures.   This market does not trade actively.

Eurodollar Futures.   The market is heavily traded by financial institutions, and although not generally known, trading volume can often be extremely large, with numerous large blocks exchanging hands. Although this is not a day trader's market—unless, of course, you are trading on the exchange floor—Eurodollar futures have been prone to establish long-lasting and technically reliable trends. They are also responsive to flight-to-quality events, although not nearly as strongly as are T-bond and federal funds futures.

Coffee.   Among the food commodities, coffee ranks as the king of the speculator's markets. It has been said that the most obstreperous nations of Europe are addicted to coffee. And coffee futures may very well be the most obstreperous of all markets. Coffee may also be the most profitable for systems trading. However, for the short-term trader coffee is not a market that I recommend. The problem with coffee is that the order fills can be disastrous.

Coffee futures are not for the thin-skinned or inexperienced trader. Volatility is substantial, seasonal factors and weather play a large part in the game, and coffee production cartels play a major role in large price moves.

Given the speculative nature of coffee trading, I recommend it only for those who have both the experience and the capital to trade effectively. I advise against day trading due to the typically poor price fills, particularly on market orders.

Cocoa.   The market tends to run in spurts of strong moves up and down with alternate periods of dormancy. While not nearly as good a market as coffee, cocoa can do well with a variety of technical trading systems, provided there is sufficient price range to limit whipsaw signals. This market is not recommended for short-term trading.

Orange Juice.   The major aspect of this market is seasonal. Typically, seasonal lows tend to develop during the summer months, although most traders are unaware of this fact. By the time many traders realize that frost or freeze conditions are developing, the market has often made its up move from humble beginnings in the summer months.

Unfortunately, trading volume is thin most of the year; I advise against day trading and against market orders unless unavoidable.

Sugar.   Sugar futures have been traded for many years and have spent much of their time languishing in a narrow price range. There have, however, been several exceptionally explosive bull markets, followed in every case by equally strong bear markets.

Day trading is not recommended; however, position trading during big bull and bear markets is advised. Short-term swings can also be traded due to each price tick's relatively high value.

Cotton.   Cotton has been a speculator's market for many years. Weather is the main determinant of price. With a 1-cent move being $500 in value, the cotton contract has been a favorite of higher-risk traders for many years. It is a market in which many legendary traders such as Jesse Livermore and Arthur Cutten learned their skills, often the hard way.

But today's cotton is not the same as yesterday's cotton. The market is still a highly speculative vehicle; however, it is not as technically reliable as it was during the 1920s and 1930s. Although this is a volatile market, it is not suitable for day trading.

Lumber.   I find it strange that more traders are not interested in this highly seasonal market. Lumber futures have exhibited some of the most reliable seasonal trends of any market and rank near number one with copper in seasonal predictability. There has also been a close relationship between lumber prices and the trend in residential building. Hence, lumber fluctuates on the basis of two powerful fundamental forces that are reflected in strong, reliable, and technically valid price trends that are amenable to systems trading. This is *not* a market for day traders.

Lumber futures are clearly the market of choice for seasonal trading when combined with technical timing indicators to fine-tune the approach of seasonal turns. Trends are relatively long lasting and are, therefore, amenable to trend-following systems.

Petroleum Complex.   Some of the better markets for technical short-term trading are the petroleum-complex markets. Trend-following systems as well as day-trading systems are often very effective, and the market is international in scope. The markets are worth trading via electronic order entry.

In addition, the highly seasonal nature of petroleum futures makes the markets ideal for the seasonal trader who can apply timing to the seasonals. The reliability of the seasonal price tendencies is truly impressive. The markets enjoy broad international participation and heavy volume—making them ideal for all types of trading and electronic order entry.

Stock Index Futures.   I've saved the best for last. However, the term *best* is clearly subjective. What's best for one trader may be worst for another trader. In this case, I define best as the most technical, most liquid, and most volatile. In spite of these outstanding features, S&P futures trading is not for everyone. There are alternatives, such as the E-Mini, NASDAQ, Dow futures, and foreign stock index markets.

The S&P has been the preeminent day trader's market of the 1980s and 1990s. The market makes large price moves during virtually each trading day, liquidity is often exceptionally good, tick value is high, and there is rarely a dearth of news to move the market. But the high margin requirement prevents many traders and floor traders from holding their positions overnight, and this contributes to the high volatility.

Furthermore, many floor traders do not own their own memberships, but rent them from other members. This forces them to trade frequently in an effort to generate sufficient profits for their monthly rental fee. The S&P futures market, therefore, is the best of all markets for day trading. S&P is the quintessential market for the e-trader, but be forewarned—it is also the market with the greatest risk. For serious e-traders, a Globex terminal will provide virtually instant order execution in the E-Mini S&P.

Note also that there are now numerous vehicles for e-trading in stock index futures. Among these are the E-Mini, Dow futures, Russell 2000 futures, and NASDAQ futures. Trading volume varies considerably in these vehicles, and not all of them are suitable for very short-term trades.

Given its dominant role, I have given considerable attention to the S&P futures market. However, the systems shown in this book should work equally well in other volatile markets, as well as in new markets not yet being traded.

System Adaptivity to Changes
in Market Personalities

Given my years of experience in the markets, I believe that good trading systems, whether long-term or short-term, must be adaptive to market considerations as well as to possible changes in market personality. We live in an ever-changing world. Since the mid-1970s virtually all financial markets have been in a state of turmoil, often making dramatic moves in response to domestic and international political changes.

While e-trading can help reduce the amount of time it takes for your order to be filled, it is not a guarantee of success. It is highly likely that such changes and accompanying volatility will continue for the foreseeable future. Hence, it is imperative for systems in markets affected by such change to be adaptive to these changes. Keep this in mind when you select your trading system. Individuals who know how to bend with the wind, changing as the tide changes, will fare well. Those who are rigid in their approach will not fare well in the long run. One key to successful trading is to be adaptable to changing market conditions.

Seat-of-the-Pants Trading: Assets and Liabilities

While some traders follow a highly disciplined approach to futures trading, there are others who insist on what I call *seat-of-the-pants trading*. They insist on following no system; rather, they rely on instinct, gut feel, intuition, and other informal, subjective evaluations of market behavior.

Yes, there are those traders who do well with such an approach. Yet, they are clearly in the minority. I caution you to avoid intuitive trading and the seat-of-the-pants approach, inasmuch as it will likely lead to losses and inconsistency. In the long run you will be much better off following a formalized, objective methodology that has specific rules of application than a method that is subjective, intuitive, and/or seat-of-the-pants.

Why Are Most Seat-of-the-Pants Traders Losers?

The answer to this question is simple. The trader who does not follow a formalized set of rules and procedures will, in the long run (and most likely in the short run) be a loser. While I have a weak spot for clairvoyance, intuition, and the power of psychic abilities, I also know that the overwhelming majority of traders do not possess these skills, no matter how much they believe that they do.

Time and time again I have seen the average trader who does not use a system get wiped out without knowing what he or she did wrong. The fact is that such losses are expensive lessons in learning nothing. Every market loss should have an explanation that helps you learn.

Whether the loss was due simply to a signal being incorrect as the natural limitation of a system or due to trader error, the lesson should be helpful in the long run. Trading without a system, method, or other form of discipline will result in losses that cannot help the trader learn anything. In fact, it could be argued that what will be learned is akin to what the behavioral psychologist B. F. Skinner termed *random reinforcement.* The trader will never know why he or she has made or lost money. The random reward of making money causes the trading behavior to be very resistant to changes.

In this respect the trader who fails to use a system is similar to the gambler whose behavior is also maintained and resistant to change as a result of the random reinforcement schedule. Skinner's work with animal and human subjects shows clearly that behaviors maintained on a random schedule are unlikely to change significantly unless the reward schedule is changed substantially. And the only way a trader can achieve this end is to use a specific trading system that allows one to understand when and how an error has been made.

The vast majority of traders, particularly those who day trade stocks via electronic order entry, tend to trade without a system. It can be arguably concluded that, given this situation, most short-term traders and day traders are losers in the market and will likely remain so unless they begin to use a trading system.

Note also that the mere use of a system does not guarantee profits, since there are other behaviors that must also be part of a trading approach. Remember that of all the tools a trader can use in the market, discipline is the single most important. Without the discipline to implement a system in its entirety, all else becomes unimportant since the trader will fail miserably in the long run and most likely in the short run.

The Psychology of Trading the News

Investors and traders have had a love/hate relationship with the news for many years. On the one hand, traders love the news since it often makes markets move, and traders want movement. On the other hand, some traders do not like the news since they feel that it distorts their chart patterns, technical indicators, cycles, and so on.

Many traders are completely in the dark as to why markets seem to move contrary to the news, and many traders capitalize on the news by following the old adage, "buy the rumor, sell the news." While the news tends to move markets, there are many things I have observed about the news that are considerably more subtle than the immediate impact of the news itself.

The following sections present a few cogent points to consider in relation to the news.

Do Markets Know the News Before the News Is the News?

In other words, does the market anticipate the news, often giving buy and sell signals before the news is generally known?

My work has shown many clear-cut instances of the markets and market timing indicators turning slightly ahead of the news. I suspect that insiders who know the news in advance do indeed take positions prior to the news becoming public.

If significantly large positions are taken, then sensitive timing indicators will respond to the insider buying or selling, and you will find it possible to enter a market in advance of the news, taking advantage of the news to exit your position.

Using the News to Evaluate Underlying Market Conditions

If, for example, a bit of bullish news comes out about a market which has been in a bear trend, then the resulting rally (if there even is a rally) will tell you a great deal about the market.

Typically, the market tends to respond upward briefly, and then sell off quickly, often falling below prenews levels rather abruptly.

If, however, the market can retain its gains, then the news is indeed important and a change in trend has likely taken place.

As a case in support of both these points, consider the behavior of wheat prices subsequent to and during the nuclear accident at Chernobyl in 1986. It is most interesting to note that the agricultural futures markets clearly anticipated some bullish news, and continued to respond to the bullish news even though reports indicated that the initial news may have been highly exaggerated.

In the event of severe environmental damage to crops or growing areas due to the radioactive fallout, wheat would have been most severely affected, since the reactor was located in a prime wheat-growing area. The actual news of this event became public late in the day on April 28, 1986, and on April 29, 1986. There were reports that the news was known to some

Europeans several days earlier and that the accident may in fact have taken place well before the news was made public.

Hence, there was ample opportunity by insiders to establish long positions. Market technicians employing even the most simple of methods of analysis, such as trendline breakouts, had signals of a change in trend as early as the close of trading on April 22, 1986, or the next day.

There was ample technical notice of the up move. The hourly wheat chart from the period in question showed how the strong indications to buy wheat developed on an intraday basis. By 12:30 Chicago time on April 28, 1986, it was evident that something important was about to happen—but the charts broke out to the upside well in advance of the news, and then again on the news.

After 3 days of frenzied activity, during which wheat regained most of the ground it had lost in 4½ months, the news was over, and reports disclaiming severe damage and claiming considerable exaggeration began to circulate. The old adage of "buy the rumor, sell the news" held true again. In this case, traders were buying on rumors (and there were many) of severe damage, and selling when the news was out.

Then, after the initial buying spree that lasted several days, the markets began to sell off just as the news reached its most dramatic levels (i.e., with the report that a second meltdown was in process). A hard decline of two days followed. On Monday, May 5, 1986, the wheat market calmed down, the trading range narrowed, and prices closed higher. On Tuesday, May 6, 1986, a strong rally developed, and prices stood poised to challenge the high of several days earlier.

The behavior of prices told us some important news about wheat prices. Specifically, it strongly suggested that the bear market was over and that postnews profit taking was likely behind us, clearing the way for prices to rise or fall on the basis of a more realistic fundamental, and a similar scenario was being played out in other agricultural commodity markets.

In other words, the news of the Chernobyl accident was initially the cause of a strong rally in a bear market. The aftermath of the news, and the failure to return to prenews levels, was taken as a bullish indication of intermediate- to long-term significance.

As you can see, the news is indeed important; however, I maintain that market response to the news is even more important than the news itself. Generally, there are several rules regarding the news which appear to have merit for all traders.

Consider the following:

- In a bear market, bullish news should have only a minor and temporary effect on prices.

- If, after the initial bullish response to the news, prices fail to return to pre-news levels or lower, then a change in trend may have taken place. The reverse can be said about bull markets.

- When major news that is consistent with the existing trend fails to evoke the appropriate response, then there is good reason to believe that the trend is changing or has changed.

- For example, in a bull market, bullish news which fails to have a bullish impact (or even has a bearish impact) is often an indication of a pending change in trend. The reverse would hold true for bear markets.

- It is not the news itself that is important; rather, it is market response to the news that is important.

- Bullish response to bearish news is bullish. Bearish response to bullish news is bearish.

- Regardless of the actual news, the astute e-trader has a clear advantage, inasmuch as the general public will respond slowly to news. By the time the average trader has taken a position, the e-trader will already be in the market, and may, in fact, be exiting as the majority of traders enter. E-traders who use such trading tools as a Globex terminal will enjoy virtually immediate price fills and, using some of the tools discussed in this book, will profit handsomely from their speed and efforts.

5

Characteristics of Effective
Short-Term Trading Systems

Trading systems that make money tend to share a number of common characteristics above and beyond the mere fact that they provide clear, consistent, and totally objective rules and signals to the trader. These aspects of a trading system are taken for granted, inasmuch as they are part of the definition of a trading system. All too often, traders erroneously assume that they are using a trading system when, in fact, they are not.

These basic characteristics of a trading system have been previously described in Chapter 4. Above and beyond these basic and necessary aspects, there are other factors that constitute an effective trading system. This chapter discusses in detail the factors that often characterize effective trading systems. As you read about these variables, please consult Figure 5-1, the Sample System Report, to see how they appear on a system back-test historical summary.

Determining If a Trading System
Is Likely to Be Effective

Accuracy

There is a tendency among traders to ask the wrong questions about systems and about trading in general. As in all aspects of life, asking the wrong questions will get you answers that are unlikely to assist you in your quest for profits. One of the most frequently asked questions about a trading system is "How accurate is the system?"

While this appears on the surface to be a reasonable question, it is not nearly as important as other questions, and without additional information

Performance Summary: All Trades

Total net profit	$ 95875.00	Open position P/L	$ 0.00
Gross profit	$ 248350.00	Gross loss	$-152475.00
Total # of trades	259	Percent profitable	85%
Number winning trades	220	Number losing trades	39
Largest winning trade	$ 7625.00	Largest losing trade	$ -10300.00
Average winning trade	$ 1128.86	Average losing trade	$ -3909.62
Ratio avg win/avg loss	0.29	Avg trade(win & loss)	$ 370.17
Max consec. winners	25	Max consec. losers	3
Avg # bars in winners	2	Avg # bars in losers	5
Max intraday drawdown	$ -29250.00		
Profit factor	1.63	Max # contracts held	1
Account size required	$ 29250.00	Return on account	328%

Performance Summary: Long Trades

Total net profit	$ 102225.00	Open position P/L	$ 0.00
Gross profit	$ 158525.00	Gross loss	$ -56300.00
Total # of trades	142	Percent profitable	89%
Number winning trades	126	Number losing trades	16
Largest winning trade	$ 6500.00	Largest losing trade	$ -10300.00
Average winning trade	$ 1258.13	Average losing trade	$ -3518.75
Ratio avg win/avg loss	0.36	Avg trade(win & loss)	$ 719.89
Max consec. winners	28	Max consec. losers	1
Avg # bars in winners	2	Avg # bars in losers	4
Max intraday drawdown	$ -16850.00		
Profit factor	2.82	Max # contracts held	1
Account size required	$ 16850.00	Return on account	607%

Performance Summary: Short Trades

Total net profit	$ -6350.00	Open position P/L	$ 0.00
Gross profit	$ 89825.00	Gross loss	$ -96175.00
Total # of trades	117	Percent profitable	80%
Number winning trades	94	Number losing trades	23
Largest winning trade	$ 7625.00	Largest losing trade	$ -6275.00
Average winning trade	$ 955.59	Average losing trade	$ -4181.52
Ratio avg win/avg loss	0.23	Avg trade(win & loss)	$ -54.27
Max consec. winners	18	Max consec. losers	3
Avg # bars in winners	3	Avg # bars in losers	5
Max intraday drawdown	$ -29450.00		
Profit factor	0.93	Max # contracts held	1
Account size required	$ 29450.00	Return on account	-22%

Figure 5-1. Sample system report. (*Reprinted with permission of Omega Research.*)

about the system, the information gleaned from the answer is essentially worthless.

There are many systems whose accuracy is very high, yet they do not make money. A system may be correct 75 percent of the time, but if the total losses exceed the total profits, then the 75 percent accuracy is essentially meaningless. Hence, accuracy is an important consideration but not the only consideration.

Maximum Consecutive Losing Trades

An important consideration in all systems is the maximum number of consecutive losing trades. A system that has had more than seven consecutive losing trades may work well in the long run; however, in the short run it may prove to be a serious test of the trader's discipline. Most traders are unable or unwilling to accept more than 3 to 4 losing trades in a row. By the time loss 4 has occurred, the trader is either ready to abandon the system or wishes to change it.

By the time loss 5 has come, the discipline of most traders is about to falter. And by the time losses 6 and 7 come, most traders have abandoned the system. Although the disciplined trader will stay with a system that has shown itself to be effective in the past, such systems can test your patience and pocketbook. Knowing this aspect of your system in advance will allow you to decide ahead of time that you don't want to use this system, or it will help you steel yourself for the losing scenario.

Maximum Consecutive Winning Trades

Just as the maximum consecutive losing trades will tell you the worst-case situation historically and prepare you for the future, the maximum consecutive winning trades number will tell you a great deal about when your system has enjoyed a greater than average winning streak.

As a rule, I like to see at least a 2:1 ratio between maximum consecutive winners and maximum consecutive losers. For example, a system that has had 13 maximum consecutive winners compared to a maximum of 4 consecutive losers is likely to be an effective system, provided other aspects are also present.

Drawdown and Upswing

Drawdown is the term used to describe a system in its losing phase. *Upswing* is the opposite of drawdown. It describes a system in its winning phase.

Maximum drawdown is defined as the maximum uninterrupted dollar decline of a system.

Assume, for example, that an examination of trading results for a system shows three consecutive losses as follows: $450, $888, and $723. The maximum drawdown of this system is now the total of these three consecutive losses, or $2061. Now comes another loss of $200, making the maximum drawdown $2261. And then comes another loss in this string of $1000.

This brings the maximum drawdown to $3261. Assume now that the next trade makes a profit of $434. The $3261 figure now stands as the maximum drawdown. It will remain the maximum drawdown until and unless a new string of consecutive losses surpasses the $3261 value.

The maximum drawdown is important in that it will give you an idea of how much pain you would have had to endure in the past had you been trading this system. Maximum drawdown can also give you an idea of when you may want to be either more or less aggressive in terms of your position size.

There is no guarantee that the maximum drawdown will not be exceeded, yet it does provide an excellent idea of the system at its worst. Some traders believe that the best time to begin using a well-established and successfully back-tested system is after it has suffered a period of drawdown. And I agree. Too many traders want to begin using a system when it has been doing well.

To a certain extent, the dollar size of the maximum drawdown will be a function of the market that is being traded. S&P trading, for example, is highly volatile; therefore, large drawdowns should be expected.

Maximum upswing is the opposite of maximum drawdown. It gives you the best-case scenario of consecutive winning trades. It can tell you a great deal about how the system has worked when it has enjoyed a major winning streak. Knowing the maximum upswing can also give you an idea of when to be either more or less aggressive in terms of your position size.

Effective trading systems may have either a very large maximum upswing or they may show a relatively small maximum upswing but with high accuracy and a large average profit per trade. To a certain extent, the maximum upswing figure is a function of market volatility. In a market such as S&P futures the maximum upswing and downswing figures will be considerably larger than they might be in a market such as oats.

Average Winning Trade and Average Losing Trade

This is a simple statistic that tells you the size of the average winning trade in dollars (or whatever currency you are using). The larger the average profit, the better the system. But note that the average profit figure is meaningless without the average loss figure.

If a system has an average winning trade of $1250 but an average losing trade of $2568, there could be a problem with the system. Most likely, the larger size of the average losing trade suggests that your stop loss may not be correct for this system to perform at its optimum.

Average Trade (Win and Lose)

This is also an important number, inasmuch as it tells you what you can expect from your average trade. If the average trade is too small, then your system may not be too effective. Even though a good system back-test will deduct slippage and commission (*slippage* is the number of ticks or dollars that a trade entry varies from the ideal or expected amount), slippage is intangible and can seriously undermine the actual performance of a system that has a marginal average trade (win and lose).

Clearly, the game must be worth playing. You are far better off with a system that trades less frequently but which has a large average trade than you are with a system that trades frequently but which has a small average trade.

Largest Winning Trade and Largest Losing Trade

These are very important variables, as well. They will tell you at least two important things:

- If the largest winning trade comprises a high percentage of the total net profit, then your system likely made most of its money on a few trades. If you subtract the largest winner from the total net profit, then you will know how the system did without the largest winner. If the statistics are still viable with the largest winner excluded, then you have something worth keeping and trading.

- If the largest losing trade is substantially larger than the stop loss, then it is likely that the system had a trade that got locked into a series of limit moves against it. It is likely that this was an unusual event. Remove this losing trade from the total and see how the system performed. If the results are significantly better, then you likely have a valid system that is worth keeping and trading.

Evaluating a Trading System

Figure 5-2 shows the performance summary of a short-term trading system based on 30-minute data. Let's evaluate the system based on the results shown.

The system showed a good total net profit of $88,000+ on 30-minute S&P futures data with slippage and commissions deducted. The 80 percent profitable trades are impressive, as is the $503+ average trade. The average losing trade is large since the system requires a $5000 stop loss (not unusual in S&P futures). The system could be back-tested using a smaller stop loss to see if this improves the data. Such a back-test with a smaller stop loss is shown in Figure 5-3.

The maximum number of consecutive losers was small at only 2, a very respectable figure, while the maximum number of consecutive winners was very large at 22, also an impressive figure.

The largest winning trade does not comprise a particularly large amount of the total net profit. Hence, one large winning trade does not skew the system. The breakdown of long trades versus short trades reveals a most interesting result. Long trades have been 87 percent correct, with a very large average profit per trade and much lower drawdown. Short trades, although 64 percent profitable, have been net losers, significantly affecting the accuracy and profitability of the system.

Without the short trades the system shows more than $103,000 in profits, a major improvement. This suggests that the system should be used only from the long side. Further testing and development could be done in order to determine why the system fails to make money on the short side, given its stellar performance on the long side. One explanation is that the market may have been in a strong underlying bull trend during this period of time.

Now, let us return to Figure 5-3. The system was retested with a smaller stop loss. As you can see, the overall accuracy was lower, but the average profit per trade improved. Hence, we know from the second test that a lower stop loss was more appropriate. We learned this by examining the system results and adjusting the stop loss accordingly.

The Good and Bad News About System Testing

System testing and development can be a good thing, or it can lead you down some dead ends. The trader is always tempted to overly optimize a system, making the input variables fit perfectly in order to generate an impressive historical trading record.

Performance Summary: All Trades

Total Net Profit	$88,062.50	Open position P/L	$3,325.00
Gross Profit	$236,412.50	Gross Loss	($148,350.00)
Total # of trades	175	Percent profitable	80.00%
Number winning trades	140	Number losing trades	35
Largest winning trade	$12,600.00	Largest losing trade	($6,100.00)
Average winning trade	$1,688.66	Average losing trade	($4,238.57)
Ratio avg win/avg loss	0.40	Avg trade (win & loss)	$503.21
Max consec. Winners	22	Max consec. losers	2
Avg # bars in winners	24	Avg # bars in losers	19
Max intraday drawdown	($23,575.00)		
Profit Factor	1.59	Max # contracts held	1
Account size required	$23,575.00	Return on account	373.54%

Performance Summary: Long Trades

Total Net Profit	$103,925.00	Open position P/L	$3,325.00
Gross Profit	$177,725.00	Gross Loss	($73,800.00)
Total # of trades	122	Percent profitable	87.00%
Number winning trades	106	Number losing trades	16
Largest winning trade	$12,600.00	Largest losing trade	($6,100.00)
Average winning trade	$1,676.65	Average losing trade	($4,612.50)
Ratio avg win/avg loss	0.36	Avg trade (win & loss)	$851.84
Max consec. Winners	21	Max consec. losers	2
Avg # bars in winners	27	Avg # bars in losers	15
Max intraday drawdown	($18,925.00)		
Profit Factor	2.41	Max # contracts held	1
Account size required	$18,925.00	Return on account	549.14%

Performance Summary: Short Trades

Total Net Profit	($15,862.50)	Open position P/L	$0.00
Gross Profit	$58,687.50	Gross Loss	($74,550.00)
Total # of trades	53	Percent profitable	64.00%
Number winning trades	34	Number losing trades	19
Largest winning trade	$8,600.00	Largest losing trade	($5,425.00)
Average winning trade	$1,726.10	Average losing trade	($3,923.68)
Ratio avg win/avg loss	0.44	Avg trade (win & loss)	($299.29)
Max consec. Winners	6	Max consec. losers	2
Avg # bars in winners	16	Avg # bars in losers	23
Max intraday drawdown	($26,500.00)		
Profit Factor	0.79	Max # contracts held	1
Account size required	$26,500.00	Return on account	-59.86%

Figure 5-2. Performance summary of a short-term trading system based on 30-minute data. (*TradeStation system report using Omega Research Portfolio Maximizer Version 5.0.*)

Performance Summary: All Trades

Total Net Profit	$104,150.00	Open position P/L	$3,325.00
Gross Profit	$228,900.00	Gross Loss	($124,750.00)
Total # of trades	176	Percent profitable	77.00%
Number winning trades	135	Number losing trades	41
Largest winning trade	$12,600.00	Largest losing trade	($4,475.00)
Average winning trade	$1,695.56	Average losing trade	($3,042.68)
Ratio avg win/avg loss	0.56	Avg trade (win & loss)	$591.76
Max consec. Winners	22	Max consec. losers	3
Avg # bars in winners	22	Avg # bars in losers	14
Max intraday drawdown	($16,550.00)		
Profit Factor	1.83	Max # contracts held	1
Account size required	$16,550.00	Return on account	629.31%

Performance Summary: Long Trades

Total Net Profit	$115,175.00	Open position P/L	$3,325.00
Gross Profit	$179,475.00	Gross Loss	($64,300.00)
Total # of trades	123	Percent profitable	86.00%
Number winning trades	106	Number losing trades	17
Largest winning trade	$12,600.00	Largest losing trade	($4,475.00)
Average winning trade	$1,693.16	Average losing trade	($3,782.35)
Ratio avg win/avg loss	0.45	Avg trade (win & loss)	$936.38
Max consec. Winners	21	Max consec. losers	2
Avg # bars in winners	26	Avg # bars in losers	15
Max intraday drawdown	($14,950.00)		
Profit Factor	2.79	Max # contracts held	1
Account size required	$14,950.00	Return on account	770.40%

Performance Summary: Short Trades

Total Net Profit	($11,025.00)	Open position P/L	$0.00
Gross Profit	$49,425.00	Gross Loss	($60,450.00)
Total # of trades	53	Percent profitable	55.00%
Number winning trades	29	Number losing trades	24
Largest winning trade	$8,600.00	Largest losing trade	($2,850.00)
Average winning trade	$1,704.31	Average losing trade	($2,518.75)
Ratio avg win/avg loss	0.68	Avg trade (win & loss)	($208.02)
Max consec. Winners	6	Max consec. losers	4
Avg # bars in winners	9	Avg # bars in losers	13
Max intraday drawdown	($25,650.00)		
Profit Factor	0.82	Max # contracts held	1
Account size required	$25,650.00	Return on account	-42.98%

Figure 5-3. Back-Test with a smaller stop loss. *(TradeStation system report using Omega Research Portfolio Maximizer Version 5.0.)*

Excessive optimization looks good on paper, but it does not carry forward in real time once the system test has been completed. Hence, the bad news is that if you overoptimize a system, you will end up with specious results. There are steps you can take to avoid this problem. They are discussed in the following section. Additional aspects of system performance and testing are discussed in Chapter 12.

Optimization: Tips and Strategies

The overly optimized system will rarely go forward profitably in real time. Therefore, it is best to avoid developing such systems, as appealing and as exciting as the challenge may be. Here are a few tips and strategies that will help you avoid the pitfalls of overoptimization:

- Begin with a concept or idea about the market that was derived from a theory or an observation about the markets. I am certain that you have many ideas worth testing.
- Develop the system code for testing.
- The system should contain the following built in features:

  Risk management stop loss for long and short positions.

  Trailing stop-loss floor amount (i.e., the level at which a trailing stop loss will be used in place of a risk management or initial stop loss).
- Input variables—for example, the length of the different moving averages you are testing, and so on.
- Begin by setting a fixed dollar amount for the risk management stop loss. Make this value realistic in terms of the kind of risk you want to take. Do not optimize these values at this time.
- Set a reasonable floor level and trailing stop-loss percentage. Generally, your trailing stop loss must be willing to give back at least 50 percent of the open profit once the floor level has been reached. Do not optimize these values at this time.
- Optimize your input values in increments of 4 units. In other words, if you are testing two moving averages, then test in increments of 4, 8, 16, 20, and so on, as opposed to increments of 1 unit. This type of testing is what I term *loose optimization*. It is much more likely to go forward in time than is a *tight optimization* in which every single input value is back-tested.
- Once the test has been completed and you have reasonable positive results, you can tighten up the variables using increments of 2. You can

go as low as an incremental step unit of 1, but if you do, then do not use a tight optimization on the stop losses.

- After you have optimized the inputs, you can run a loose optimization on the trailing stop and floor level, and then on the dollar risk stop.

- *Do not* set an optimization of all the variables at once in small increments. You do not need hundreds of thousands of iterations of the data in order to arrive at a good system.

The process of learning how to develop effective systems that are not overly optimized takes time, trial, and error, but it can pay off handsomely provided you follow the rules. Fortunately, software developers such as Omega Research have provided excellent tools for back-testing, system writing, and optimization. Do not abuse these tools by attempting to create a perfect system.

As a final caveat, be particularly cautious when using a trailing stop loss in system testing. There are significant limitations in how trading systems back-test such stops. Typically, a trading system that uses trailing stops on daily data (as opposed to tick-by-tick data) may make incorrect assumptions about the sequence of events regarding daily open, high, and low prices. In such cases, the results may be misleading. Tick-by-tick data is less likely to yield misleading results for trailing stops. In addition, more precise definitions in system programming code can minimize such problems using daily data.

6

Basic Categories
of Trading Systems

Trend-Following Systems

Trend-following systems attempt to do what their name implies. They seek out the start of a new trend, and they follow that trend until either they are stopped out or the trend changes. While such systems seek to fulfill a lofty goal, many fail in their efforts. The reason for their failure is simply that the logic of most trend-following systems is not valid.

Trend-following systems have difficulty in determining when a trend has really changed or when the apparent change in trend is merely a blip. Hence, such systems tend to be low in accuracy due to the many false starts. Trend-following systems can do extremely well when they can get you onboard a trend and ride it. But the problem with many such systems is that they cannot reliably grab onto a new trend. I believe that this is due to the fact that many traders do not have the necessary tools to evaluate a trend correctly or, for that matter, to spot a new trend reliably early in its inception.

Another problem with trend-following systems is that once they have gotten hold of a trend, they tend to wait too long to change direction. I will give you some suggestions for improving the performance of your trend-following systems, and I will give you some examples of trend-following systems that can be used in e-trading. Note that I am not opposed to the use of such systems. However, I do believe that many traders cannot use such systems effectively since they do not incorporate effective and appropriate risk management procedures.

Moving-Average-Based Systems

The vast majority of trend-following systems are based on moving averages or a combination of various moving averages. These systems are notoriously poor in their accuracy and timing since they are essentially lagging systems. In other words, they lag behind the market. As an example, consider the system report shown in Figure 6-1. This is typical of most moving-average-based trend-following systems.

As you can see under Performance Summary: All Trades, the results show an accuracy of 46 percent over 432 trades. The system trades on 15-minute S&P 500 data. The string of nine consecutive losing trades makes this system unpalatable and difficult to implement. The average trader would have had difficulty following such a system since the nine consecutive losing trades would have severely tested his or her patience.

Yes, the system does show more than $344 in average profit [Avg trade (win & loss)]; however, as you will see from the systems presented later on, we can do much better. Finally, note that the system shown in Figure 6-1 was created with very tight optimization. My mission was to produce the best system possible by repeatedly optimizing the variables. This report, therefore, represents a best-case scenario.

The Parabolic Method

Parabolic is a trend-following method developed by veteran trader Welles Wilder. Parabolic tracks the market exponentially. It is highly sensitive to reversals in price that occur subsequent to a period of strong acceleration up or down. Parabolic provides a specific price for each time unit (i.e., daily, weekly, monthly, and hourly) which, if penetrated, most likely signals a change in trend. You can use the parabolic indicator as a stop-loss method.

As long as the market is rising at a steady rate, the market will remain above the trigger number generated by the parabolic method. Once this number has been penetrated on the downside, the trend is considered down. The reverse holds true for markets that are in downtrends. In other words, when a trend is down, there will be a parabolic buy-stop number above the market. In this case, a change in trend occurs when the parabolic buy stop has been penetrated.

Parabolic is an excellent method, provided it can be harnessed into a system using risk management and an effective trailing stop-loss procedure. I have developed a short-term trading system that uses the parabolic indicator as its timing method.

There are many other trend-following indicators, systems, and methods. Chapter 7 presents my system development in two of the better trend-following indicators. While trend-following systems have their distinct limitations, I believe that I have overcome many of these by the judicious use of indicators, timing methods, and risk management.

Performance Summary: All Trades

Total Net Profit	$148,775.00	Open position P/L	$5,050.00
Gross Profit	$460,250.00	Gross Loss	($311,475.00)
Total # of trades	432	Percent profitable	46.00%
Number winning trades	198	Number losing trades	234
Largest winning trade	$14,400.00	Largest losing trade	($8,350.00)
Average winning trade	$2,324.49	Average losing trade	($1,331.09)
Ratio avg win/avg loss	1.75	Avg trade (win & loss)	$344.39
Max consec. Winners	9	Max consec. losers	9
Avg # bars in winners	24	Avg # bars in losers	9
Max intraday drawdown	($23,875.00)		
Profit Factor	1.48	Max # contracts held	1
Account size required	$23,875.00	Return on account	623.14%

Performance Summary: Long Trades

Total Net Profit	$103,675.00	Open position P/L	$5,050.00
Gross Profit	$266,275.00	Gross Loss	($162,600.00)
Total # of trades	218	Percent profitable	50.00%
Number winning trades	108	Number losing trades	110
Largest winning trade	$14,400.00	Largest losing trade	($8,350.00)
Average winning trade	$2,465.51	Average losing trade	($1,478.18)
Ratio avg win/avg loss	1.67	Avg trade (win & loss)	$475.57
Max consec. Winners	6	Max consec. losers	5
Avg # bars in winners	27	Avg # bars in losers	11
Max intraday drawdown	($18,725.00)		
Profit Factor	1.64	Max # contracts held	1
Account size required	$18,725.00	Return on account	553.67%

Performance Summary: Short Trades

Total Net Profit	$45,100.00	Open position P/L	$0.00
Gross Profit	$193,975.00	Gross Loss	($148,875.00)
Total # of trades	214	Percent profitable	42.00%
Number winning trades	90	Number losing trades	124
Largest winning trade	$13,775.00	Largest losing trade	($5,075.00)
Average winning trade	$2,155.28	Average losing trade	($1,200.60)
Ratio avg win/avg loss	1.80	Avg trade (win & loss)	$210.75
Max consec. Winners	8	Max consec. losers	10
Avg # bars in winners	20	Avg # bars in losers	8
Max intraday drawdown	($23,675.00)		
Profit Factor	1.30	Max # contracts held	1
Account size required	$23,675.00	Return on account	190.50%

Figure 6-1. Performance summary of simple moving-average-based trend-following system in S&P 500 on 15-minute data. *(TradeStation system report using Omega Research Portfolio Maximizer Version 5.0.)*

Breakout Systems

A breakout system attempts to overcome the limitations of trend-following systems by trading only when the market overcomes a predetermined resistance point (*buy breakout*) or falls below a predetermined support point (*sell breakout*). These systems tend to be considerably more accurate than do trend-following systems, and they tend to produce larger average profits.

Strengths and Weaknesses of Breakout Systems

Breakout systems are also subject to the limitations inherent in trend-following systems. They can be victims of false breakouts. If, however, the logic used in defining a breakout for the purpose of generating a signal is faulty, then there will be numerous false signals. Notwithstanding these limitations, breakout systems are particularly effective in today's volatile markets, such as treasury bonds, currencies, and stock index futures.

Chapter 9 provides examples of two breakout systems and their application in short-term e-trading. As you will see from these examples, the accuracy of these systems tends to be quite high without excessive optimization.

Range Breakout Systems

Such systems focus on buying (and/or reversing positions) when prices penetrate certain levels of resistance and selling short (and/or reversing positions) when prices penetrate certain levels of support. Inherent in this idea is the belief that markets move through levels of resistance and support, and that once these levels have been penetrated, fairly strong moves in the direction of the penetration can be expected.

The belief is likely a correct one, based not only on observational experience but also on valid systems that have been developed on the basis of this concept. The most well-known breakout systems were developed by Chester Keltner. Also noteworthy in the original work on this type of system is Nicholas Darvas, who expounded on the *box theory* of price movement in stocks. The concept of such systems is simple. Once prices have made a new high for a given period of time or a new low for a given period of time, buy or sell signals are triggered accordingly.

Range Relationships

During every trading day or time frame (i.e., month, week, year, hour, and minute), there are four prices that describe or summarize the price activity. Each time segment yields an *opening, closing, high* and *low* price. These prices are very important, inasmuch as they tell us who is in control of the market. By *control* I do not mean control in the sense of manipulation, but rather in the sense of who has the upper hand in terms of the trend. In addition to these four prices, the *range* or average price of the day is important.

When the bulls are in control of a market, prices tend to close near their high of the day more often than they tend to close near their low of the day. When the bears are in control, prices tend to close near their low of the day more often than they close near their high of the day.

While the relationship between the closing price and the opening price is very important, the relationship between the range over several days is also important. Markets that are in bull trends, as well as markets that are about to enter new bull trends, tend to show a specific range relationship. Range breakout systems attempt to take advantage of these relationships, producing buy and sell signals depending upon the exact configuration range and its derivatives.

As examples of how a range breakout system generates buy and sell signals, consider the illustrations in Figures 6-2 and 6-3.

There is much more to these systems. Chapter 9 shows the detailed historical summary of a system I have developed for this type of trading. Chapter 9 also discusses the parameters of the system so that you may research it for yourself.

Market Pattern Systems

Trading systems based on market patterns have received insufficient attention over the years, because in the past back-testing was laborious and frequently insufficient due to the difficulty of writing objective algorithms and the limited computer power then available to test such systems. Virtually unlimited computer power can now be applied to thorough system testing

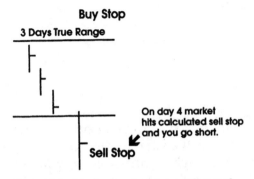

Figure 6-2. Ideal range breakout sell signal.

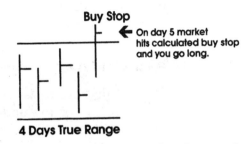

Figure 6-3. Ideal range breakout buy signal.

over millions of combinations and iterations to adequately quantify the performance characteristics of pattern-based systems.

As an example of a pattern-based system, consider the following algorithm:

> **If Tuesday's high is greater than Monday's open and last Friday's high, then buy on a two-tick penetration of Monday's high on Tuesday. Use a 2-point sell stop below the lowest low of the last 10 trading sessions and exit on the nth profitable opening.**

This is an example of a fairly elementary market pattern that can be quickly tested via computer but which was exceedingly difficult to validate or even back-test prior to the development of today's advanced computer systems. Among today's most effective market pattern systems we find methods that compare multiple-day open, high, close, and low relationships with timing indicators and a variety of trend filters.

Strengths and Weaknesses of Market Pattern Systems

Chapter 8 illustrates the performance and application of an open-pattern versus a closed-pattern system for electronic short-term stock index futures trading. The good news about pattern-based systems is that they frequently *anticipate* market moves, as opposed to lagging indicators, such as moving indicators, which usually follow market moves.

Furthermore, pattern-based indicators tend to reveal subtle changes in the underlying indication and distribution of contracts and/or shares by market professionals, large traders, managed funds, and insiders. The bad news about market pattern systems is that there are literally thousands of combinations that can be tested. The trader could easily spend a lifetime researching different patterns and combinations of patterns.

Support and Resistance Systems

Systems that are based on support and resistance depend on an active determination of the underlying trend and then take action depending upon the trend. In a market that is trending higher, these systems will buy when prices decline to predetermined support levels, while in a declining market, they will sell short at a predetermined resistance levels. The success of these systems is a direct function of how accurate the determination of trend, support, and resistance have been.

The vast majority of methods available today for making such determinations either are inaccurate, are based on myth, as opposed to fact, or are otherwise specious. Chapter 10 presents a method for accurately determining the variables, as well as support and resistance methods that will effectively allow you to trade on a short-term basis using this approach.

Strengths and Weaknesses of Support and Resistance Systems

Clearly, the limitation of such systems is their ability, or lack thereof, to accurately determine the three major variables necessary for success. Furthermore, such methods frequently fail to capture major market moves, but rather focus their attention on short-term swings.

Arguably, such an approach can be criticized for failing to fulfill the dictum that the big money is made in the big move. By focusing on the smaller moves, the trader may miss the bigger move. I believe, however, that it is possible to capture both moves with a good degree of accuracy.

Artificial Intelligence (AI) Systems

Although an entire book (or for that matter, several books) could be written on the subject of artificial intelligence (AI), I will make this coverage brief and to the point. The essence of AI-based systems is that they attempt to combine a multiplicity of indicators, inputs, systems, and methods in order to arrive at the best combination.

Then, by analyzing previous losses, these systems supposedly *learn* from their mistakes and *correct* their mistakes. In the future, AI systems will become increasingly complex and may even prove successful in generating profits. Today, I am unimpressed with such methods, with the exception of a few that seem to hold promise as the systems of tomorrow.

The elements of contemporary artificial intelligence systems are as follows:

- A learning model that comprises the brain of the neural net
- Layers of analysis in which the variables are weighted as to their effect on the overall learning

Iterations: 2302   Last Learning Dif: 378.00
Last date trained: 7/29/99
Start date: 1/6/99   Report date: 8/18/99
End date: 8/18/99   Report time: 15:06

Trade	Date	Entry	Date	Exit	Drawdown Intraday	Closing	Profit
Short*	3/01/99	1252.00	3/02/99	1253.20	12.50	10.90	-1.20
Long	3/02/99	1253.20	3/03/99	1255.50	9.30	0.00	2.30
Short	3/03/99	1255.50	3/04/99	1268.00	2.30	2.30	-12.50
Long	3/04/99	1268.00	3/05/99	1293.00	13.20	0.00	25.00
Long	3/08/99	1302.00	3/09/99	1308.00	4.50	0.00	6.00
Short	3/09/99	1308.00	3/26/99	1301.00	42.00	36.00	7.00
Long	3/26/99	1301.00	4/01/99	1317.50	0.50	0.00	16.50
Short	4/01/99	1317.50	4/05/99	1330.90	0.00	0.00	-13.40
Long	4/05/99	1330.90	4/08/99	1353.00	0.00	0.00	22.10
Short	4/08/99	1353.00	4/20/99	1317.00	32.50	32.10	36.00
Long	4/20/99	1317.00	4/27/99	1391.50	8.00	0.00	74.50
Short	4/27/99	1391.50	4/30/99	1367.00	0.50	0.00	24.50
Long	5/03/99	1351.50	5/13/99	1390.00	15.50	0.00	38.50
Short	5/14/99	1364.00	5/18/99	1357.50	4.00	0.00	6.50
Long	5/18/99	1357.50	5/19/99	1360.50	17.50	3.00	3.00
Short	5/20/99	1364.50	5/21/99	1356.50	4.00	0.00	8.00
Long	5/21/99	1356.50	5/24/99	1351.00	14.00	8.40	-5.50
Long	5/25/99	1323.00	5/26/99	1307.00	28.00	25.70	-16.00
Short	5/27/99	1308.50	5/28/99	1300.00	5.50	0.00	8.50
Long	5/28/99	1300.00	6/08/99	1344.00	9.50	0.00	44.00
Short	6/09/99	1335.00	6/16/99	1331.00	5.00	0.00	4.00
Long	6/16/99	1331.00	6/18/99	1350.50	1.50	0.00	19.50
Short	6/21/99	1357.50	6/28/99	1335.50	7.50	2.50	22.00
Long	6/28/99	1335.50	6/29/99	1341.50	0.00	0.00	6.00
Short	6/29/99	1341.50	6/30/99	1356.80	21.00	15.20	-15.30
Long	6/30/99	1356.80	7/02/99	1392.50	7.50	0.00	35.70
Short	7/02/99	1392.50	7/15/99	1414.50	25.50	21.20	-22.00
Short	7/19/99	1429.00	7/23/99	1371.00	0.80	0.00	58.00
Long	7/23/99	1371.00	7/26/99	1355.20	13.20	8.20	-15.80
Short	7/28/99	1368.00	7/29/99	1354.00	10.50	0.00	14.00
Long	7/29/99	1354.00	7/29/99	1349.80*	16.00	4.20	-4.20

Total trades: 29
No. of Gains: 22   Avg Gain: 21.89   Maximum Gain: 74.50
No. of Losses: 7   Avg Loss: 14.36   Maximum Loss: 22.00

	Average Drawdown	Maximum
Intraday:	10.46	42.00
Closing:	5.33	36.00

Percent Gains: 75%   Avg. Trade Length:
Percent Losses: 250-.   3.2 days
Gain/Loss Ratio: 3.0 to 1

Total Net Profit 381.10
Total Drawdown 100.50

Figure 6-4. Sample neural system report.

- A learning mode in which the system is trained
- A forward mode during which the neural system goes ahead trading on its own with the base of knowledge that it has accumulated during its training period.

As an example of the output derived from an AI program, consider the illustration in Figure 6-4.

Strengths and Weaknesses of AI Systems

It has been said that current AI systems are nothing more than sophisticated optimization programs that curve-fit the market's past behavior perfectly, but which do not perform up to expectations. The reality of such systems is that they are still in their infancy and cannot yet be fully judged as to their future performance.

More time is needed to develop and evaluate neural nets. I believe that as we learn more about the variables and components that comprise market behavior, we will also learn more about developing effective and profitable AI and neural net systems for trading stocks and commodities. The future of e-trading in stocks and futures may well rest with these systems, but much more progress is needed. Chapter 15 discusses AI and neural net systems in detail.

7

Two Trend-Following Strategies for the E-Trader

The next few chapters are dedicated to a detailed examination of various systems and methods that can be used effectively by the e-trader. The methods presented herein can be programmed and developed into systems. The systems are complete (as defined in Chapter 4). Note that the systems have been back-tested using OmegaResearch TradeStation and TradeStation 2000 software. Optimization has been fairly loose rather than tight, thereby suggesting strongly that the systems are likely to go forward effectively in real time. Note also that back-testing results are hypothetical and based on the underlying variables and assumptions indicated in the text.

The Essence of Trend-Following Systems

As noted in Chapter 6, trend-following systems are designed to do what their name implies. Rather than attempting to get into a market move before it occurs, the trend-following system attempts to get into a move that is just beginning. It attempts to get out of a market move after it has ended, or it allows itself to get stopped out if the move fails to develop as anticipated.

The vast majority of market systems and methods are trend-following. Because they *follow* trends, they tend to be late in entry and late in exit. As a result, some traders become frustrated with such systems, since they often have generally lower accuracy than other methods.

The good news about trend-following systems is that when they work they tend to get a good portion of market moves, and they do so repeatedly within existing trends. While trend-following systems are not a panacea to the problems of trading, they can afford a sense of security in that they do not buck trends; rather, they take the path of least resistance once they have discerned that a trend exists.

The Parabolic System for Short-Term Trading

The parabolic indicator is explained in Chapter 6. I believe that the parabolic method can be used very effectively, not only as a timing indicator, but also in trading systems and risk management as a trailing stop methodology. The parabolic indicator is a daily buy or sell stop number based on the parabolic formula.

Details of the parabolic formula calculation and its suggested applications can be found in the writings of J. Welles Wilder, developer of the parabolic method. Consult his book *New Concepts in Technical Trading Systems* (Trend Research, Greensboro NC, 1978). Most trading software contains parabolic as one of its resident indicators. Critical to the profitable use of parabolic is selection of the correct acceleration factor (AF) length.

Figure 7-1 shows a sample daily chart with the parabolic indicator. The parabolic indicator appears as a small line under prices as the market is trending higher and as a small line above the market when prices are trending lower. Penetration of the parabolic number on the upside is considered a buy signal, whereas penetration on the downside is considered a sell signal. Figure 7-2 shows the actual prices and the parabolic number for each day.

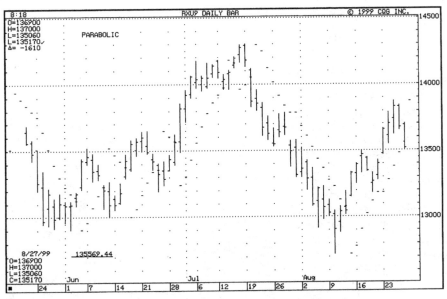

Figure 7-1. Daily parabolic chart. *(Copyright © 1999 CQG Inc.)*

RXU9 DAILY BAR
RXU9 PARABOLIC

DATE	OPEN	HIGH	LOW	CLOSE	PARABOL
07/01/99	138200	139550	137170	139210	133024.00
07/02/99	139250	140650	139000	140590	134329.19
07/06/99	140150	141750	139750	140350	135593.34
07/07/99	140000	140650	139520	140450	136824.67
07/08/99	139850	141600	139720	140500	137809.73
07/09/99	140800	141500	140520	141370	138597.78
07/12/99	141750	141800	140460	140910	139228.22
07/13/99	140200	140750	139650	140370	139742.56
07/14/99	140800	141050	139600	140920	141800.00
07/15/99	141450	142080	141200	141940	141580.00
07/16/99	142220	142950	141640	142750	139600.00
07/19/99	142900	142980	141350	141800	139935.00
07/20/99	141050	141150	138300	138750	140544.00
07/21/99	138950	139550	138050	138550	142980.00
07/22/99	138250	138600	136150	136780	142487.00
07/23/99	137100	137600	135780	136280	141219.59
07/26/99	135520	136700	135310	135480	140131.67
07/27/99	136550	137760	136000	136370	139167.33
07/28/99	136800	137850	136200	136770	138395.86
07/29/99	135400	135740	133800	134980	137850.00
07/30/99	135210	135800	133000	133180	137850.00
08/02/99	133360	135200	133050	133620	136880.00
08/03/99	134110	134250	132020	132880	136104.00
08/04/99	132950	133700	130800	130900	135287.19
08/05/99	131200	132200	129200	132120	134389.75
08/06/99	131300	132300	129820	130700	133700.00
08/09/99	130850	131280	130060	130300	132800.00
08/10/99	130200	130450	127200	129050	132300.00
08/11/99	129600	130750	128860	130400	131280.00
08/12/99	130700	131950	130200	130470	130750.00
08/13/99	131550	133350	131500	133290	127200.00
08/16/99	133250	134000	132520	133940	127815.00
08/17/99	134550	134950	133320	134700	129052.00
08/18/99	134450	134500	133400	133460	130231.59
08/19/99	132500	133300	131850	132700	131175.27
08/20/99	133100	134250	132770	134020	131850.00
08/23/99	134750	136650	134680	136620	131850.00
08/24/99	136100	137850	135500	137050	132770.00
08/25/99	137400	138740	136210	138300	133786.00
08/26/99	138300	138390	136550	136780	134776.80
08/27/99	136900	137000	135060	135170	135569.44

Figure 7-2. Raw data for Figure 7-1.

System Basics, Logic, and Description

The system I developed for e-trading S&P futures on a short-term basis using the parabolic system employs the following rules:

- *Buy.* Buy when price penetrates its parabolic buy number.
- *Sell.* Sell short or reverse position when price penetrates its parabolic sell number.
- *Money management stop.* Use an initial money management stop.
- *Floor level.* When profit has reached this level, use a trailing stop.
- *Trailing stop.* Use a trailing stop of the open profit at *x* percent once the *floor level* has been reached
- *Data.* Use either 15-minute or 60-minute data (can be adapted for shorter or longer time frames based on your needs).
- *Parameters.* Note the specific parameters listed on each of the system reports (historical performance records).

Historical Performance Records

Figure 7-3 shows a chart of the parabolic system's signals as I developed it using the TradeStation 2000i software, as previously explained. Note the following abbreviations.

- Pblc 1 = long side entry and/or reverse to long from short
- Pblc – 1 = short side entry and/or reverse to short from long
- sx.tStop% = exit short on trailing stop percentage
- lx.tStop% = exit long on trailing stop percentage

How the System Works

The parabolic system is simple and straightforward. At the end of the time segment you are using (e.g., 5 minutes, 15 minutes, or 60 minutes), the system calculates a parabolic buy or sell stop number based on the AF that has been entered as part of the system. You place a buy stop to go long or a sell stop to go short at the indicated parabolic number. If your system is operating in real time, updating on a tick-by-tick basis, and if your system allows you to set an audible or visible alert for new signals, then you will be notified when a new signal has been triggered.

Once a trade has been entered, a given money management stop loss is used. If the stop loss is hit, then the loss must be taken and the system goes

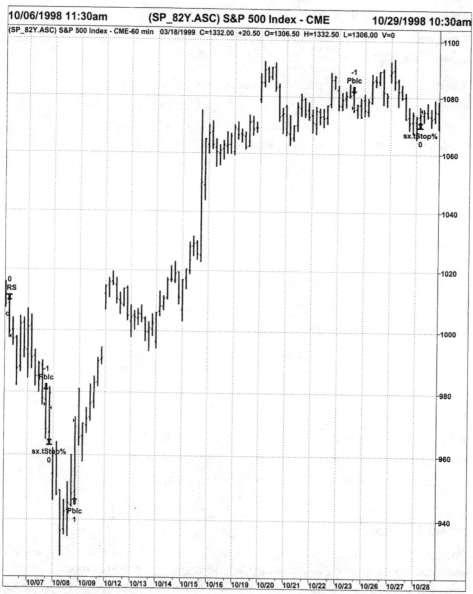

(SP_82Y.ASC) S&P 500 Index - CME-60 min   03/18/1999   C=1332.00 +20.50 O=1306.50   H=1332.50   L=1306.00   V=0

Figure 7-3. Example of parabolic system signals on S&P 60-minute chart, October 6 to 29, 1998. *(TradeStation chart © 1999 Omega Research, Inc.)*

flat (i.e., no position). If the trade is not stopped out, then a trailing stop is used as soon as the minimum profit target is hit. This target is called the *floor level*. Once the floor level has been hit, a *trailing stop loss* is used. The trailing stop loss is a percentage of the open profit. The trailing stop changes daily as a function of the open profit. As soon as a new high is made in the open profit, the trailing stop changes. If the trade is stopped out, then the system goes flat until the next signal develops.

Figure 7-4 shows the historical system report for S&P 500 futures based on 15-minute data from October 7, 1998, to March 18, 1999. The test covers 101 trades. The results show 72 percent accuracy with an average profit per trade of more than $1340. As you can see, this is a higher-risk trading method since it is used in S&P 500 futures. Note that performance across short and long trades is fairly even in accuracy and average profit per trade. Drawdown is somewhat high, although this is to be expected with S&P futures. Finally, the number of consecutive losses (five) is acceptable.

Here are the system inputs:

- AF for buy signals: .0171
- AF for sell signals: .0015
- Money management stop loss for long and short positions: $5000
- Floor amount: $2500 with trailing stop 62 percent

The results shown deduct $75 for slippage and commission.

Now let's take a look at the back-test in the 60-minute time frame for S&P futures. These results are shown in Figure 7-5. As you can see, the accuracy of the system is 70 percent across 117 trades spanning the time frame from November 27, 1997, to March 18, 1999. Note that the hourly time frame, although showing slightly less in net profit and a smaller average profit per trade, shows fewer consecutive losing trades and much smaller drawdown. The system is clearly favored for long trades. And this is no surprise, given the bullish underlying trend of stock index futures during the time frame of the test.

Here are the system inputs:

- AF for buy signals: .026
- AF for sell signals: .006
- Money management stop loss: short positions, $5300; long positions, $3500
- Floor amount: $2600 with trailing stop 90 percent

The results shown deduct $75 for slippage and commission.

Performance Summary: All Trades

Total Net Profit	$135,600.00	Open position P/L	$7,800.00
Gross Profit	$241,650.00	Gross Loss	($106,050.00)
Total # of trades	101	Percent profitable	72.00%
Number winning trades	73	Number losing trades	28
Largest winning trade	$24,450.00	Largest losing trade	($6,350.00)
Average winning trade	$3,310.27	Average losing trade	($3,787.50)
Ratio avg win/avg loss	0.87	Avg trade (win & loss)	$1,342.57
Max consec. Winners	12	Max consec. losers	5
Avg # bars in winners	19	Avg # bars in losers	7
Max intraday drawdown	($32,350.00)		
Profit Factor	2.28	Max # contracts held	1
Account size required	$32,350.00	Return on account	419.17%

Performance Summary: Long Trades

Total Net Profit	$110,500.00	Open position P/L	$7,800.00
Gross Profit	$197,950.00	Gross Loss	($87,450.00)
Total # of trades	80	Percent profitable	75.00%
Number winning trades	60	Number losing trades	20
Largest winning trade	$24,450.00	Largest losing trade	($6,350.00)
Average winning trade	$3,299.17	Average losing trade	($4,372.50)
Ratio avg win/avg loss	0.75	Avg trade (win & loss)	$1,381.25
Max consec. Winners	12	Max consec. losers	4
Avg # bars in winners	21	Avg # bars in losers	8
Max intraday drawdown	($25,350.00)		
Profit Factor	2.26	Max # contracts held	1
Account size required	$25,350.00	Return on account	435.90%

Performance Summary: Short Trades

Total Net Profit	$25,100.00	Open position P/L	$0.00
Gross Profit	$43,700.00	Gross Loss	($18,600.00)
Total # of trades	21	Percent profitable	62.00%
Number winning trades	13	Number losing trades	8
Largest winning trade	$20,750.00	Largest losing trade	($4,400.00)
Average winning trade	$3,361.54	Average losing trade	($2,325.00)
Ratio avg win/avg loss	1.45	Avg trade (win & loss)	$1,195.24
Max consec. Winners	3	Max consec. losers	2
Avg # bars in winners	7	Avg # bars in losers	5
Max intraday drawdown	($10,650.00)		
Profit Factor	2.35	Max # contracts held	1
Account size required	$10,650.00	Return on account	235.68%

Figure 7-4. Parabolic system 15-minute data report, October 7, 1998, to March 18, 1999. *(TradeStation system report using Omega Research Portfolio Maximizer Version 5.0.)*

Performance Summary: All Trades

Total Net Profit	$132,175.00	Open position P/L	$3,450.00
Gross Profit	$231,500.00	Gross Loss	($99,325.00)
Total # of trades	117	Percent profitable	70.00%
Number winning trades	82	Number losing trades	35
Largest winning trade	$26,275.00	Largest losing trade	($5,375.00)
Average winning trade	$2,823.17	Average losing trade	($2,837.86)
Ratio avg win/avg loss	0.99	Avg trade (win & loss)	$1,129.70
Max consec. Winners	14	Max consec. losers	3
Avg # bars in winners	20	Avg # bars in losers	6
Max intraday drawdown	($12,500.00)		
Profit Factor	2.33	Max # contracts held	1
Account size required	$12,500.00	Return on account	1057.40%

Performance Summary: Long Trades

Total Net Profit	$118,750.00	Open position P/L	$3,450.00
Gross Profit	$164,775.00	Gross Loss	($46,025.00)
Total # of trades	70	Percent profitable	77.00%
Number winning trades	54	Number losing trades	16
Largest winning trade	$26,275.00	Largest losing trade	($4,600.00)
Average winning trade	$3,051.39	Average losing trade	($2,876.56)
Ratio avg win/avg loss	1.06	Avg trade (win & loss)	$1,696.43
Max consec. Winners	12	Max consec. losers	3
Avg # bars in winners	25	Avg # bars in losers	7
Max intraday drawdown	($12,675.00)		
Profit Factor	3.58	Max # contracts held	1
Account size required	$12,675.00	Return on account	936.88%

Performance Summary: Short Trades

Total Net Profit	$13,425.00	Open position P/L	$0.00
Gross Profit	$66,725.00	Gross Loss	($53,300.00)
Total # of trades	47	Percent profitable	60.00%
Number winning trades	28	Number losing trades	19
Largest winning trade	$11,600.00	Largest losing trade	($5,375.00)
Average winning trade	$2,383.04	Average losing trade	($2,805.26)
Ratio avg win/avg loss	0.85	Avg trade (win & loss)	$285.64
Max consec. Winners	6	Max consec. losers	4
Avg # bars in winners	10	Avg # bars in losers	5
Max intraday drawdown	($16,850.00)		
Profit Factor	1.25	Max # contracts held	1
Account size required	$16,850.00	Return on account	79.67%

Figure 7-5. Parabolic system 60-minute data report, November 27, 1997, to March 18, 1999. *(TradeStation system report using Omega Research Portfolio Maximizer Version 5.0.)*

Assets and Liabilities

We have here the basics of a valid system. The results here have been optimized, but not to an absurd extent. Before you use this system, take a little time to get it running on TradeStation or other software. Also take the time to adjust the optimum parameters, taking care not to overly curve-fit the inputs. The assets of this approach are simply that it is mechanical and totally objective. The liability is that trading S&P futures is risky, no matter what your system may be. The parabolic system is easily used for e-trading and can be adapted for use with stocks.

The Momentum System: Jake's MOM/MA

Momentum and Moving Average

This use of momentum (MOM) is among my favorite indicators. Not only is the concept of momentum logical and simple to understand, but it is easily employed as a viable trend indicator. Momentum in its several forms is discussed in my earlier book, *The Compleat Day Trader* (McGraw-Hill, 1995). However, the current discussion provides a more detailed examination of momentum as employed in a support and resistance approach. Since momentum can be plotted in many different lengths, the key issue is determining the optimum length for the given stock or commodity you want to day trade. In most cases, the length of the indicator will be a function of the market or stock you are day trading.

For day trading volatile markets I recommend a length of 7 to 14 periods, while for less-volatile markets a length of 14 to 28 periods is recommended. The time segment used for trading must be long enough for valid signals to occur but short enough to provide both an entry opportunity and an exit opportunity before the day is over. When momentum crosses above its zero line for at least two consecutive readings, the trend is defined as up, or bullish. When momentum falls below zero for at least two consecutive postings, the trend is defined as down, or bearish. Figure 7-6 shows this relationship.

Momentum can yield good average profits per trade when used by itself as a buy or sell signal as just described, but often with only mediocre accuracy. In order to improve accuracy, we add one more indicator. We take a *moving average* (MA) of the momentum, which improves accuracy considerably.

Buy signals are generated when the momentum crosses *above* its moving average and remains there for at least two consecutive postings. Sell signals are generated when momentum crosses *below* its moving average and remains there for at least two consecutive postings. This is my MOM/MA system.

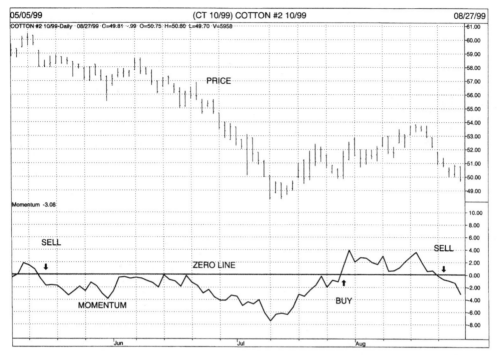

Figure 7-6. Example of momentum on a daily chart. Note buy and sell signals. *(TradeStation chart © 1999 Omega Research, Inc.)*

The results of this methodology are shown in Figure 7-7, which illustrates how the buy and sell signals are generated. Note that at point A on the chart the crossover was a false one, in that the indicators crossed back into the sell position again. Shortly thereafter, however, they again crossed to the bullish pattern. I believe that this method of using momentum ultimately produces much better results than using momentum alone. And it appears to be a much more effective trend-following system.

System Basics, Logic, and Description

The system I developed for using the MOM/MA indicator on an intraday basis is simple but very effective. The rules are as follows:

- If momentum crosses above its MA for at least two consecutive postings, *buy.*

- If momentum crosses below its MA for at least two consecutive postings, *sell.*

Figure 7-7. Example of momentum and moving average (MOM/MA) on a daily chart. Note buy and sell signals. *(TradeStation chart © 1999 Omega Research, Inc.)*

■ Use an initial risk management stop loss, a floor amount, and a percentage trailing stop.

Figures 7-8 and 7-9 illustrate the signals as well as the indicator lines on 60-minute S&P data.

Historical Performance Record

The historical record for this system is shown in Figure 7-10. As you can see, the results are good, with 60 percent accuracy and an average trade of more than $705 after slippage and commission. Long trades were clearly superior to short trades. The data used is 60-minute S&P. Results from this system can be improved significantly by using different time lengths. The parameters used are as follows:

■ Momentum length: 16
■ MA length: 19

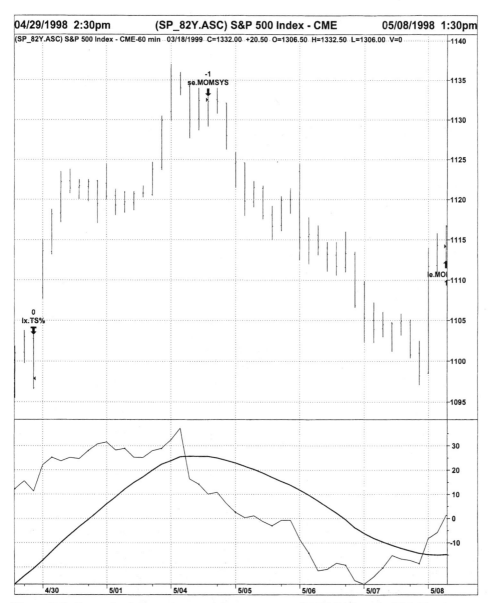

Figure 7-8. Example of momentum and moving average (MOM/MA) on an S&P 60-minute chart. Note buy and sell signals. *(TradeStation chart © 1999 Omega Research, Inc.)*

Figure 7-9. Example of momentum and moving average (MOM/MA) on an S&P 60-minute chart. Note buy and sell signals. *(TradeStation chart © 1999 Omega Research, Inc.)*

Performance Summary: All Trades

Total Net Profit	$124,200.00	Open position P/L	$1,050.00
Gross Profit	$269,350.00	Gross Loss	($145,150.00)
Total # of trades	176	Percent profitable	60.00%
Number winning trades	105	Number losing trades	71
Largest winning trade	$21,775.00	Largest losing trade	($4,525.00)
Average winning trade	$2,565.24	Average losing trade	($2,044.37)
Ratio avg win/avg loss	1.25	Avg trade (win & loss)	$705.68
Max consec. Winners	11	Max consec. losers	6
Avg # bars in winners	11	Avg # bars in losers	5
Max intraday drawdown	($23,850.00)		
Profit Factor	1.86	Max # contracts held	1
Account size required	$23,850.00	Return on account	520.75%

Performance Summary: Long Trades

Total Net Profit	$71,125.00	Open position P/L	$1,050.00
Gross Profit	$122,425.00	Gross Loss	($51,300.00)
Total # of trades	82	Percent profitable	70.00%
Number winning trades	57	Number losing trades	25
Largest winning trade	$10,850.00	Largest losing trade	($4,525.00)
Average winning trade	$2,147.81	Average losing trade	($2,052.00)
Ratio avg win/avg loss	1.05	Avg trade (win & loss)	$867.38
Max consec. Winners	9	Max consec. losers	4
Avg # bars in winners	11	Avg # bars in losers	4
Max intraday drawdown	($11,400.00)		
Profit Factor	2.39	Max # contracts held	1
Account size required	$11,400.00	Return on account	623.90%

Performance Summary: Short Trades

Total Net Profit	$53,075.00	Open position P/L	$0.00
Gross Profit	$146,925.00	Gross Loss	($93,850.00)
Total # of trades	94	Percent profitable	51.00%
Number winning trades	48	Number losing trades	46
Largest winning trade	$21,775.00	Largest losing trade	($3,425.00)
Average winning trade	$3,060.94	Average losing trade	($2,040.22)
Ratio avg win/avg loss	1.50	Avg trade (win & loss)	$564.63
Max consec. Winners	8	Max consec. losers	7
Avg # bars in winners	11	Avg # bars in losers	5
Max intraday drawdown	($26,300.00)		
Profit Factor	1.57	Max # contracts held	1
Account size required	$26,300.00	Return on account	201.81%

Figure 7-10. MOM/MA system 60-minute data report in S&P futures. *(TradeStation system report using Omega Research Portfolio Maximizer Version 5.0.)*

Performance Summary: All Trades

Total Net Profit	$160,825.00	Open position P/L	$3,125.00
Gross Profit	$271,425.00	Gross Loss	($110,600.00)
Total # of trades	171	Percent profitable	65.00%
Number winning trades	111	Number losing trades	60
Largest winning trade	$25,475.00	Largest losing trade	($4,925.00)
Average winning trade	$2,445.27	Average losing trade	($1,843.33)
Ratio avg win/avg loss	1.33	Avg trade (win & loss)	$940.50
Max consec. Winners	9	Max consec. losers	4
Avg # bars in winners	12	Avg # bars in losers	4
Max intraday drawdown	($15,675.00)		
Profit Factor	2.45	Max # contracts held	1
Account size required	$15,675.00	Return on account	1026.00%

Performance Summary: Long Trades

Total Net Profit	$110,150.00	Open position P/L	$3,125.00
Gross Profit	$160,600.00	Gross Loss	($50,450.00)
Total # of trades	86	Percent profitable	70.00%
Number winning trades	60	Number losing trades	26
Largest winning trade	$25,475.00	Largest losing trade	($4,750.00)
Average winning trade	$2,676.67	Average losing trade	($1,940.38)
Ratio avg win/avg loss	1.38	Avg trade (win & loss)	$1,280.81
Max consec. Winners	10	Max consec. losers	3
Avg # bars in winners	17	Avg # bars in losers	4
Max intraday drawdown	($11,925.00)		
Profit Factor	3.18	Max # contracts held	1
Account size required	$11,925.00	Return on account	923.69%

Performance Summary: Short Trades

Total Net Profit	$50,675.00	Open position P/L	$0.00
Gross Profit	$110,825.00	Gross Loss	($60,150.00)
Total # of trades	85	Percent profitable	60.00%
Number winning trades	51	Number losing trades	34
Largest winning trade	$19,375.00	Largest losing trade	($4,925.00)
Average winning trade	$2,173.04	Average losing trade	($1,769.12)
Ratio avg win/avg loss	1.23	Avg trade (win & loss)	$596.18
Max consec. Winners	6	Max consec. losers	3
Avg # bars in winners	6	Avg # bars in losers	4
Max intraday drawdown	($10,975.00)		
Profit Factor	1.84	Max # contracts held	1
Account size required	$10,975.00	Return on account	461.73%

Figure 7-11. Rising and falling momentum system 60-minute data report in S&P futures. (*TradeStation report using Omega Research Portfolio Maximizer Version 5.0.*)

■ Money management stop loss: long positions, $3100; short positions, $4400

■ Floor amount: $2100 with trailing stop 66 percent

The results shown deduct $75 from each trade for slippage and commission.

Another approach to momentum is to use rising and falling momentum (i.e., bullish and bearish momentum) to generate buy and sell signals without using the moving average of momentum. The results shown in Figure 7-11 were generated using a system developed with Omega Research 2000i. This approach to momentum uses the following parameters:

■ Buy signal MA: 7 periods of the closing price

■ Sell signal MA: 28 periods of the closing price

■ Money management stop loss: long positions, $4400; short positions, $4200

■ Floor amount: $2000 with trailing stop 63 percent

The results shown deduct $75 for slippage and commission.

This variation on the theme of momentum produces better results than the MOM/MA application. As Figure 7-11 shows, the accuracy has increased to 65 percent over 171 trades with a $940+ profit per trade and a considerable improvement in the performance of short-side trades. The maximum number of consecutive losers also decreases, while the net profit improves substantially.

Assets and Liabilities

Momentum-based systems have good potential for profit on a short-term basis. They are, therefore, well worth considering as part of your e-trading work.

8
Two Market Pattern Systems

The Open/Close Oscillator System: Short-Term Version

The relationship between opening and closing prices is very important. Frequently, a bull market is characterized by closing prices that are consistently higher than opening prices. A count of days in which the closing price of a market was higher than the opening price of the market during virtually any given time frame will confirm this relationship. Figure 8-1, for example, shows a daily price chart of October 1999 crude oil futures with days when the close was greater than the open highlighted in bold. As you can see, the big bull market from June through mid-August 1999 was characterized by a vast majority of days when the close was greater than the open.

Conversely, in bear markets there is a fairly consistent relationship wherein closing prices are consistently lower than opening prices. Furthermore, large trading range days in bear markets tend to close lower than they opened, whereas in bull markets the opposite is true. Figure 8-2 illustrates this relationship in a stock. The downtrend from nearly $60 to under $42 per share was accompanied by numerous days when the close was less than the open.

While there is no one relationship in the stock or futures markets which occurs with 100 percent consistency, the open/close relationship is, I believe, one of the most reliable. It is possible to use this relationship as the basis of a trading system and with it to develop effective short-term trading strategies for the e-trader. The most effective way to achieve this end is to compare opening and closing prices using several moving averages in the form of an oscillator. The first step in this process is to construct a moving average of the open and a moving average of the close. The second step is to subtract the moving average of the open from the moving average of the close. And

Figure 8-1. Days with the close greater than the open (bold bars), October 1999 crude oil futures. *(TradeStation chart © 1999 Omega Research, Inc.)*

Figure 8-2. Days with the close less than the open (bold bars) in a bear market for a stock. *(TradeStation chart © 1999 Omega Research, Inc.)*

the third step is to construct a moving average of the difference between these two.

Buy and sell signals are generated when the moving average of the open minus the close and its moving average cross one another. Figure 8-3 illustrates this relationship on intraday S&P data. As you can see from this illustration, when the MA of the open minus the MA of the close crosses above its moving average, the market tends to move higher. When the MA of the open minus the MA of the close moves below its moving average, a sell signal develops and the market moves lower. Many times, this relationship produces high-probability up and down trends even on an intraday basis.

Extending this relationship to a system, the addition of risk management and trailing stop procedures results in a complete system. Figure 8-4 illustrates this system as back-tested on 15-minute S&P data from March 1 to November 1, 1997. The results show 62 percent accuracy for 135 trades, with even performance across long and short trades. The average profit per trade of $858 after slippage and commission is a very respectable figure with acceptable drawdown. This system is based on the following parameters:

- Money management stop on short position: $3500
- Money management stop on long position: $3700
- Moving average of open: 46
- Moving average of close: 34
- Moving average of difference: 39
- Floor level: $3900
- Percent trail: 75

While the open/close oscillator can be used in virtually any time frame, it appears to have its best results on short-term data, and is therefore well suited to use for short-term e-trading.

Assets and Liabilities

Assets of the open/close oscillator are twofold. First, it is very responsive to market turns early in their inception. Second, it is easily applicable to short-term trading using intraday data. One liability of this approach is a function of the tick-by-tick data that you collect in relation to the speed of your computer.

Since the closing of one intraday time segment is essentially similar to the opening of the next time segment, the amount of time it takes your com-

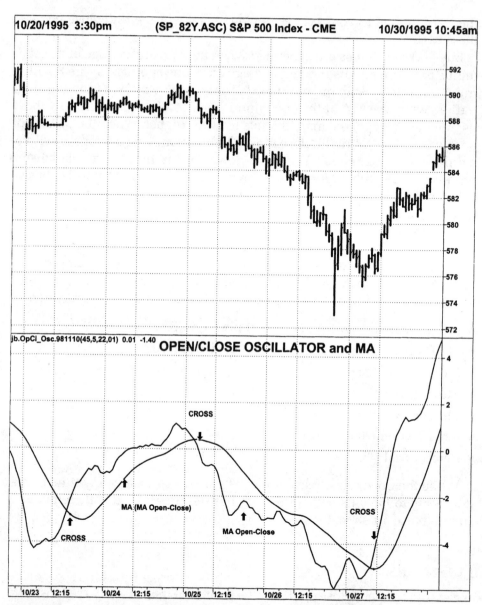

Figure 8-3. Open/close oscillator and moving average on intraday S&P futures.
(TradeStation chart © 1999 Omega Research, Inc.)

Performance Summary: All Trades

Total Net Profit	$115,925.00	Open position P/L	$0.00
Gross Profit	$268,500.00	Gross Loss	($152,575.00)
Total # of trades	135	Percent profitable	62.00%
Number winning trades	84	Number losing trades	51
Largest winning trade	$16,650.00	Largest losing trade	($5,850.00)
Average winning trade	$3,196.43	Average losing trade	($2,991.67)
Ratio avg win/avg loss	1.07	Avg trade (win & loss)	$858.70
Max consec. Winners	8	Max consec. losers	5
Avg # bars in winners	29	Avg # bars in losers	12
Max intraday drawdown	($27,650.00)		
Profit Factor	1.76	Max # contracts held	1
Account size required	$27,650.00	Return on account	419.26%

Performance Summary: Long Trades

Total Net Profit	$65,900.00	Open position P/L	$0.00
Gross Profit	$137,250.00	Gross Loss	($71,350.00)
Total # of trades	67	Percent profitable	64.00%
Number winning trades	43	Number losing trades	24
Largest winning trade	$14,650.00	Largest losing trade	($5,850.00)
Average winning trade	$3,191.86	Average losing trade	($2,972.92)
Ratio avg win/avg loss	1.07	Avg trade (win & loss)	$983.58
Max consec. Winners	9	Max consec. losers	3
Avg # bars in winners	29	Avg # bars in losers	13
Max intraday drawdown	($20,250.00)		
Profit Factor	1.92	Max # contracts held	1
Account size required	$20,250.00	Return on account	325.43%

Performance Summary: Short Trades

Total Net Profit	$50,025.00	Open position P/L	$0.00
Gross Profit	$131,250.00	Gross Loss	($81,225.00)
Total # of trades	68	Percent profitable	60.00%
Number winning trades	41	Number losing trades	27
Largest winning trade	$16,650.00	Largest losing trade	($3,600.00)
Average winning trade	$3,201.22	Average losing trade	($3,008.33)
Ratio avg win/avg loss	1.06	Avg trade (win & loss)	$735.66
Max consec. Winners	7	Max consec. losers	3
Avg # bars in winners	27	Avg # bars in losers	11
Max intraday drawdown	($15,375.00)		
Profit Factor	1.62	Max # contracts held	1
Account size required	$15,375.00	Return on account	325.37%

Figure 8-4. Open/close oscillator system report, 15-minute data, March 1 to November 1, 1997. *(TradeStation system report using Omega Research Portfolio Maximizer Version 5.0.)*

puter to post the next opening price could have a significant impact on how your results compare with the results generated on another computer. E-traders with slow computers, take note! End-of-day data is not subject to a similar limitation, since there is a delay from the closing time of one day to the opening time of the next.

The S&P Day-of-Week System

Traders have long maintained that markets exhibit day-of-week patterns. My work with day-of-week patterns suggests that they do indeed exist; however, they are not nearly as strong as many would have us believe. I have found that a combination of patterns combined with day-of-week studies can yield extremely reliable results. I have studied the relationship between the open/close relationship, day-of-week, support and resistance penetration, and market exit techniques. I have developed a short-term trading system based on the following facts and factors:

- Many markets exhibit specific tendencies to move higher or lower on given days of the week. This was demonstrated by Yale Hirsch in his classic book, *Don't Sell Stocks on Monday* (Facts on File, 1986). While the percentages are not dramatic, the database is large and the tendencies are definitely real and valid. The key issue until now has been how to take advantage of these tendencies. My S&P day-of-week system begins with this basic fact and modifies it with filters in order to extract the maximum benefit from these patterns.

- Beginning with the basic day-of-week pattern, apply the first filter. One of the most reliable filters to use is the relationship between the open and the close on any given day. If a market closes *higher* than it opens, then the odds are that the market will trend higher the next day, particularly if it penetrates the previous day's high. If a market closes *lower* than it opens, then the odds are that the market will trend lower the next day, particularly if it penetrates the previous day's low. This is an important relationship that I use in conjunction with the day-of-week pattern.

- The third aspect of my S&P day-of-week system is to buy on a stop *x* ticks above the previous daily high *if* the close was greater than the open or to go short on a stop *x* ticks below the previous daily low *if* the close was less than the open. This filter helps you stay out of trades that may be random, as opposed to those that are consistent with the day-of-week and open/close pattern.

- The fourth aspect of my S&P day-of-week method is the exit. If you exit the trade on the same day as you enter, then your percentage accuracy is acceptable, but *not* great. If, however, you exit on the *first profitable opening* (FPO), then your accuracy becomes very high. In effect, you *force* the system to take a profit in order to keep accuracy high. With the software provided, you could test different exit scenarios if you like.

- The last aspect is the stop loss. Use a dollar risk stop loss in the event that your trade goes against you. You may also vary the stop loss using the software provided if you want to test different scenarios.

Results

Figure 8-5 shows the results of this approach from 1982 to 1997 using the Genesis Financial Data continuous contracts for S&P. Note that in November of 1997 the $500 point value in S&P was changed to $250. There are, therefore, two records for S&P. The 1982 to 1997 results are based on the Friday open/close relationship with the trade trigger on Monday a 3-tick penetration of Friday's high for buy signals and a 26-penetration of Friday's low for sell signals, with a $3400 stop loss. The results speak for themselves. Remember that exit is on FPO.

Figure 8-6 illustrates the same approach on S&P from November 3, 1997, through August 3, 1999, using the $250 per 100 points S&P value. The results are considerably better in terms of average profit per trade, but there have been only 50 trades, which means that more time is needed to evaluate performance. The parameters here are a 4-tick penetration of Friday's high on Monday for buy signals and a 2-tick penetration of Friday's low on Monday for sell signals, with a $5500 stop loss. The larger stop is necessary due to increased volatility since 1997.

Although these are optimized results, I believe that the system will continue to perform well over time. Remember that volatility is an integral aspect of system performance. If volatility increases, the stop loss will need to increase in order to accommodate the volatility. Conversely, less volatility will mean a lower stop loss. Accordingly, the stop loss should be adjusted to accommodate such changes. *Trading systems must be dynamic if they are to produce profitable results for the e-trader.*

It should be noted that the Friday-Monday relationship is not the only valid one. Other sequential combinations (Monday-Tuesday, Tuesday-Wednesday, etc.) also yield valid results in some cases. Furthermore, I have not investigated nonsequential relationships such as Monday-Wednesday or Wednesday-Friday. Figure 8-7 shows the Wednesday-Thursday relationship in S&P from 1982 to 1997. Clearly, the performance here dollarwise is not as impressive as the Friday-Monday relationship; however, the percentage accuracy is very high.

```
          S&P 500 INDEX 55/99-Daily    04/21/82 - 10/31/97
                Performance Summary:  All Trades

Total net profit       $ 166825.00   Open position P/L       $        0.00
Gross profit           $ 422900.00   Gross loss              $-256075.00

Total # of trades             392    Percent profitable              78%
Number winning trades         305    Number losing trades            87

Largest winning trade  $  39425.00   Largest losing trade    $  -5725.00
Average winning trade  $   1386.56   Average losing trade    $  -2943.39
Ratio avg win/avg loss        0.47   Avg trade(win & loss)   $    425.57

Max consec. winners            21    Max consec. losers               4
Avg # bars in winners           2    Avg # bars in losers             2

Max intraday drawdown  $ -27325.00
Profit factor                 1.65   Max # contracts held             1
Account size required  $  27325.00   Return on account             611%
```
— — — — — — — — — — — — — — — — —
```
                Performance Summary:  Long Trades

Total net profit       $ 109200.00   Open position P/L       $        0.00
Gross profit           $ 248925.00   Gross loss              $-139725.00

Total # of trades             258    Percent profitable              81%
Number winning trades         209    Number losing trades            49

Largest winning trade  $  13525.00   Largest losing trade    $  -3825.00
Average winning trade  $   1191.03   Average losing trade    $  -2851.53
Ratio avg win/avg loss        0.42   Avg trade(win & loss)   $    423.26

Max consec. winners            18    Max consec. losers               3
Avg # bars in winners           2    Avg # bars in losers             2

Max intraday drawdown  $ -13600.00
Profit factor                 1.78   Max # contracts held             1
Account size required  $  13600.00   Return on account             803%
```
— — — — — — — — — — — — — — — ‥
```
                Performance Summary:  Short Trades

Total net profit       $  57625.00   Open position P/L       $        0.00
Gross profit           $ 173975.00   Gross loss              $-116350.00

Total # of trades             134    Percent profitable              72%
Number winning trades          96    Number losing trades            38

Largest winning trade  $  39425.00   Largest losing trade    $  -5725.00
Average winning trade  $   1812.24   Average losing trade    $  -3061.84
Ratio avg win/avg loss        0.59   Avg trade(win & loss)   $    430.04

Max consec. winners            12    Max consec. losers               4
Avg # bars in winners           2    Avg # bars in losers             3

Max intraday drawdown  $ -19000.00
Profit factor                 1.50   Max # contracts held             1
Account size required  $  19000.00   Return on account             303%
```

Figure 8-5. Performance summary of the day-of-week system in S&P, 1982 to 1997.
(*Reprinted with permission of Omega Research.*)

```
      S&P 500 INDEX 55/99-Daily CME-Daily   11/03/97 - 08/31/99
                    Performance Summary:  All Trades

Total net profit       $   53325.00  Open position P/L    $       0.00
Gross profit           $  114650.00  Gross loss           $  -61325.00

Total # of trades              50    Percent profitable          78%
Number winning trades          39    Number losing trades         11

Largest winning trade  $   12675.00  Largest losing trade  $   -5575.00
Average winning trade  $    2939.74  Average losing trade  $   -5575.00
Ratio avg win/avg loss        0.53   Avg trade(win & loss) $    1066.50

Max consec. winners            10    Max consec. losers            2
Avg # bars in winners           2    Avg # bars in losers          2

Max intraday drawdown  $  -20950.00
Profit factor                 1.87   Max # contracts held          1
Account size required  $   20950.00  Return on account           255%
```

- - - -- -- - - ·· - ·

```
                    Performance Summary:  Long Trades

Total net profit       $   13825.00  Open position P/L    $       0.00
Gross profit           $   64000.00  Gross loss           $  -50175.00

Total # of trades              37    Percent profitable          76%
Number winning trades          28    Number losing trades          9

Largest winning trade  $   12675.00  Largest losing trade  $   -5575.00
Average winning trade  $    2285.71  Average losing trade  $   -5575.00
Ratio avg win/avg loss        0.41   Avg trade(win & loss) $     373.65

Max consec. winners             9    Max consec. losers            2
Avg # bars in winners           2    Avg # bars in losers          2

Max intraday drawdown  $  -25625.00
Profit factor                 1.28   Max # contracts held          1
Account size required  $   25625.00  Return on account            54%
```

- - · -- - - - - - - - - - - - - -- - - - - - - - - - - - - - - - - -- - · - · -

```
                    Performance Summary:  Short Trades

Total net profit       $   39500.00  Open position P/L    $       0.00
Gross profit           $   50650.00  Gross loss           $  -11150.00

Total # of trades              13    Percent profitable          85%
Number winning trades          11    Number losing trades          2

Largest winning trade  $   12425.00  Largest losing trade  $   -5575.00
Average winning trade  $    4604.55  Average losing trade  $   -5575.00
Ratio avg win/avg loss        0.83   Avg trade(win & loss) $    3038.46

Max consec. winners             5    Max consec. losers            1
Avg # bars in winners           2    Avg # bars in losers          1

Max intraday drawdown  $   -5575.00
Profit factor                 4.54   Max # contracts held          1
Account size required  $    5575.00  Return on account           709%
```

Figure 8-6. Performance summary of the day-of-week system in S&P, 1997 to 1999. (*Reprinted with permission of Omega Research.*)

```
            S&P 500 INDEX 55/99-Daily    04/21/82 - 10/31/97
                  Performance Summary:  All Trades

Total net profit        $ 142125.00   Open position P/L    $       0.00
Gross profit            $ 387250.00   Gross loss           $-245125.00

Total # of trades             384     Percent profitable           80%
Number winning trades         308     Number losing trades          76

Largest winning trade   $  11175.00   Largest losing trade  $  -7900.00
Average winning trade   $   1257.31   Average losing trade  $  -3225.33
Ratio avg win/avg loss         0.39   Avg trade(win & loss) $    370.12

Max consec. winners            17     Max consec. losers             5
Avg # bars in winners           2     Avg # bars in losers           3

Max intraday drawdown   $ -28225.00
Profit factor                  1.58   Max # contracts held           1
Account size required   $  28225.00   Return on account           504%
```

- -

```
                  Performance Summary:  Long Trades

Total net profit        $ 113400.00   Open position P/L    $       0.00
Gross profit            $ 246000.00   Gross loss           $-132600.00

Total # of trades             259     Percent profitable           83%
Number winning trades         216     Number losing trades          43

Largest winning trade   $   8025.00   Largest losing trade  $  -7900.00
Average winning trade   $   1138.89   Average losing trade  $  -3083.72
Ratio avg win/avg loss         0.37   Avg trade(win & loss) $    437.84

Max consec. winners            20     Max consec. losers             2
Avg # bars in winners           2     Avg # bars in losers           3

Max intraday drawdown   $ -15825.00
Profit factor                  1.86   Max # contracts held           1
Account size required   $  15825.00   Return on account           717%
```

- -

```
                  Performance Summary:  Short Trades

Total net profit        $  28725.00   Open position P/L    $       0.00
Gross profit            $ 141250.00   Gross loss           $-112525.00

Total # of trades             125     Percent profitable           74%
Number winning trades          92     Number losing trades          33

Largest winning trade   $  11175.00   Largest losing trade  $  -5075.00
Average winning trade   $   1535.33   Average losing trade  $  -3409.85
Ratio avg win/avg loss         0.45   Avg trade(win & loss) $    229.80

Max consec. winners            13     Max consec. losers             6
Avg # bars in winners           2     Avg # bars in losers           3

Max intraday drawdown   $ -35875.00
Profit factor                  1.26   Max # contracts held           1
Account size required   $  35875.00   Return on account            80%
```

Figure 8-7. Performance summary of the Wednesday-Thursday relationship in the day-of-week system in S&P, 1982 to 1997. (*Reprinted with permission of Omega Research.*)

The performance history in Figure 8-7 is based on a 6-tick penetration of Wednesday's high on Thursday and a 22-tick penetration of Wednesday's low on Thursday, with a $3850 stop loss.

Other Markets

I believe that the methodology presented for day-of-week-based trading using the paradigm just explained will also be applicable to other markets, such as bonds, currencies, and petroleum futures. Additional research should be conducted in these areas in order to determine the validity of the approach. In addition, the relationship should be tested on other stock index markets, such as FTSE, DAX, CAC-40, Hang Seng, and so on.

Inputs and Variables

The S&P day-of-week system uses the following input variables in generating signals:

- Day of week
- Penetration of high by x ticks
- Penetration of low by x ticks
- Exit on nth profitable opening
- Stop loss

In order to follow the procedures indicated here without a computer, the following steps should be observed. Given, however, the ultimate simplicity of this system, it should be tracked by computer, automatically generating signals for you as they occur.

- Check Friday open/close relationship in S&P 500.
- If the close on Friday is *greater than* the open on Friday, then a *buy* condition is set for Monday.
- If the close on Friday is *less than* the open on Friday, then a *sell* condition is set for Monday.
- If a *buy* condition is set, then on Monday *buy* on stop x ticks above the Friday high.
- If a *sell* condition is set, then on Monday *sell short* on stop x ticks below the Friday *low.*
- Exit either at the indicated *stop loss* or on the *first profitable opening.*

By *first profitable opening* I mean simply the first opening after you enter that gives you a profit compared to your entry price. This is a key element of the system since it forces high accuracy. Naturally, if you are stopped out first you cannot exit on the first profitable opening, since you are already out.

In time, these values may change slightly. Therefore, if you have TradeStation or ProSuites2001 you may wish to rerun the optimum values. If you do not have these programs, simply contact me and I will give you the new values. *Do not* overly optimize the suggested values. Although this will make the back-tested performance better, it will create a system that will look good on paper but will not go forward in time with similar results.

9

Two Breakout Systems

The Channel Break System: Short-Term Model

Breakout systems have been described in Chapter 6. The simple methodology here is that prices move in ranges, and when these ranges are penetrated by a given amount, then the market is likely to make a move in the direction of the breakout. These are essentially simple systems that are designed to follow trends when they begin and to stay generally on the sidelines when a market is trendless. Although they do not always accomplish this goal, they tend to do well in the more active markets, such as the financials and stock index futures markets. Breakout systems are not only logical but are highly applicable to today's volatile markets. Furthermore, they are extremely simple to implement and yield consistent results in active markets.

The channel break approach to price breakout trading is a variation on the theme originally presented by Keltner in the 1960s. The concept is simply to buy when prices exceed a given price level or to sell when prices fall below a given price level. The price level is most often either the high or the low of the last x number of days. In the case of short-term trading that uses intraday data, penetration would be on x number of price bars as opposed to days. Furthermore, there are three types of channel break methods, as follows:

- *Channel break on close.* This approach buys on a closing penetration of the high of the last x number of bars. It sells on a close below the low of the last x number of bars.

- *Intrabar channel break.* This approach is the same as the previous method; however, it buys and sells on any intraday or intrabar penetration, as opposed to waiting for the close.

■ *Channel break percentage penetration.* This method is a variation of volatility breakout. This approach requires a breakout above the high of *x* bars by a given amount and likewise below the low of X bars.

Finally, the number of bars penetration for a buy signal and the number of bars penetration for a sell signal need not be the same, since markets are not linear. In other words, since markets tend to go down much faster then they tend to go up, the number of bars penetration to trigger a sell should be shorter than the number of bars penetration to trigger a buy.

This is the approach that I used in developing the channel break system for short-term trading. In addition, the method employs the usual dollar risk stop management and trailing stop procedure. This approach can be used by the e-trader for short-term market swings in active markets such as S&P futures. Figure 9-1 shows an intraday S&P chart with the channel break sell and buy signals.

Note that the channel break indicator used is intrabar as written in Omega TradeStation els code. The following parameters apply to this system as developed:

■ Stop loss short exit: $2900

■ Stop loss long exit: $3400

■ Bars of low: 12

■ Bars of high: 8

■ Floor level: $1500

■ Percent trailing stop: 90

■ Period covered: January 27, 1998, to March 18, 1999, 60-minute data

Figure 9-2 shows the system report for the channel breakout method. As you can see, the results are highly impressive. Over a span of 136 trades, covering 14 months of a highly volatile S&P market, the system generated 75 percent overall accuracy with an amazing 83 percent accuracy and nearly $1400 per average trade on long positions. The average trade on all positions was more than $1030, also extremely good. These results were based on only $9275 in drawdown. On the short side, the system was also profitable 66 percent of the time, with more than $532 per average trade on short positions.

This method, although optimized, has not been overly optimized and should continue to work well in the future. However, I recommend checking the variables from time to time to make certain that they are correctly optimized. Furthermore, different time frames should also produce good results.

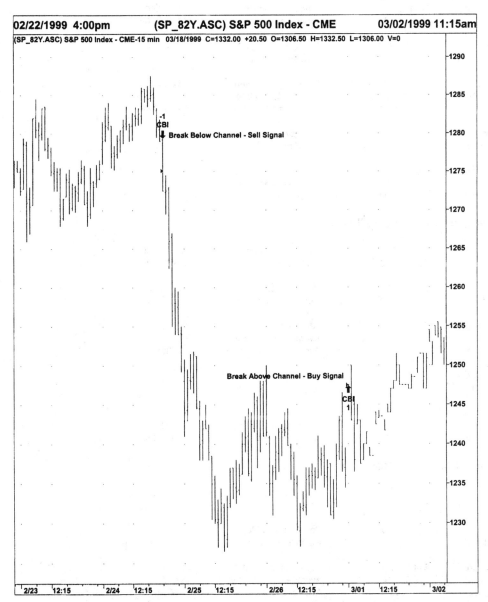

Figure 9-1. Channel break signals on an intraday S&P chart. *(TradeStation chart © 1999 Omega Research, Inc.)*

Assets and Liabilities

The channel break method is not only simple to understand and apply, it is also easy to program, simple to test, and highly effective, as you can see from the foregoing analysis. Based on the performance history and reasonable drawdown, the only realistic liability of this approach is the possibility

Performance Summary: All Trades

Total Net Profit	$140,200.00	Open position P/L	$3,125.00
Gross Profit	$216,700.00	Gross Loss	($76,500.00)
Total # of trades	136	Percent profitable	75.00%
Number winning trades	102	Number losing trades	34
Largest winning trade	$14,750.00	Largest losing trade	($4,850.00)
Average winning trade	$2,124.51	Average losing trade	($2,250.00)
Ratio avg win/avg loss	0.94	Avg trade (win & loss)	$1,030.88
Max consec. Winners	13	Max consec. losers	3
Avg # bars in winners	14	Avg # bars in losers	5
Max intraday drawdown	($9,275.00)		
Profit Factor	2.83	Max # contracts held	1
Account size required	$9,275.00	Return on account	1511.59%

Performance Summary: Long Trades

Total Net Profit	$99,100.00	Open position P/L	$3,125.00
Gross Profit	$127,800.00	Gross Loss	($28,700.00)
Total # of trades	71	Percent profitable	83.00%
Number winning trades	59	Number losing trades	12
Largest winning trade	$14,400.00	Largest losing trade	($4,850.00)
Average winning trade	$2,166.10	Average losing trade	($2,391.67)
Ratio avg win/avg loss	0.91	Avg trade (win & loss)	$1,395.77
Max consec. Winners	16	Max consec. losers	2
Avg # bars in winners	17	Avg # bars in losers	6
Max intraday drawdown	($9,825.00)		
Profit Factor	4.45	Max # contracts held	1
Account size required	$9,825.00	Return on account	1008.65%

Performance Summary: Short Trades

Total Net Profit	$41,100.00	Open position P/L	$0.00
Gross Profit	$88,900.00	Gross Loss	($47,800.00)
Total # of trades	65	Percent profitable	66.00%
Number winning trades	43	Number losing trades	22
Largest winning trade	$14,750.00	Largest losing trade	($3,125.00)
Average winning trade	$2,067.44	Average losing trade	($2,172.73)
Ratio avg win/avg loss	0.95	Avg trade (win & loss)	$632.31
Max consec. Winners	6	Max consec. losers	3
Avg # bars in winners	11	Avg # bars in losers	4
Max intraday drawdown	($12,550.00)		
Profit Factor	1.86	Max # contracts held	1
Account size required	$12,550.00	Return on account	327.49%

Figure 9-2. Channel break method system report using 60-minute S&P data. *(TradeStation system report using Omega Research Portfolio Maximizer Version 5.0.)*

Performance Summary: All Trades

Total Net Profit	$83,100.00	Open position P/L	$3,850.00
Gross Profit	$184,175.00	Gross Loss	($101,075.00)
Total # of trades	72	Percent profitable	72.00%
Number winning trades	52	Number losing trades	20
Largest winning trade	$36,550.00	Largest losing trade	($12,150.00)
Average winning trade	$3,541.83	Average losing trade	($5,053.75)
Ratio avg win/avg loss	0.70	Avg trade (win & loss)	$1,154.17
Max consec. Winners	9	Max consec. losers	2
Avg # bars in winners	28	Avg # bars in losers	15
Max intraday drawdown	($30,000.00)		
Profit Factor	1.82	Max # contracts held	1
Account size required	$30,000.00	Return on account	277.00%

Performance Summary: Long Trades

Total Net Profit	$58,775.00	Open position P/L	$3,850.00
Gross Profit	$120,450.00	Gross Loss	($61,675.00)
Total # of trades	40	Percent profitable	75.00%
Number winning trades	30	Number losing trades	10
Largest winning trade	$36,550.00	Largest losing trade	($12,150.00)
Average winning trade	$4,015.00	Average losing trade	($6,167.50)
Ratio avg win/avg loss	0.65	Avg trade (win & loss)	$1,469.38
Max consec. Winners	6	Max consec. losers	2
Avg # bars in winners	35	Avg # bars in losers	15
Max intraday drawdown	($26,350.00)		
Profit Factor	1.95	Max # contracts held	1
Account size required	$26,350.00	Return on account	223.06%

Performance Summary: Short Trades

Total Net Profit	$24,325.00	Open position P/L	$0.00
Gross Profit	$63,725.00	Gross Loss	($39,400.00)
Total # of trades	32	Percent profitable	69.00%
Number winning trades	22	Number losing trades	10
Largest winning trade	$24,450.00	Largest losing trade	($11,475.00)
Average winning trade	$2,896.59	Average losing trade	($3,940.00)
Ratio avg win/avg loss	0.74	Avg trade (win & loss)	$760.16
Max consec. Winners	6	Max consec. losers	2
Avg # bars in winners	19	Avg # bars in losers	15
Max intraday drawdown	($18,625.00)		
Profit Factor	1.62	Max # contracts held	1
Account size required	$18,625.00	Return on account	130.60%

Figure 9-3. Breakout system historical summary. *(TradeStation system report using Omega Research Portfolio Maximizer Version 5.0.)*

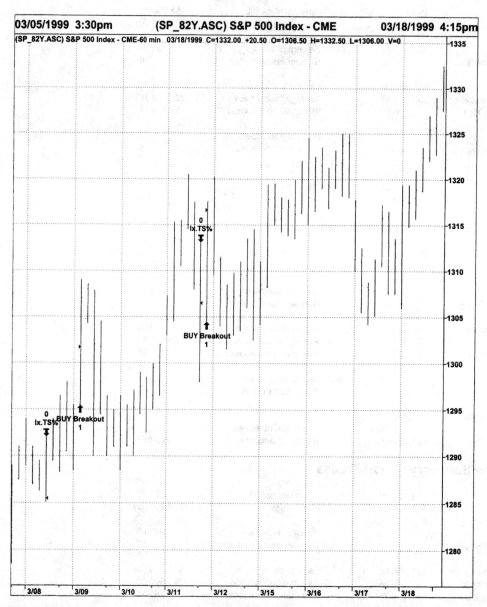

Figure 9-4. Intraday chart with breakout signals. (*TradeStation chart © 1999 Omega Research, Inc.*)

of false signals if a market becomes trendless. In such cases, numerous false breakouts are likely.

The Range Breakout System

To a certain extent, this approach is similar to the channel breakout system just described; however, it trades less frequently and produces essentially similar results, but with slightly lower accuracy. This method is also applicable to daily price data, with excellent results. The range breakout method is essentially a volatility breakout system that buys or sells on a penetration above or below the true range of a give number of price bars.

The parameters used to generate the results in Figure 9-3 are as follows:

- Number of bars in volatility window: 15
- Percentage penetration: 96
- Momentum filter: 21 bars
- Floor level: $2200
- Percent trailing stop: 74

Figure 9-4 shows an intraday chart with the breakout signals and stop loss follow-ups. The historical summary (Figure 9-3) shows an overall accuracy of 72 percent, with more than $1154 per average trade from November 2, 1997, through March 18, 1999, on hourly data. Both systems can be used for e-trading.

10

Two Support and Resistance Methods

Computerized Short-Term Trading with Support and Resistance

Perhaps one of the most effective ways to trade for the short term is by using support and resistance methods. The various approaches to using support and resistance all involve an essentially similar approach. The approach consists of two aspects. The first aspect requires an evaluation of the current *trend*, while the second aspect involves the determination of support and resistance.

In a market that is in an uptrend, the day trader will want to buy at support (as defined). In a market that is in a downtrend, the short-term trader will want to go short at resistance. These procedures are self-evident. The key issues here are severalfold, as follows:

- How is the trend determined?
- How can the short-term trader know when the trend is changing?
- How can support be objectively determined in an uptrend?
- How can resistance be objectively determined in a downtrend?
- How can the short-term trader know when the market is essentially trendless and thereby not suitable for short-term trading using support and resistance methods?

The Traditional Method

The traditional method for determining support, resistance, and trend was, for many years, the domain of the chartist. Using methods that had been developed over the course of many years, the chartist employed paper charts, either hand drawn or commercially published, to find a variety of chart patterns that purportedly would give clues as to market direction, strength, weakness, and potential changes in trend, support, and resistance.

While these methods had their heyday from the 1950s through as late as the mid-1980s, the growth of computerized trading has given rise to a host of mathematical models that appear to give better results. Furthermore, the methods of old are more subject to interpretation than are the more operationalized methods in use today. Bear in mind that there are still many e-traders traders who find the traditional methods helpful and who use them daily.

Most trading software programs contain tools that allow the user to draw and highlight various chart formations. These methods are not discussed here, inasmuch as *they are subject to individual interpretation and, therefore, are not easily taught.* They are perhaps as much art as they are science. Several traders looking at the same information could easily reach several different conclusions.

However, the methods discussed in this chapter are primarily objective and easily defined in operational terms so that they may be readily duplicated by other traders. While objectivity does not necessarily lead to profits or 100 percent agreement among traders, it does go a long way toward formalizing procedures. And formalized procedures will be reproducible, as well as ultimately profitable, provided that the underlying assumptions of the approach are correct.

Determining the Trend

The first issue that confronts the short-term e-trader, whether in stocks or commodities, is to determine the existing trend. There are many methods for doing so. Ultimately, traders will have their pet methods; however, it is not the method so much as how it is used that is important in the final analysis. I could write an entire book on methods that are valid approaches to determining trends and changes in trends.

This book, however, discusses only those that I feel have better potential for profit in short-term time frames. Note that the indicators discussed are my favorites but certainly not the only ones you can employ for the purpose of determining trend and trend changes. You could, in fact, use virtually any method that is sensitive enough to detect a change in the intraday trend as well as reliable enough to correctly define the trend as either up, down, or sideways.

For the purpose of this approach, trend is defined by using a 14-period momentum. If momentum is positive and has been so *for at least two consec-*

utive postings, then the trend is defined as up. If momentum is negative and has been so *for at least two consecutive postings,* then trend is defined as down. Once the trend has been so defined, we can employ support and resistance as the buy and sell method. Figure 10-1 shows 14-period momentum trends.

After Defining the Trend

Once the trend has been defined there are essentially two issues. The first issue is whether to take a position using timing alone (i.e., the cross above or below zero) or to take a position based on a support and resistance method. In actuality, both methods could be employed; however, if the trader wishes to use only support and resistance, then the crossing of momentum above or below zero will be only the first step in the procedure. The next step is to define support and resistance levels.

The method I prefer for accomplishing this purpose is to use a moving average of lows for support and a moving average of highs for determining resistance. Remember that *in order to use this method, there must be sufficient market volatility to make the game worthwhile.* There are only several commodity markets that make large enough intraday moves to allow for sufficient profit potential in trading support and resistance methods on an intraday basis.

On the other hand, there are many stocks that offer sufficient opportunities for such moves. And this is one of the reasons that many traders have been attracted to stocks for the purpose of day trading. Yet, futures markets such as S&P, T-bonds, some of the petroleum markets, and some of the currency markets offer excellent opportunities. As a rule, the higher-tick-value futures markets are the ones that will be viable using this approach.

The 3/3 High/Low Channel

The method I suggest is to use a three-period intraday moving average of the high and the low. The computerized short-term trader will find this method easily available on most software systems. The rules of application are simple. Remember that the *shorter* the time frame you use (i.e., 50-minute, 20-minute, 10-minute), the *more* signals you will get and the *smaller* the price moves will be.

Your job is to determine the optimum frame as a function of market volatility. The moving average length I recommend is three units of the high and three units of the low. To some traders this will be reminiscent of my

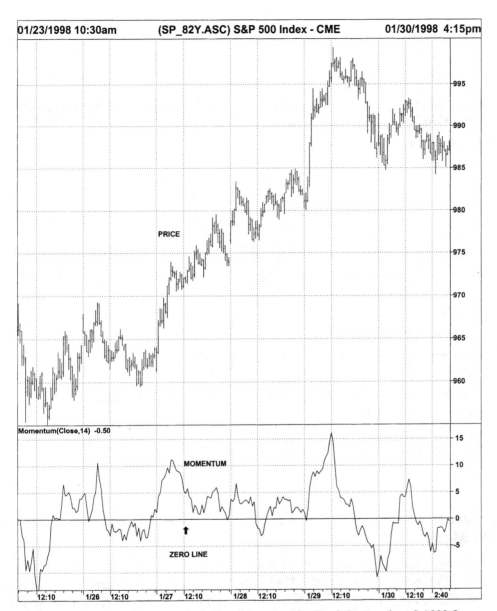

Figure 10-1. 14-period momentum bull and bear trends. *(TradeStation chart © 1999 Omega Research, Inc.)*

10/8 moving average channel, but I assure you it is very different in its application. Figure 10-2 illustrates the 3/3 channel on an intraday chart showing support and resistance.

The rules are as follows:

- If momentum has been above the zero line for at least two postings, then the trend is considered up.
- If the trend is up, then buy at support.
- *Support* is defined as the three-period moving average of lows.
- If you buy at support, take profit at resistance.
- Use a stop loss that is 100 percent of the average of the last 3 trading ranges—close only.
- *Resistance* is defined as the three-period moving average of the highs.
- If you buy at support and exit at resistance and the trend as defined is still up, then place another order to buy at support and repeat the same procedure.
- Do the opposite for sell signals.
- Do not trade signals that occur close to the end of the trading day, since there will not be enough time for a profit to be made.
- Be out of all trades by the end of the day, win, lose, or draw.

As noted earlier, longer time frames give larger moves and fewer trades. Figures 10-3 through 10-6 show how this method works. Support, resistance, entries, and exits are marked accordingly.

The Momentum and Moving Average (MOM/MA) Method

A more sensitive approach to this methodology is to use the momentum and its moving average (MOM/MA) for the purpose of determining timing. Generally, this approach will show a change in trend faster than will momentum alone. When momentum crosses above its own moving average, an uptrend is signaled, and when momentum crosses below its moving average, a downtrend is indicated.

This method is also viable as a buy and sell method; however, in the current application it is used simply for determining when the trend of a market has changed so that the 3/3 channel may be employed as a means of

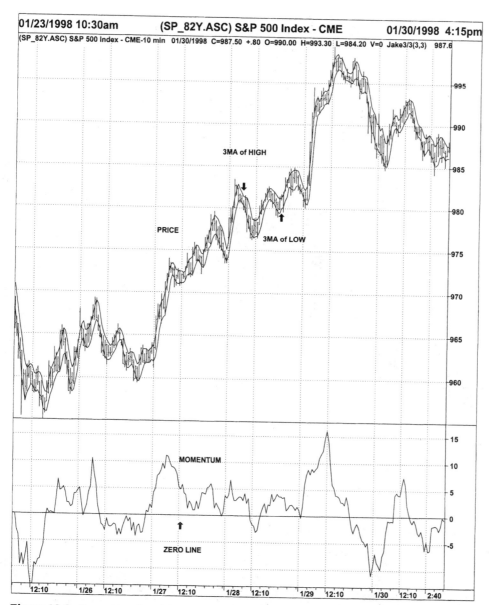

Figure 10-2. Support and resistance using the 3/3 high/low channel method. *(TradeStation chart © 1999 Omega Research, Inc.)*

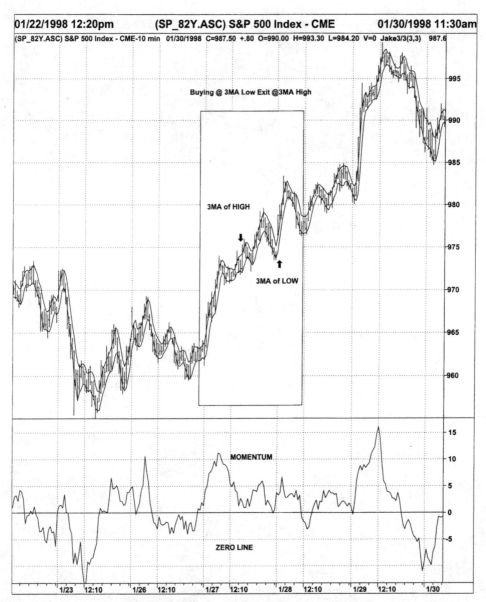

Figure 10-3. Momentum and 3/3 channel on an intraday S&P chart. Momentum was positive during the highlighted period; as a result, longs would have been taken at 3MA of low and closed out at 3MA of high. *(TradeStation chart © 1999 Omega Research, Inc.)*

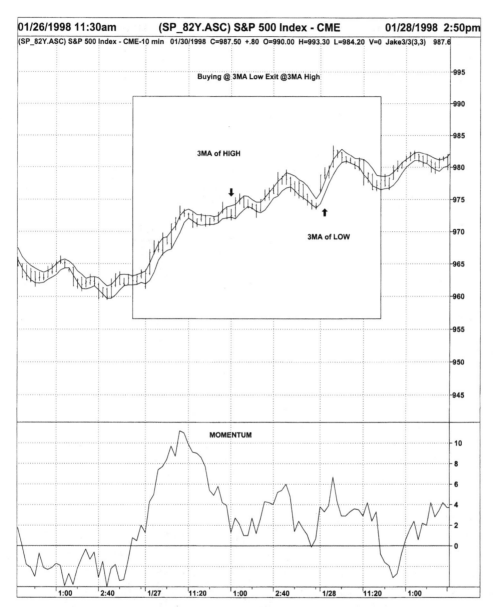

Figure 10-4. Momentum and 3/3 channel on a close-up intraday S&P chart. This is a closer look at the chart segment shown in Figure 10-3. Note at least seven signals. *(TradeStation chart © 1999 Omega Research, Inc.)*

01/28/1998 10:30am   (SP_82Y.ASC) S&P 500 Index - CME   01/30/1998 4:15pm

(SP_82Y.ASC) S&P 500 Index - CME-10 min 01/30/1998 C=987.50 +.80 O=990.00 H=993.30 L=984.20 V=0 Jake3/3(3,3) 987.6

3MA of HIGH

3MA of LOW

Selling 3MA High Exit 3MA Low

Figure 10-5. Momentum and 3/3 channel on a close-up intraday S&P chart, showing a closer view of 3/3 sell signals during a negative momentum period. *(TradeStation chart © 1999 Omega Research, Inc.)*

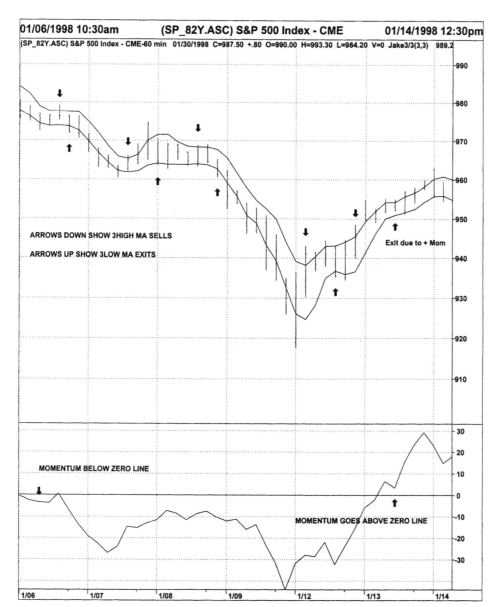

01/06/1998 10:30am   (SP_82Y.ASC) S&P 500 Index - CME   01/14/1998 12:30pm

(SP_82Y.ASC) S&P 500 Index - CME-60 min 01/30/1998 C=987.50 +.80 O=990.00 H=993.30 L=984.20 V=0 Jake3/3(3,3)   989.2

ARROWS DOWN SHOW 3HIGH MA SELLS

ARROWS UP SHOW 3LOW MA EXITS

Exit due to + Mom

MOMENTUM BELOW ZERO LINE

MOMENTUM GOES ABOVE ZERO LINE

Figure 10-6. Momentum and 3/3 channel on a close-up intraday S&P chart, showing actual market entry and exit points. Down arrows show sells, whereas up arrows show exits of short positions. *(TradeStation chart © 1999 Omega Research, Inc.)*

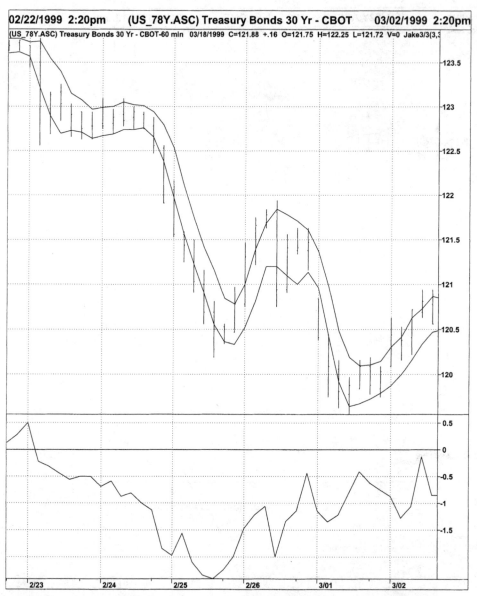

02/22/1999 2:20pm   (US_78Y.ASC) Treasury Bonds 30 Yr - CBOT   03/02/1999 2:20pm

(US_78Y.ASC) Treasury Bonds 30 Yr - CBOT-60 min   03/18/1999 C=121.88 +.16 O=121.75 H=122.25 L=121.72 V=0 Jake3/3(3,3

Figure 10-7. Example of the 3/3 channel sells with bearish momentum. *(TradeStation chart © 1999 Omega Research, Inc.)*

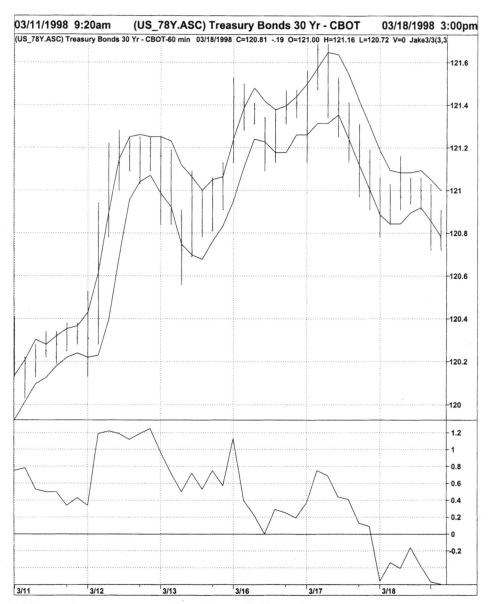

Figure 10-8. Example of the 3/3 channel buys with bullish momentum. *(TradeStation chart © 1999 Omega Research, Inc.)*

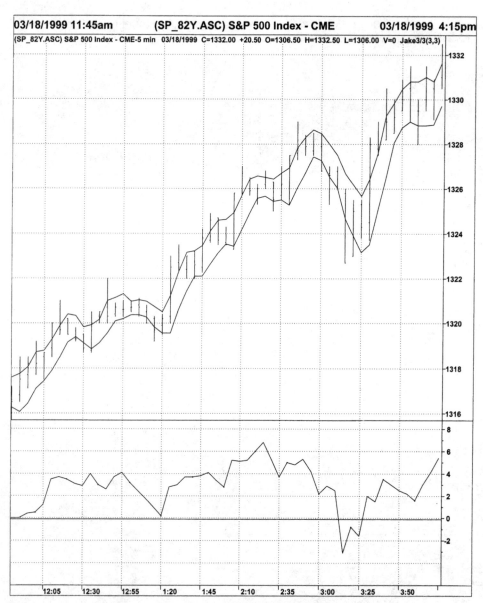

Figure 10-9. Example of the 3/3 channel buys with bullish momentum. *(TradeStation chart © 1999 Omega Research, Inc.)*

buying at support and selling at resistance, or vice versa. This method is also applicable to the computerized short-term and day trading of stocks.

Numerous Trades

Due to the short-term nature of this approach, it is possible—indeed, highly likely—that the day trader, whether in stocks or commodities, will have many opportunities to buy and sell. It must be remembered, above all, that these opportunities must have a sufficiently large profit potential to make the game worthwhile. The day trader must always be cognizant that there are costs involved in trading.

Do not confuse the *quantity* of trades with the *quality* of trades. You are far better off having 2 highly profitable day trades than 15 marginal or poor trades. Because you will need to exit by the end of the day, your trades must have sufficient profit potential to make them worthwhile.

Conclusions

The use of momentum or MOM/MA for determining the trend combined with the 3/3 channel can be an effective method for intraday and short-term trading in stocks and commodities. This chapter outlines the methodology, provides some specific examples, and lists a few caveats that must be considered when trading this approach.

Due to its intensive nature, it is a method that is well suited for the computerized day trader, since numerous trades and signals are possible during any given day. The art of the science is to have enough day trades to yield a profit but not so many as to result in more heat than light.

Examples and Illustrations

Figures 10-7 through 10-9 illustrate a few more examples of the 3/3 channel method on various intraday charts.

Caveats

The 3/3 channel method is not a trading system per se. It is a method that will work well for you if you use it carefully and in active markets only. The method is designed for short-term trading on daily data; however, it could be used on intraday data in active markets with large trading ranges.

11
Trading Example: The MOM/MA

As noted in Chapter 10, another method of using momentum is by combining it with its moving average (MA). The method is simple. When the 28-period momentum crosses above its 28-period MA for at least 2 consecutive closes, a buy is triggered. Sell signals occur on the opposite configuration. The best way to illustrate this method (note that this is not a system) is with a series of actual signals.

This chapter provides a running synopsis of an S&P short-term trade using the momentum and moving average (MOM/MA) method just described. In this case, the inputs used were a 28-period momentum and a 28-period moving average of the momentum. The time frame used was 1-minute S&P 500 data.

Figure 11-1 shows 1-minute S&P data with the MOM/MA indicator. Toward the end of the hour, from 9 to 10 A.M., a sell signal occurred. The arrow pointing up shows the sell signal at that time. The sell signal was triggered at approximately 1333.

Thereafter, a buy signal was triggered, and the trade was closed out at about 1332 and reversed to long. This was followed by another sell signal at approximately 1328 (see Figure 11-2).

The short position was then closed out at approximately 1329 and reversed to long (see Figure 11-3).

Figures 11-4, 11-5, and 11-6 show the subsequent signals through the end of the day using this approach.

Figures 11-7 and 11-8 show similar signals in NASDAQ futures. Figure 11-9 shows signals on 5-minute T-bond futures.

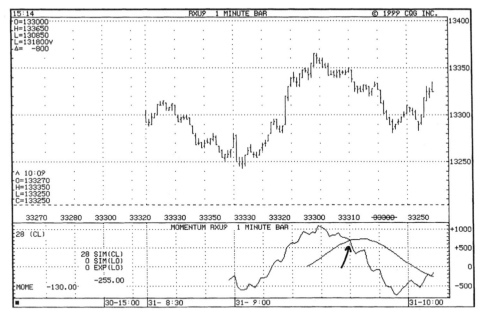

Figure 11-1. Sell signal in S&P. *(Chart copyright © 1999 CQG Inc.)*

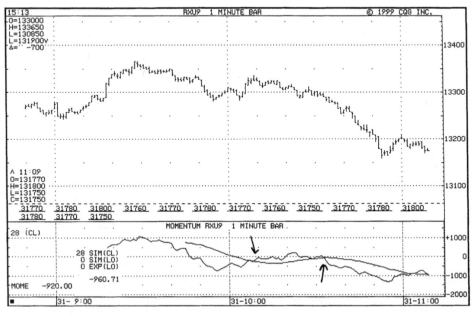

Figure 11-2. Reversal back to buy signal and subsequent sell signal in S&P. *(Chart copyright © 1999 CQG Inc.)*

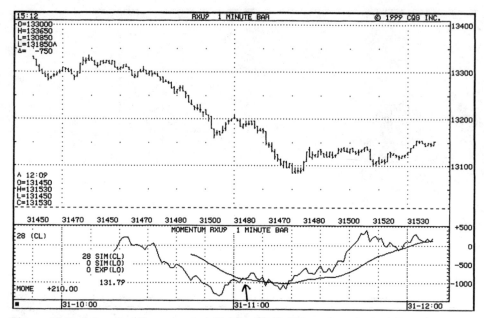

Figure 11-3. Subsequent buy signal at 11:00 in S&P. *(Chart copyright © 1999 CQG Inc.)*

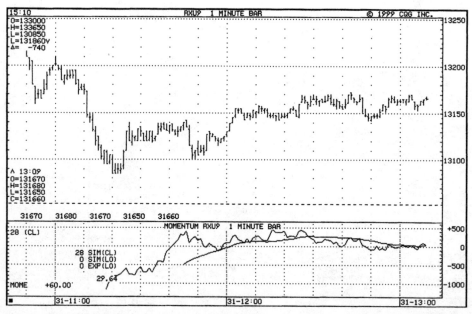

Figure 11-4. Subsequent sell signal at about midday in S&P. *(Chart copyright © 1999 CQG Inc.)*

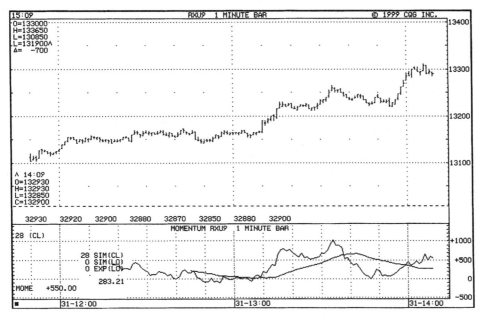

Figure 11-5. Signals in S&P during the 13:00 to 14:00 time frame. *(Chart copyright © 1999 CQG Inc.)*

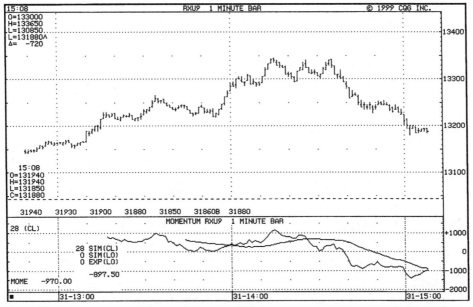

Figure 11-6. Subsequent signals in S&P during the 14:00 to 15:00 time frame. *(Chart copyright © 1999 CQG Inc.)*

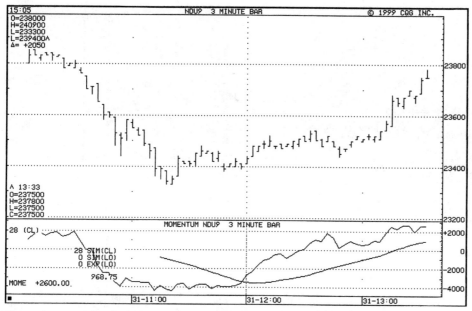

Figure 11-7. Buy signal in NASDAQ futures at the end of the 11:00 hour. *(Chart copyright © 1999 CQG Inc.)*

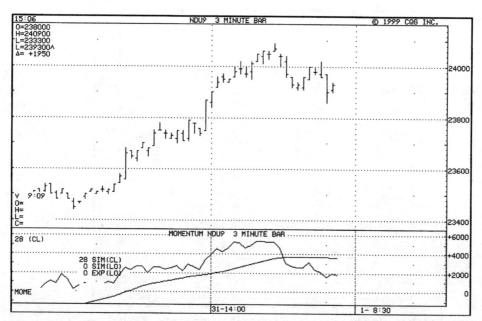

Figure 11-8. Sell signal in NASDAQ futures during the 14:00 hour. *(Chart copyright © 1999 CQG Inc.)*

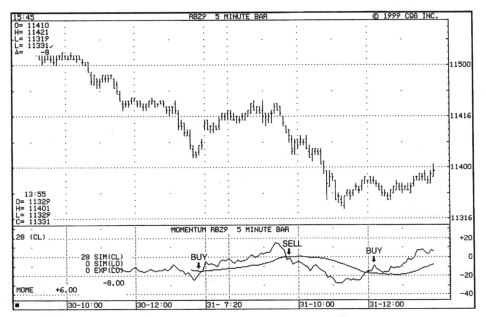

Figure 11-9. Signals in 5-minute T-bond futures using MOM/MA. *(Chart copyright © 1999 CQG Inc.)*

12

Additional Methods
and Issues

In addition to the indicators, systems, and methods already discussed, there are a number of other issues that deserve consideration. These are reviewed in this chapter.

Systems, Methods, Indicators, and Techniques: Similarities and Differences

One of the problems often encountered by traders is that they fail to implement their trading systems consistently and/or effectively. There are many reasons for this, not the least of which are psychological. But in part, one of the major reasons is that traders tend to misunderstand the similarities and differences between a trading system, a timing indicator, a trading method, and a trading technique. The explanations that follow may assist you in understanding some of the similarities and differences among these trading approaches.

Timing Indicators

A timing indicator does exactly what its name suggests. It indicates timing in the market. It answers the questions, "Is it time to buy? Is it time to sell? Is it time to go short? Is it time to cover a short position? Is it time to enter a spread? Is it time to exit a spread?" A timing indicator that works is an excellent tool to have at your disposal. However, do *not* confuse a timing indicator with a trading system. A timing indicator is only one part of a trading system. And it may not necessarily be the most important part of the system.

Therefore, if you're trading the markets with timing indicators only, you may find that *timing indicators alone are often not enough to keep you in a profitable position* when all is said and done. In order to achieve their full efficacy, timing indicators must also include a system for managing losses when they are wrong and for exiting profitable trades either at an objective, on an opposite signal, or on a trailing stop-loss procedure. Moving averages, stochastics, RSI, accumulation/distribution, ADX, and DMI, are all examples of timing indicators. It should be noted that many timing indicators look good on paper; however, they lose their reliability when subjected to the acid test of trading with stops and other risk management methods.

Trading Methods

A trading method usually consists of several timing indicators that are applied in unison, or of one timing indicator that includes with it a set of application rules that are often, but not always, objective. A trading method is somewhat more complicated than a timing indicator. It is often based on a particular market theory or analysis method.

For example, the Elliott wave can be considered as a trading method. It provides buy and sell indications, but it must be interpreted by the application of trading rules. Some Elliott wave analysts and theorists have highly objective rules, while others have subjective rules. Gann analysis and Fibonacci analysis can also be used as trading methods. Candlesticks can be used as a trading method, and so can point and figure charting. All of these must contain specific methods of risk management in order to be elevated to the status of a trading system. However, they will not rank as trading systems unless they have objective rules that are not subject to interpretation.

Analytical Methods

An analytical method consists of various inputs that allow the analyst to determine the strength, weakness, trend, price objective, or anticipated direction of a market. By studying a variety of inputs, the market analyst will arrive at a conclusion or at a series of conclusions or at an "if-then" scenario for a given market or markets.

Such analytical approaches often yield forecasts and suggestions as to which side of a market one should trade. They may also include a general idea of risk and reward; however, they rarely include specific recommendations to enter or exit at certain prices, and they do not include any risk management rules or recommendations (other than general ones at best).

Trading Systems

This is the highest and most specific level of market approaches. A trading system provides the following features that make it preferable to any of the approaches cited previously:

- It contains purely objective rules for market entry and exit.
- It contains risk management rules such as stop loss, trailing stop loss, and so on.
- It tells you which markets to trade and when to trade them.
- It can be back-tested using the indicated rules in order to test its validity.
- Its signals are not subject to interpretation—they are operational and repeatable.
- Historical back-testing performance provides key statistics and hypothetical results.
- Different traders should be able to get exactly the same signals using similar inputs.

There are other fine details that characterize a trading system; however, the ones just indicated are the most salient. Clearly, the good news about trading systems is that they can be implemented specifically and without interpretation. The bad news is that many traders are unable to follow a trading system due to their lack of discipline. They would much rather wallow in subjective indicators than have the self-confidence and self-discipline to trade a mechanical system.

The Current Trend

While totally mechanical trading systems were popular in the 1970s, 1980s, and early 1990s, there are many professional traders who have recently turned away from such systems in favor of trading methods. They feel that human input is vital in making trading decisions.

It should also be noted that the recent trend toward neural networks (i.e., artificial intelligence) often takes many different technical indicators and timing signals into account when developing a smart system that is likely to go forward in time with good results. This is not necessarily a negative thing; however, it does tend to test the resolve and self-discipline of the analyst.

For the newcomer to trading, I think that a trading system approach is often the best thing. But remember that trading systems will require you to be consistent, thorough, and disciplined.

System Testing and Optimization: Friend or Foe?

The days of untested systems are gone forever. In fact, the pendulum is now swinging in the other direction. While unscrupulous operators in the days of old sold systems and methods for which they claimed fantastic results, today's unethical operators use *statistics* as a tool of deception.

These individuals—who, paradoxically, will benefit from the trend toward the statistical validation of systems—can easily dupe the public. Manipulating statistics is not difficult. Just as Archimedes once said, "Give me a place to stand on and I can move the earth," the modern systems promoter would likely say, "Give me enough statistics and I can prove anything."

This sermonette on system validation makes the point that merely testing a system and generating highly favorable hypothetical results does not guarantee success with that system. Nor should such statistics be used as a security blanket or crutch by traders. Statistics can easily be manipulated, systems can be (and are) curve-fitted, and results, unless realistic, will not reflect actual performance when the system is implemented. While many systems are developed to show optimum performance, it is imperative that systems be tested to show the worst-case performance. This is especially important to the e-trader.

Why Test Trading Systems?

Traders test systems for various reasons. Some test a system merely to say they've done so, only to disregard the outcome or to accept mediocre results, rationalizing the negative aspects of their "system." Other traders test systems in order to sell them to the public—their goal is to optimize systems in order to show maximum performance. Then there's the serious futures trader who tests systems to achieve several goals, including but not limited to the following:

- To determine whether a theory or hypothetical construct is valid in historical testing
- To summarize the overall hypothetical performance of a system and to analyze its various aspects in order to isolate its strong and weak points
- To determine how different timing indicators interact with one another to produce an effective trading system

■ To explore the interaction of risk and reward variables (i.e., stop loss, trailing stop loss, position size, etc.) that would have returned the best overall performance with the smallest drawdown

Testing Your Trading System

While it may seem that the last item in the preceding list refers to optimization, you will see from the discussion of optimization later in this chapter that it is not optimization according to my definition of the term. The purpose of testing systems is simply to find what will work best for you, based on what appears to have worked best in the past. In so doing, you must remember that what worked in the past in hypothetical testing may not necessarily work in the future.

A thorough test of your trading system should include at least the following information:

Number of Years Analyzed. Although it is desirable to test as much data as possible, many trading systems and indicators do not withstand the test of time. The farther back you test, the less effective most systems will be. Many system developers test only 10 years of historical data since that best shows their systems. You must make your own decision regarding the length of your test.

Number of Trades Analyzed. More important than the number of years analyzed is the number of trades. You need not analyze many years of data if you have a large sample size of trades. I recommend at least 100 trades, provided your system will generate this number of trades in back-testing. If you are truly interested in determining the effectiveness of your system, the more trades you test the better. Remember that there will always be a tendency to test fewer trades when you realize that the system is not holding up under back-testing.

Some traders argue that the factors underlying futures market trends 25 years ago were distinctly different from those during the past 10 years. They feel that testing 25 years of data distorts the picture. If they are correct, how would we know when the current market forces change and that we must therefore change our trading systems? We are much better off finding systems that work in all types of markets.

Maximum Drawdown. This is one of the most important aspects of a trading system. A very large drawdown is a negative factor, since it eliminates most traders from the game well before the system would have turned in its positive performance. Since most traders are not well capitalized, they cannot withstand a large drawdown. However, drawdown is a function of account size. Obviously, a $15,000 drawdown in a $100,000 account is not unusual; however, the same drawdown in a $35,000 account is serious. You may decide to risk large drawdown in order to achieve outstanding performance, but this is your decision.

Consider also the source of the drawdown by examining the largest losing trade. If the majority of the drawdown occurred on only one trade, you would be better off than if the drawdown were spread out over numerous successive losses.

Maximum Consecutive Losses. This performance variable is more psychological than anything else is. An otherwise excellent trading system may have lost money on many trades in succession. Few traders can maintain their discipline through four or more successive losing trades. Even after the third loss, many traders are ready to either abandon their system or find ways of changing it.

However, at times it is necessary to weather the storm of 10 or more successive losses. If you know ahead of time what the worst-case scenario has been, you will be prepared. That's why it's important for your system test to give you this information.

Largest Single Losing Trade. This important piece of information indicates how much of the maximum drawdown is the result of a single losing trade. And this allows you to adjust the initial stop loss in retesting the system so as to see how large the average losing trade has been. If the average losing trade, for example, was $1055, and the largest single loser was $8466, you can readily see that a good portion of the average losing trade was a function of the largest loser. This shows that if you had had a better way of managing the largest loser (in hindsight, of course), your overall system performance would have been considerably better.

I strongly recommend close examination of the trade that resulted in the single largest loss if this loss is clearly much higher than the average losing trade. Another question to ask is why the largest single losing trade was so much larger than the stop loss selected. A single largest losing trade that is several times larger than your selected stop loss points to a potential problem, perhaps with the system test. You must investigate further in such cases.

Largest Single Winning Trade. Perhaps more important than the largest single losing trade is the largest single winning trade. If, for example, your hypothetical profits total $96,780, and $33,810 of this is attributed to only one trade, you have a distorted average trade figure. It's often a good idea to remove this one trade from the overall results and recompute them in order to show the performance without this extraordinary winner.

You may find that the system you have tested is mediocre, perhaps even a loser, when the single largest trade has been eliminated from the performance summary. If you can wait 10 years for the one big trade, then use the system—but do so against my advice. What you're looking for in any system with regard to average winning and losing trades is consistency—far more important than one or two extremely large winning trades that give a distorted performance picture.

On occasion, only two trades may account for a considerable portion of the net system profits. While some traders feel that this somehow diminishes the value of the system, I disagree. As long as at least one-half of the overall system performance is due to trades other than the largest single winning long and short trade combined, the system is valid. As far as numbers are concerned, I would not use any system that, after deducting reasonable slippage and commission as well as the largest single long and short winners, does not show at least $100 average profit per trade.

More important, because a large portion of profits in many systems derives from a very small number of trades, it is imperative that you follow each and every trade as closely to the rules as possible. Trading systems are not money machines; they don't grind out one profit after another. Trading systems make their money on the bottom line. There are many losers and few winners. The losers are kept in check by using money management stop losses that must, in most cases, be reasonably large.

And the winners, only a few of which are very large, make the game worth the candle. The trader who can't stick with a position, or let it ride, is the trader who will be sorely disappointed with the results, because the big winners will be cut short.

Percentage of Winning Trades.   This statistic is not nearly as important as one might think. In actuality, few systems have more than 65 percent winning trades, and the more trades in your sample, the smaller this figure will be. Systems that are correct as little as 30 percent of the time can still be good systems, and systems that are accurate as much as 80 percent of the time can be bad systems. It's easy to see that even a high degree of accuracy with a large average losing trade and small average winning trade does not make a good system.

Average Trade.   This statistic will tell you what the average hypothetical trade has been. You must make certain that when you test your system you deduct slippage and commission from your average trade. Commissions add up, even discount commissions. And slippage is an important factor when determining system performance.

As a rule of thumb, I recommend deducting between $75 and $100 per trade for slippage and commission. Once this has been done, you will often significantly reduce the average trade figure. As pointed out earlier, you must also pay close attention to the largest winning trade and the largest losing trade when evaluating the average trade. The average trade figure is important since it considers all profits, all losses, slippage, and commission.

Optimization. There has been considerable controversy about trading system optimization. What exactly is wrong with optimizing systems? Can you go too far? Is there a happy medium?

The real issues in system optimization are complex, and they've been exacerbated by the tendency of systems developers to optimize their programs above and beyond any reasonable degree. To optimize a system is to discover the parameters that provide the best results in hypothetical backtesting. In other words, optimization is a form of discovering what would have produced the best results using numerous if-then scenarios.

Before affordable computer hardware and software were available, optimization was a long and laborious procedure. To discover the best fit, the systems developer would need to repeatedly backtrack and test several variables. If the system parameters were numerous, the process was virtually impossible. Obviously, computers have made this a quick and efficient task. Now any trader with several thousand dollars can develop optimized systems.

Such ease of testing and optimizing is both good and bad. On one hand, it allows traders to develop, test, and refine (i.e., optimize) systems much more rapidly. On the other hand, it has opened the door to what is called *curve-fitting*. The simple fact is that the powerful system-testing programs now available allow traders as well as systems vendors to repeatedly test a host of timing variables, stop losses, and other risk management schemes in order to determine which combinations would have produced the best results. In effect, this procedure fits the best parameters on historical data to produce the best hypothetical results. However, the conclusions reached by such methods are often specious.

The trader who tests and retests to find the best fit will eventually reach his or her goal, but the goal itself may be nothing more than a reflection of the curve-fitted results. Tests tell us what has worked in the past, but may not reveal anything worthwhile about the future. Since the past is not a carbon copy of the future, it is doubtful that the optimized parameters will work in the future. The more parameters in the decision-making model, the less likely they are to work in the future.

Overly optimized results lead to false conclusions. The result will likely mean losses. For those who develop and sell futures trading systems as a business, optimization is an amazing tool that allows the creation of outstanding hypothetical performance results that, in turn, allow systems developers to make incredible claims. And claims sell systems.

Time will tell if I am wrong about overly optimized systems. Vast personal experience, however, strongly validates my conclusions. I recall recent developments regarding several popular trading systems sold by a software developer. The advertised claims were fantastic. Systems were sold for T-bond futures, S&P, and currency futures. The outstanding performance claims provided a strong media campaign.

Naturally, all of the proper disclaimers were made to comply with the then-current regulatory requirements. There were no disclaimers regarding optimized results, however, nor was it disclosed that not all buyers of the systems would be using the same system parameters. Because the systems were continually optimized for best results, the hypothetical track records were truly impressive.

However, the results did not jibe with results experienced by those who had old versions of the software—versions that did not reflect the new optimized parameters. This is high-tech deception. Recognizing that there might be legal liability, the systems developers eventually disclosed this fact in small print. Few buyers understood the meaning of the disclosure and even fewer cared, given the impressive hypothetical performance record. Naturally, buyers of the software felt that they could match the hypothetical performance.

In many cases, these traders did well initially. A customer in my brokerage firm purchased one of these programs and began trading it strictly according to the rules. The results were impressive. I began to watch intently every time a trade was made. It was uncanny how well the system entered and exited trades. It was as if the system had internalized a sixth sense about the market.

Then, after several months of excellent results, the system began to unravel. Numerous large losses occurred, and performance deteriorated more rapidly than it had climbed. The dangers of an overly optimized system became apparent once again.

A Rational Approach to System Development

I do not oppose optimizing trading systems; however, I do favor a rational approach to this procedure. My rule of thumb is simple: your trading system should have no more than 4 to 6 variables. Search for the best combination of entry and exit variables, as well as a reasonable combination of stop-loss and trailing stop-loss amounts. But this is where the optimization should end. The more variables you build into the system, the less likely will be the future performance of the parameters.

Another aspect of system development relates to market personality—a topic that has received little attention by most traders and market analysts. Rather than heavily optimizing a system, I recommend tailoring your system to the personality characteristics of the individual markets, provided that such characteristics exist and that they are sufficiently stable.

Market Sentiment

On April 1, 1987, several associates and I initiated the *daily sentiment index* (DSI) market survey. DSI is based on contrary opinion. In other words, when DSI is very high, we expect a top. When it is very low, we expect a bottom. The DSI has been provided daily since 1987, and has become one of the leading market sentiment services in the world. Figure 12-1 shows a sample DSI report.

My historical database of daily market sentiment now covers over 10 years of history on virtually all active U.S. markets and 5 years on European markets. Given the vast amount of data, as well as my experience in preparing, using, understanding, and studying the DSI, I would like to share the following conclusions:

- The long-standing belief that a relationship exists between high bullish sentiment and market tops, and between low bullish sentiment and market bottoms, appears to be valid and correct. This is especially true for the short term and therefore is highly important to the e-trader.
- In order for these relationships to be reasonably correct, we must consider trading based on market sentiment *only when market sentiment is at an extreme level*.
- The definition of *extreme* is subject to some degree of interpretation. I prefer to use the 90 and 10 percent *levels* as trigger points.
- When market sentiment is at or above 90 percent, meaning that the majority of traders are probably bullish, I consider the short side as the better side of the market. At this point, the short-term e-trader is likely best off looking for short-term *sell* signals on intraday data.
- When market sentiment is at or below 10 percent, meaning that the majority of traders are probably bearish, I consider the long side as the better side of the market. At this point, the short-term e-trader is likely best off looking for short-term *buy* signals on intraday data.
- Market sentiment is merely an indicator, and, as a result, it is not always correct. There are times when it will be totally incorrect.

Market	08-30-1999					08-27-1999					08-26-1999					08-25-1999					08-24-1999				
	Raw %Up	3ma %Up	5ma %Up	9ma %Up	18ma %Up	Raw %Up	3ma %Up	5ma %Up	9ma %Up	18ma %Up	Raw %Up	3ma %Up	5ma %Up	9ma %Up	18ma %Up	Raw %Up	3ma %Up	5ma %Up	9ma %Up	18ma %Up	Raw %Up	3ma %Up	5ma %Up	9ma %Up	18ma %Up
T-Bonds	8	34	50	58	47	15	60	61	66	49	78	76	73	71	49	87	71	71	70	46	62	67	68	63	42
Euro Dollar	32	40	45	48	39	36	48	51	49	39	53	53	55	49	39	56	55	54	47	37	49	55	51	44	36
S&P Index	13	33	49	52	51	21	58	65	60	51	65	71	74	67	51	89	80	66	71	48	58	73	56	66	44
Swiss Franc	28	23	22	32	32	25	17	18	30	34	16	19	27	30	36	9	16	36	29	39	32	36	41	32	42
Deutsche Mark	37	28	28	34	33	32	20	24	32	35	16	23	30	31	37	13	24	39	31	40	41	41	42	33	43
Japanese Yen	73	53	54	65	58	45	44	54	66	58	41	51	60	70	58	47	62	67	70	60	64	71	76	70	62
British Pound	45	36	28	38	40	41	25	23	38	41	23	18	29	38	42	12	18	40	40	45	18	37	45	44	49
Canadian Dollar	54	46	45	35	46	62	41	37	37	47	23	36	28	37	48	39	34	27	44	50	45	26	28	48	51
Dollar Index	57	67	70	54	58	61	77	74	53	56	82	78	66	54	54	87	76	53	55	51	65	53	41	52	47
Crude Light	88	57	43	53	59	59	32	39	50	57	23	22	39	49	57	15	37	49	53	58	29	53	58	59	60
Heating Oil	88	58	44	55	61	60	33	40	53	59	27	25	41	51	58	13	37	51	55	60	34	56	61	61	62
Unleaded Gas	92	69	49	56	59	71	42	43	53	57	43	27	42	49	57	13	34	48	50	58	25	51	57	55	60
Natural Gas	65	35	28	55	58	22	18	34	52	58	18	18	47	55	60	15	43	62	60	62	22	67	74	65	65
Gold	34	26	21	18	36	25	19	15	21	36	19	15	13	26	37	14	11	13	30	39	11	11	14	35	40
Silver	29	27	24	26	32	27	23	21	26	34	26	22	25	25	36	15	17	25	25	37	24	27	27	28	40
Platinum	39	33	28	35	37	34	27	27	35	38	25	23	30	33	40	21	25	34	33	41	23	35	39	36	42
Copper	36	37	44	33	42	45	40	41	34	43	31	46	38	35	43	43	44	35	38	44	65	38	29	39	46
Corn	44	34	39	40	48	31	40	35	42	50	27	40	36	46	52	62	39	39	45	56	31	30	39	39	55
Wheat	31	38	44	55	55	35	48	53	57	57	48	51	60	60	57	60	60	64	61	59	46	65	65	56	60
Oats	37	41	41	38	48	44	45	39	39	49	41	42	37	40	50	49	37	35	42	51	35	32	35	42	50
Soybean	57	52	52	55	57	54	54	50	56	59	45	49	51	57	60	63	50	56	54	63	39	49	56	48	61
Soybean Oil	35	32	40	50	54	38	40	41	54	56	23	43	46	57	59	60	48	57	56	62	45	50	58	51	60
Soybean Meal	43	31	36	47	50	29	32	38	49	52	22	36	44	52	55	45	47	53	52	59	41	52	56	48	57
Orange Juice	36	49	48	54	64	58	52	52	57	65	53	48	53	60	64	45	50	56	63	63	46	55	60	69	62
Coffee	19	22	33	29	35	25	31	36	27	36	21	40	37	25	37	47	45	36	32	38	52	38	29	30	36
Cocoa	38	29	40	31	27	34	34	37	28	26	16	43	34	29	26	53	45	35	30	27	59	33	27	28	26
Sugar	86	69	67	64	59	63	63	63	60	58	57	62	61	60	58	68	64	62	60	58	61	60	60	56	58
Lumber	53	48	37	30	42	47	39	35	28	42	45	28	30	30	43	26	28	23	32	45	12	26	20	38	47
Cotton	18	32	34	40	52	23	40	35	46	53	54	44	40	51	54	42	33	40	54	53	35	34	44	58	55
Live Cattle	61	63	57	51	52	65	60	50	51	52	63	52	46	51	52	53	40	43	51	52	41	37	44	47	50
Live Hogs	44	32	41	44	54	28	38	47	42	56	25	45	54	46	58	62	61	58	51	61	47	61	47	52	60
Pork Bellie	63	72	61	52	52	75	61	61	50	52	78	56	54	49	53	29	51	41	47	54	62	55	44	48	58
CRB Index	44	29	33	48	58	25	26	38	49	60	19	33	45	54	63	35	48	55	59	66	44	57	61	63	67
Nikkei Index	65	68	69	71	67	67	70	71	72	67	72	70	72	72	67	70	71	73	72	67	69	73	74	71	66

* = Market Closed Copyright 1999 MBH   (847) 291-1870   There is a risk of loss in futures trading.

Figure 12-1. Sample DSI report. *(Report copyright © 1999, MBH Inc.)*

- The disciplined e-trader is always best off using risk management methods to protect his or her position, since there are times when the market sentiment will be wrong. The DSI has its limitations, as do all market indicators, systems, and trading methods.

- DSI is always at its best when it is used in combination with short-term timing indicators. I have found that 30-minute and 60-minute data and indicators are often best when attempting to time short-term market swings with the DSI.

- DSI is primarily a short-term indicator. It is therefore best used for assistance in timing short-term market swings. I define *short term* in this case as from 2 to 15 trading sessions. This does not mean that DSI cannot catch market swings that are of longer or shorter duration. My definition is merely a guideline.

- It is possible to use moving averages of market sentiment. I use a 3-, 5-, 9-, and 18-day moving average of the DSI in my analyses.

- When the actual daily number and *all* of the moving averages are at an extreme, the odds appear to be more favorable for a significant and longer-lasting move in the opposite direction.

Accumulation Distribution Derivative

For many years traders have attempted to find a method that would give insight as to the locus of control in a market. The question as to whether the bulls or the bears are in control of a market is an important one, particularly for the day trader. If we know that the bulls are in control of a market, then we will do well to buy on declines, knowing that the market is likely to recover from its drop.

In a market that is controlled by the bears, rallies will be relatively short lived, as sellers overpower buyers and the market returns to its declining trend. By "control" I do not mean to imply that there is an actual group of buyers or sellers who are conspiring to control the direction of a market. By control I mean essentially *balance of power*.

In a perfect world, we would like to see markets follow our model or theory as closely as possible. While this would make our task as traders more definitive, it would likely mean an end to free markets, since virtually every market trend and trend change would be predictable, and there would, therefore, be no market.

Theoretically, as a market that has been in a bull trend moves sideways, a change of control is taking place as the bears gain the upper hand. One interpretation is that selling pressure outweighs buying power. During this sideways phase, the bears are *distributing* contracts to the bulls. The bulls eventually reach a point where their cumulative buying can no longer sustain an uptrend, and the market drops as the bears continue their selling.

At a market bottom, the reverse holds true. In theory, buying power outweighs the selling pressure. There is cumulatively more buying than selling. Eventually, the balance is overcome as buying demand outpaces the supply of selling, and the market surges higher. The bulls gain firm control. Theoretically, the bulls are slowly but surely gaining control of the market during the bottoming or *accumulation* phase.

Markets do not always follow their ideal situations. At times a market will change trend almost immediately and seemingly without notice. Purists will argue that in such cases markets do give advance warnings but that the signs are subtle. I do not disagree. But I note that if the signs cannot be found, then the theory, no matter how seemingly valid, will not help us.

The Accumulation/Distribution Indicator

What the preceding section describes is the theory of accumulation and distribution. The theory has face validity and is certainly easy to understand. The difficult part is finding methods, indicators, and technical trading systems that will allow traders to take advantage of the hypothetical constructs.

One such indicator is the advance/decline (A/D) oscillator originally developed by Larry Williams and James J. Waters in 1972. Their article, entitled "Measuring Market Momentum," appeared in the October 1972 issue of *Commodities* magazine. It introduced their A/D oscillator.

The purpose of the oscillator was to detect changes in the balance of power from buyers to sellers and vice versa. Calculation of the A/D oscillator is a relatively simple matter. A thorough explanation and critical evaluation of the A/D oscillator can be found in *The New Commodity Trading Systems and Methods* by Perry Kaufman (John Wiley & Sons, 1987, pages 102–106).

The A/D oscillator is also available in preprogrammed form on many of the popular software analysis systems, such as Commodity Quote Graphics (CQG). The formula for calculating A/D can be obtained either in the original Williams and Waters article or in Kaufman's book.

Using the A/D Oscillator

There are several potential applications of the A/D oscillator for position and day trading. They range from the artistic and interpretive to the mechanical and objective. While my application may not be as scientific as one would like, my efforts are in the correct direction. One method I have worked with extensively is to buy and sell based on A/D oscillator crosses above and below the zero line.

The construction of the oscillator suggests that when the A/D value is above zero, the market is under accumulation, and the bulls are in control. Conversely, when the A/D value is below zero, the bears are in control of the market. Theoretically, when the A/D crosses from plus to minus a market crosses from bullish to bearish, and vice versa.

All too often, markets move higher and higher while the A/D is in negative ground, and vice versa. Such situations not only confuse the trader into thinking that the theory is incorrect, but they are also costly since they produce losses. Yet another limitation of the A/D—and, indeed, of all oscillators—is that they can frequently move back and forth above and below the zero line numerous times before a sustained trend emerges.

Traders who buy and sell on such frequent crosses above and below the zero line will suffer numerous repeated losses, not to mention the cost of commissions and slippage.

The Advance/Decline Derivative (ADD)

The term *derivative* means exactly what it says. The first derivative of any value is a new value that is derived from the initial value. If, for example, I have a 24-day moving average as my original value, and I calculate a 20-day moving average of the 24-day moving average, then the 20-day moving average is the first derivative of the 24-day moving average.

If I calculate a moving average of the A/D oscillator, then the moving average I calculate is termed the *first derivative* of the A/D, since it is derived from the A/D value. One purpose of calculating a derivative is to smooth the values of the original data. Our purpose is to do this as well as to use the derivative value and the A/D value for generating signals that will help overcome the limitations of the A/D oscillator when used alone (as cited earlier).

Caveats and Considerations

As presented here the ADD method is objective, but *not entirely systematic.* In order to use it as a system, you will need to add a risk management stop loss and/or a trailing stop loss (if you prefer). This will make the method useful as a system. Naturally, you will want to trade the ADD in active and volatile markets only. The ADD method also has potential for use in day trading.

The A/D oscillator is a powerful oscillator that has considerable potential for use in day trading flat positions as well as volatile spreads. The ADD is a highly versatile indicator lending itself to use in all time frames. Traders interested in using this approach are encouraged to research it more thoroughly as a trading system with risk management rules before using it extensively for day trading.

13

How to Capitalize on Market Volatility

Whether we like it not, markets are becoming more volatile every day. News that had only a minor impact on the markets in the 1980s can now send the markets into a downward spiral or into a buying frenzy. It seems as if traders are sitting on the edge of their seats, fingers on the keyboard, ready to hit the buy or sell button in an instant. The pace of trading has increased on all world exchanges. And this is true for stocks as well as commodities.

Electronic trading has increased the speed of order entry as well as of order execution (in some cases). Market volatility is a two-edged sword. On one hand, it can lead to many trading opportunities as well as profits if you are experienced in trading volatile markets. However, such markets can be a thorn in the side of traders who either are newcomers or are otherwise unable to cope with, let alone take advantage of, the volatility.

There are a number of ways in which market volatility can be used to the advantage of the short-term trader and day trader. Here are a few guidelines and suggestions that may help you take advantage of increased market volatility.

Techniques to Capture Volatile Intraday Market Moves

As you know, today's markets are highly volatile. Large intraday price swings occur quite frequently, particularly in the interest-rate, stock index, and currency futures markets. Some of the swings are very large. Figure 13-1 shows a 2-minute chart of the Dow Jones Industrial Average on August 24,

1999, when the market reacted first down, the sharply up, then sharply down, and then higher again within the time span of 90 minutes to news about interest rates.

Such moves, while clearly volatile, offer opportunities for the e-trader who seeks to capitalize on significant volatility. Note from the chart of the move shown in Figure 13-2 that the move was clearly tradable using the 3/3 high/low channel momentum technique (as described in Chapter 10). The market dropped to its 3-low MA (A) and then rallied to its 3-high MA (B) on the hourly chart while momentum was still reading positive. The move was about a full 10-point profit based on the system.

Bull and Bear Market Strategies

Many traders believe that systems are linear. In other words, they believe that a system should give you buy and sell signals alike. I do not agree. We know that some systems work better in bear markets than they do in bull markets. We also know that stop losses are not linear. Some systems require different stop losses for longs than they do for shorts. Hence, you might want to use certain indicators and trading systems for trading bullish

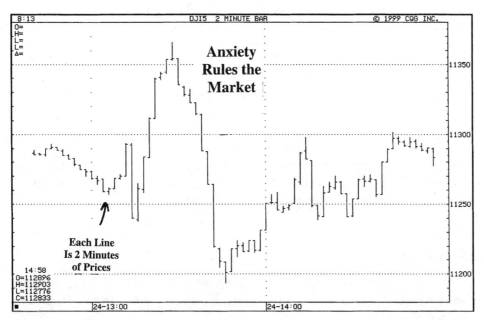

Figure 13-1. Intraday price swing in the Dow Jones, August 24, 1999. *(Chart copyright © 1999 CQG Inc.)*

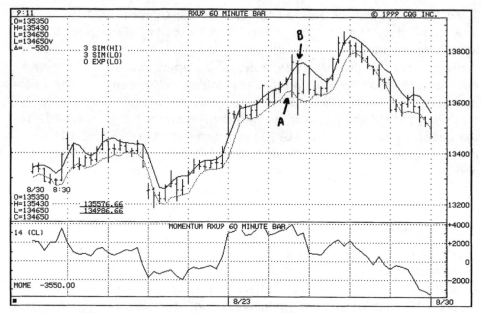

Figure 13-2. 3/3 high/low channel momentum strategy in S&P hourly data, August 24, 1999. *(Chart copyright © 1999 CQG Inc.)*

trends and others for trading bearish trends. By breaking out the buy and sell signal performance of a given system into longs and shorts, you can find a combined approach that works best for you.

As an example, consider the historical summary of results shown in Figure 13-3. As you can see, this system shows excellent results for all trades combined. The results are 78 percent accuracy with more than $1015 per trade average profit. But the long trades show only $351 profit. The short trades, however, show a whopping $3311 in profit with 82 percent accuracy. Although there were only 11 trades from November 3, 1997, to August 27, 1999, their total profit was almost 3 times larger than the total profit from long trades. This is an example of where you might want a larger position on short trades in order to capitalize on the historical tendency.

Unexpected News

When the unexpected happens, it is often an opportunity for the e-trader who is aware of underlying trends. Here are some points and strategies to consider:

```
                    Performance Summary:  All Trades

Total net profit     $   49775.00    Open position P/L     $       0.00
Gross profit         $  112750.00    Gross loss            $  -62975.00

Total # of trades           49       Percent profitable           78%
Number winning trades       38       Number losing trades          11

Largest winning trade $  12675.00    Largest losing trade  $   -5725.00
Average winning trade $   2967.11    Average losing trade  $   -5725.00
Ratio avg win/avg loss      0.52     Avg trade(win & loss) $    1015.82

Max consec. winners         10       Max consec. losers             2
Avg # bars in winners        2       Avg # bars in losers           2

Max intraday drawdown $  -21550.00
Profit factor               1.79     Max # contracts held           1
Account size required $   21550.00   Return on account            231%
```

```
                    Performance Summary:  Long Trades

Total net profit     $   13350.00    Open position P/L     $       0.00
Gross profit         $   64875.00    Gross loss            $  -51525.00

Total # of trades           38       Percent profitable           76%
Number winning trades       29       Number losing trades           9

Largest winning trade $  12675.00    Largest losing trade  $   -5725.00
Average winning trade $   2237.07    Average losing trade  $   -5725.00
Ratio avg win/avg loss      0.39     Avg trade(win & loss) $     351.32

Max consec. winners          9       Max consec. losers             2
Avg # bars in winners        2       Avg # bars in losers           2

Max intraday drawdown $  -26375.00
Profit factor               1.26     Max # contracts held           1
Account size required $   26375.00   Return on account             51%
```

```
                    Performance Summary:  Short Trades

Total net profit     $   36425.00    Open position P/L     $       0.00
Gross profit         $   47875.00    Gross loss            $  -11450.00

Total # of trades           11       Percent profitable           82%
Number winning trades        9       Number losing trades           2

Largest winning trade $  12075.00    Largest losing trade  $   -5725.00
Average winning trade $   5319.44    Average losing trade  $   -5725.00
Ratio avg win/avg loss      0.93     Avg trade(win & loss) $    3311.36

Max consec. winners          5       Max consec. losers             1
Avg # bars in winners        2       Avg # bars in losers           1

Max intraday drawdown $   -5725.00
Profit factor               4.18     Max # contracts held           1
Account size required $    5725.00   Return on account            636%
```

Figure 13-3. Historical trade summary comparing buy and sell trades.

- Unexpected news is usually not unexpected. Frequently the market is prepared for news, and prices usually discount news before it happens. If the market is waiting for an announcement and the announcement is expected to be bearish for prices, then the market will likely adjust itself lower in anticipation of the news, and once the news is out the market will react higher rather than lower. This often proves frustrating to traders who are not aware of the relationship between news and the markets. But it creates wonderful opportunities for the e-trader.

- News is often a chance to enter the market at support and/or resistance levels consistent with the underlying trend. Such moves are the bread and butter of e-traders.

- When bearish news develops in an uptrend, it is usually an opportunity to buy at support. Several methods for doing so are described in this book.

- When bullish news develops in a downtrend, it is usually an opportunity to sell short at resistance.

- If you take a position based on news, whether expected or unexpected, do not wait too long to be correct. *Reactions based on news are usually fast and furious.* You will be right or wrong quickly. Do not linger in a losing position.

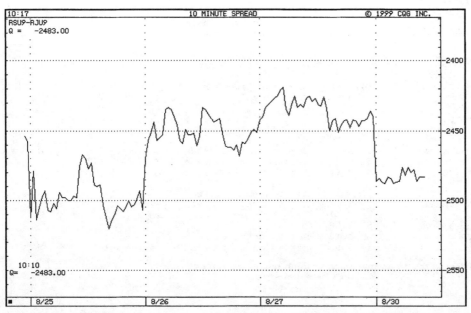

Figure 13-4. Large intraday price swings of the Swiss franc–Japanese yen spread in 10-minute data. *(Chart copyright © 1999 CQG Inc.)*

■ Use short-term data such as 5- or 10-minute data for trading news. You might even use 2- or 3-minute data for this purpose.

■ Support and resistance methods, as well as volatility breakout methods, work well in the case of news-inspired moves. A number of these methods are discussed in Chapters 9 and 10.

■ If you plan to capitalize on market volatility, then do so in volatile markets. While it may be overstating the obvious, I believe that many traders who want to take advantage of price swings do not do so in the proper vehicles.

■ Do not discount the overseas futures markets for short-term e-trades. Markets traded at the LIFFE (London) are among the best ones for this purpose. Many of them trade actively and have excellent price swings, as well as outstanding order execution.

■ Condiser short-term spread trading, particularly in currency futures. Although many traders tend to shy away from spreads because they do not understand them, I believe that short-term spread trading can be very effective. As an example, note the 10-minute chart of the Swiss franc versus the Japanese yen in Figure 13-4. As you can see, the intraday swings have been quite large. And they will likely continue that way.

14

Aspects of Risk Management and Portfolio Development

The Myth of Small Stop Losses

Of all the important aspects in futures trading, I rank risk management as the single most significant. Notwithstanding the importance of a trader's experience, risk management is an issue with which all traders must deal at one time or another, preferably sooner rather than later. Various and sundry techniques have been employed in the quest for effective risk control. Some work well; most fail miserably.

Among the methods most used are stop losses, futures options, spreads, position size, and asset allocation. The key is to find those methods and techniques that are the most productive and to *use* them consistently. Of these methods, the most obvious is the stop loss.

The Good News/Bad News Stop Loss

What makes stop losses difficult, if not at times seemingly impossible, to use is the fact that they're a double-edged sword. You know that their use is necessary if losses are to be minimized, yet you also know that you've been stopped out of positions many times only to see the market go your way *after* you've been stopped out.

What to do? Some of the ideas that follow will help you limit your exposure more effectively. I don't ask you to agree with my ideas, but I *do* ask you to keep an open mind and open eyes. Observe my ideas in real time and see if they can be valuable in your trading.

Smaller Stops Equal Smaller Profits

Perhaps one of the best lessons I have learned about stop losses is that they have to be large enough to permit the market reasonable movement. Stop losses that are too close to the market (otherwise known as *too tight*) are not recommended other than under very special circumstances.

Many traders are fascinated with the idea of using extremely small stop losses in order to limit risk. Their intentions are good, but the end result is that the accuracy of their trading may be very low, since stops will be hit very frequently.

A stop loss must be large enough to allow the market its reasonable movement, but small enough to protect you. If, for example, S&P futures have shown an average daily range of 500 points, then a stop loss of 100 points may be much too small, since the random behavior of the market will stop you out more often than not. *No* trading system is immune to the deteriorating effects of random market behavior.

My long-time friend and business associate, Larry Williams, said it best when he told me, "I use very large stop losses when day trading S&P futures because I have to give the market enough breathing room . . . when I take a loss I want to *really* feel it. . . ."

At first blush, Larry's penchant for large stop losses rubs us all the wrong way. Yet you will likely learn to respect it as I have. And after trading with Larry during the more than 30 real-time trading seminars we've done together, I've come to respect the value of wide stops.

Side-by-Side Comparison

Figure 14-1, which shows the historical performance of a trading system I developed quickly using Omega TradeStation, illustrates my point strongly. The tabular presentation shows historical back-testing of the same market entry and exit rules with 11 different stop loss levels. Here are my conclusions:

- As stop loss increases, so does net profit per trade.
- As stop loss increases, so does system accuracy, until it peaks and can no longer increase.
- As stop loss increases, drawdown remains fairly stable. Hence, more risk per trade does *not* increase drawdown.
- As stop loss increases, the largest losing trade increases minimally.
- As stop loss increases, overall profit for the system nearly doubles.

Initial Stop $	Total Profit	Average Trade	% Correct	Draw Down	Largest Loss $	Largest Win $	Consec Losers
500	34,715.00	257.15	39%	-7,155.00	-875	15,775.00	7
750	46,910.00	350.07	44%	-5,965.00	-1,645.00	15,775.00	7
1000	48,730.00	363.66	49%	-6,650.00	-1,825.00	15,775.00	6
1200	52,940.00	395.07	51%	-5,955.00	1,825.00	15,775.00	5
1400	57,395.00	431.54	52%	-2,175.00	-2,175.00	15,775.00	5
1600	57,815.00	434.7	53%	-5,655.00	-2,175.00	15,775.00	4
1800	56,475.00	424.62	53%	-5,635.00	-2,175.00	15,775.00	4
2200	58,470.00	442.95	53%	-5,145.00	-2,175.00	15,775.00	4
2800	57,480.00	435.45	53%	-5,480.00	-2,775.00	15,775.00	4
3500	57,590.00	436.29	53%	-6,180.00	-2,875.00	15,775.00	4
4500	60,720.00	460	54%	-6,165.00	-2,765.00	15,775.00	4

Figure 14-1. System back-test using 11 different initial stop-loss levels.

- Stop loss increases to a point of diminishing return and system performance peaks.
- The smallest stop losses produce the worst results.
- The largest stop losses produce the best results.
- As stop losses increase, the number of successive losing trades decreases considerably.

As you can see, small stop losses *do not* do what you'd expect them to do. Big stop losses work better.

Trailing Stop Losses

Another form of stop loss is the trailing stop. The trailing stop loss has been a favorite among traders for many years. Simply explained, the trailing stop loss trails market moves.

As a profit continues to mount, the stop loss is continuously changed to reflect the increased profit. While this sounds like a reasonable and rational methodology, it is also a flawed methodology as most often used by traders. The reason it is flawed is that, once again, traders do not allow the market sufficient space to allow the random movements breathing room.

Most often, traders are stopped out of their positions with trailing stops because their trailing stops are *too close to the market*. When the market responds to a piece of emotional news—news unrelated to the underlying trend—they are stopped out. It is *not* the trailing-stop concept that's at fault; rather, it's the *placement* of the trailing stop that's at fault.

Here is yet another experiment based on trailing stops. Figure 14-2 shows the same system as in the preceding example for 10 different levels of trailing stop losses using a fixed initial stop loss. The conclusions are as follows:

- Trailing stop losses must also be larger rather than smaller.
- There is an optimum point for trailing stop losses.
- The smaller the trailing stop, the smaller the average profit per trade.

The only exception I know to these conclusions is in S&P futures, where a small trailing stop is preferable since the market is highly volatile.

Consider the following "logic" used for stop placement:

- Use a stop loss below the low of the day.
- Use a stop loss above the high of the day.
- Get out if the market makes a new contract low.
- Exit on close below or above a trendline.

% Stop Trail	Total Profit	Average Trade $	% Correct	Draw Down $	Largest Loss $	Largest Loss $	Consec Losers
10	35,760.00	262.94	54%	-5,860.00	-2,775.00	5,735.00	3
20	32,190.00	236.69	54%	-6,195.00	-2,775.00	5,735.00	3
30	31,420.00	231.03	54%	-6,195.00	-2,775.00	5,735.00	3
40	32,255.00	238.93	55%	-5,975.00	2,775.00	5,735.00	3
50	28,930.00	215.9	55%	-5,750.00	-2,775.00	5,735.00	3
60	35,645.00	268.01	55%	-5,910.00	-2,775.00	5,735.00	3
70	44,815.00	336.95	54%	-5,780.00	-2,775.00	5,735.00	3
80	54,420.00	412.27	55%	-5,780.00	-2,775.00	5,735.00	3
90	57,560.00	436.06	53%	-5,780.00	-2,775.00	5,735.00	4
100	56,610.00	428.86	51%	-5,780.00	-2,775.00	5,735.00	7

Figure 14-2. Trailing stop losses.

The problem with all of these is that *they're way too obvious and reflect the herd mentality of the market*. The fact is that most traders think the same way about stop losses (and many other things).

In the market, *contrary* thinking pays off, whereas herd mentality tends to increase losses. The fact is that in order to use trailing stop losses effectively, you must place them where they won't have much company.

Position Size and Profits

System performance can be improved considerably by varying the number of contracts traded as a function of equity in your account, accuracy of your system, and risk level of a given trade. In other words, after a series of winning trades you may want to increase the number of contracts you trade, and vice versa for a series of losing trades. The performance differences between this approach and trading the same number of contracts each time can be and often are dramatic. There are various software programs that can tell you exactly how many contracts to trade based on the variable cited. I urge you to check them out.

15

Artificial Intelligence (AI) and Neural Network (NN) Systems for E-Trading

With increased processing speeds and larger memories, it is possible to run highly complex real-time trading programs that employ the concepts and learning models of artificial intelligence (AI). Since the early 1990s such programs, now called neural network (NN) systems, have been gaining in popularity. I believe that such systems are the wave of the future for e-traders. And their time may come very soon.

As always, the trader must be highly selective in separating the claims of promoters from the realities of the systems. As you well know, there are many outrageous claims for systems that in real-time application fail to live up to the promises. *Caveat emptor* is the key concept in all cases. However, armed with some knowledge of NN and AI you may make more informed decisions, since such information will help you ask the right questions before you spend what could be a large amount of money on a system and the data feed it requires.

The Goals of AI- and NN-Based Systems

Simply stated, the goal of such systems is to learn. If the systems are sound and the learning models upon which the systems are based are valid, and if the data or inputs the NN system examines are effective in assisting the learning process, then profits will be the end result. But there exists a vast expanse between the design of an NN system and its profitable application. There are numerous learning models that may be employed as the core or brain of an NN system.

The developer of such a system has many choices. Some are applicable to the financial markets, while others are more suited to industrial or manufacturing models. Still others are suitable for scientific applications. The stock and commodity markets are unique, inasmuch as their price movements are affected and influenced by a variety of factors. Some of the factors are known, many are not, and still others are purely random.

An NN trading system that is well designed will theoretically perform better over time, since it will ideally learn from its mistakes as well as from its successes. But in order for this learning process to occur, it must first be true that actual learning *can* occur. And for learning to occur, there must be discernible patterns that can be extracted from market behavior by the application of various inputs, indicators, and analytical techniques. Hence, all NN programs thrive on information. The classical garbage in, garbage out (GIGO) syndrome can easily be achieved with a NN trading system if the information (inputs) fed to the system is ineffective.

In working with NN-based system development for well over six years, I have discovered that aside from the learning model one chooses for the NN system, the next most important consideration is the type of inputs that should be fed into the program. Ideally, the inputs should have some degree of relevance to market movements. In the case of the stock market, for example, an NN-based system might thrive on interest-rate data, since, to a given extent, the magnitude and direction of stocks and stock futures is related to the magnitude and direction of interest rates.

In examining these relationships, the NN could find very complex patterns with predictive validity. Other important inputs might include a few traditional timing indicators, such as moving averages, momentum, RSI, stochastics, and others. An input I have found to be especially useful is market sentiment data, given the inverse relationship between sentiment and market highs and lows.

But these inputs are essentially longer-term ones. The computerized day trader using an NN approach will need to examine other inputs that may lead to more meaningful results. Among these I again include daily market sentiment, as well as a variety of intraday price pattern relationships that examine the last few days' market activity, trading volume, and even market-generated data such as tick, up volume, down volume, advancing issues, declining issues, and so on. Such combinations are ideal for the e-trader. Given the fact that the use of NN-based systems is still in its early stages for application in position-trading systems, its use in day trading is even less well developed. As noted earlier, the claims may be fantastic; however, the results are what you should be concerned about.

What to Look For in an NN System

There is a fine but readily discernible line between an optimized trading system and an NN system. An optimized system merely examines a number of relationships using various indicators and makes an assumption that the future will be the same as the past. If a system fails to be profitable, then the system developer will reoptimize the system until the results look favorable again. But the key question is whether the system will go forward profitably over time.

In most cases, such highly optimized and reoptimized systems will not produce profits. But how do they differ from NN systems? The answer is simple if you ask an NN programmer. You will be told that the optimized system has not learned anything about the behavior of a market when it spits out its results. It merely curve-fits the market by working backward and finding the best fit for various indicators. If the system fails to perform in the future, then the developer will optimize it again.

The NN system, on the other hand, develops a theory of market behavior by observing the numerous complex relationships and levels of relationships between the market and the inputs that it has been given. The NN system actually combines the different inputs in a variety of ways in order to discern the true nature of the market and then gives a specific forecast or timing signal based on what it has learned. When a trade has been completed, the NN system then evaluates the results and, theoretically, learns from them, as well.

The method by which an effective NN system is best tested is by using *out-of-sample* data. Assume, for example, that an NN day-trading system has been developed over a period of 600 trading days. A variety of inputs was given to the system. The learning model has produced a historical record of back-tested trades showing 71 percent accuracy with an average trade minus slippage and commission of $884 and acceptable drawdown and other performance statistics. The NN system, having been trained, is now given a new set of data that it has not seen before. This data was not in the original learning sample, which is why it is termed *out-of-sample* data.

The NN system now attempts to go forward a trade at a time in order to determine if it can match its trained performance. In most cases, this is where the NN model collapses if it is an essentially ineffective method. However, if the learning model holds promise, the results will approach what has been achieved in the training session and a viable method will have been discovered.

In practice, I have seen many NN models be highly effective during the training period. They develop excellent track records with outstanding results. However, in the forward mode on out-of-sample data they fail to go forward and must therefore be either radically altered or discarded. Sadly, this has been the fate of most NN systems I have seen to date. In order to prevent you from being caught in the trap of an ineffective NN system, the next section provides a list of things to watch for and questions to ask if and when you are looking either to develop such a system or to buy one that has already been programmed.

What to Ask and What to Watch For

The first thing to determine is whether you want to buy an existing NN system or develop one on your own. To develop a system on your own is a costly proposition requiring the services of a highly skilled programmer who is also conversant in NN and AI techniques. Such programmers are few and far between, and once you find them their services are very costly. In addition, your programmer will need to have some degree of facility with the stock/and or futures markets in order to understand and allow for some of the basic aspects and considerations involved in trading. In most cases, you will be better off buying an existing program. In this case there are a number of questions to ask and a number of considerations to evaluate.

Buying an NN program is not like buying a piece of canned software at your local computer store. In order for the NN program to function effectively, either it must be trained to suit your particular needs or you must trade according to its dictates. You must have the appropriate inputs to make it run, and you must learn how to run it correctly if your investment is to be worthwhile. This means that you will need considerable technical support from the software seller. Before you spend even $1 on an NN program, take the time to determine how readily available support will be and whether there are any additional or hidden charges for technical assistance. Many NN programs assume a certain level of expertise on the part of the end user, but this is not always true.

Determine the type of learning model that comprises the brain of the NN program. Some learning models are of questionable efficacy, while others are more suited to the task. In order to keep abreast of current events in the field of AI and NN, spend some time and do a little reading. There are literally thousands of locations on the Internet where you can learn about NN and where you can find software for a variety of applications, including trading.

Many of these locations will help educate you on what is considered state-of-the-art. Since this is a rapidly changing area of computerized trading and day trading, I urge you to keep up to date by visiting a variety of websites. They have developed and are developing numerous applications, from architecture to S&P futures trading, and from medical applications to the social sciences.

Before you buy a program for NN day trading (or, for that matter, any type of NN e-trading), ask for references and performance histories. If the developer has a good product, you may be offered a free trial of the software. If this is the case, take your time and give the system a good test on out-of-sample data. But be careful, since the NN may already have been trained on the data you are using, and what you think to be out-of-sample data may really not be. Once an NN system has been trained by the developer, you will not be able to get into the brain of the system to determine if your out-of-sample test is *truly* an out-of-sample test.

Use several out-of-sample tests. Test the efficacy of the NN during a period of bullish market activity, during a period of bearish activity, and during a period of sideways movement. This well-rounded testing will help you see if the NN has a bias toward one type of market trend or another. An effective NN system should be reasonably stable across all types of markets.

Find out if the system developers are traders, have ever been traders, or have consulted with traders in developing their software. All too often, software developers have no idea what trading is all about and, as a result, develop systems that are essentially untradable since they either make unrealistic assumptions or are just not practical in terms of market realities. In addition, ask for examples of the output provided by the program. As a trader you will need specific output or instructions, not vague generalities or unspecified forecasts.

Make certain that the NN has provided for stop losses and/or trailing stop losses. Frequently, NN system developers will not consider the stop loss, even though it is an integral aspect of risk management. This is a very important consideration in the use of any trading system, whether NN based or not. Many systems can test extremely well without stop losses, but when stops are added in their performance deteriorates.

Determine the types of orders you will need to place as a function of the kind of information provided by your NN. Some systems assume order executions based on their historical testing that might not be capable of being filled in actual trading. This may be one of the most serious drawbacks of an NN system. It could mean the difference between a profit and an overall loss.

Remember that in using NN for short-term or day trading, your orders will be filled either at the market or at specified prices. The mere fact that a market touches your price order does not guarantee a fill. The NN may, however, assume a fill. It is therefore in your best interest to find out what assumptions the NN makes regarding price fills for both entry and exit.

Inquire about the data and data types that will be needed in order to keep your program working properly. Many NN systems use data that is readily available from various data vendors; however, some use data that is proprietary and available only on a subscription or purchase basis. This could add considerably to the cost of your operations and must be considered in advance.

Determine the applicability of the NN to various markets. While most NN systems will focus exclusively on one specific market, there are some that are versatile enough to accommodate many different types of markets. What you decide to do will depend upon what kind of a trader you want to be and which markets you want to trade. Not all day traders are S&P traders. Some will want to day trade T-bond futures or even some of the overseas financial markets. Find out from the software seller or developer if the NN is flexible enough to trade in different markets.

Ask how the NN system handles risk. A system that produces excellent winning trades but which has severe drawdowns in equity, or which uses a stop loss that is beyond your means, is a system that will not work for you. You must determine how the NN makes its decisions regarding risk and stop loss, or, at the very minimum, you must ask the developer or system seller to provide you with a listing of trades so that you may determine for yourself the degree of risk the system takes.

Finally, note that within a few years NNs may be the most successful approach to e-trading. Pursue this area of market analysis and trading aggressively. The technology to create such systems is now available. Progress is developing at a rapid rate.

16

Practical Trading Considerations

In addition to the mechanical requirements of trading, the startup capital you will need, and the systems you plan to use, there are numerous psychological and practical considerations that must be taken into account no matter what your time frame may be. This chapter discusses many of these considerations.

Trader Psychology and Short-Term Trading

Systems Versus Traders

Nowadays there is a wealth of information available on how you may improve your relationship with the markets, as well as your relationship with yourself. In more than 25 years as a futures trader I've found, time and time again, that the weakest link in the chain of market success is the *trader*, not the system. Systems are a dime a dozen. Most good systems are not very different from one another in terms of their performance. But what *is* different is the level of skill that the trader possesses.

Can a Good System Be Your Answer?

While it's certainly true that a good system can help an e-trader, it is also true that a good system in the hands of a poor trader is a losing proposition. On the other hand, even a relatively poor system in the hands of a good trader can do well. The simple and undeniable fact of the matter is that winners and losers are distinguishable by their discipline, persistence, and self-image. These are the ultimate variables that contribute to consistent market success. But the key question is whether they can be learned.

Great Traders Are Created, Not Born

I have long maintained that great traders are not born great; rather, they learn to be great. I do not deny that every now and then an individual seems to have the knack, the inherent ability to do well as a trader, but I assure you that these qualities are not inborn, that they are not genetic.

They are qualities most likely learned at a very early age which have now become reflexive, so entrenched in the repertoire of the trader that they cannot be distinguished from what is inborn. They are as natural to the trader as a reflex; as a blink of the eye; as an involuntary response to the outer and inner environment. Such traders make things look easy.

What to Do?

What can we do to improve our results in the markets? What can we do to improve our skills as traders? How do we know where to begin? How can we separate the small amount of useful information that's available to the trader from the mountains of worthless information? Are there sources for honest and useful information?

These are the important questions that face all traders nowadays. And they are questions made even more pressing by the fact that the consumer market has, in recent years, been deluged with an avalanche of trading systems and software programs, each claiming to be better than the next. All of this tends to confuse the trader.

Some Valuable Suggestions

Based on my many years of experience as a trader, market analyst, system developer, and writer, I've reached some important conclusions about trader psychology, and I've developed a support network of individuals and resources that can help overcome the problems of weak trader discipline. To be honest, most of the stuff that's being sold to the public under the guise of market psychology is written merely for the purpose of selling yet another book, for the purpose of conducting yet another seminar.

The sad fact is that individuals who are essentially unqualified to do anything but market seminars are offering some of these courses.

Here are some suggestions that may help you wade through the quagmire of misinformation, disinformation, and worthless information as you attempt to teach a safe haven of solid information.

1. *Before you even think about buying a trading system, make certain you have mastered the basics of self-discipline.* Read the writings of the great masters; study the chapters in this book for a variety of tools designed to help you achieve this goal.

2. *View with considerable suspicion all fantastic claims.* Be wary not only of claims by system sellers but also of those made by brokers, friends, and market advisors. More often than not, such claims cannot be backed up with real-time performance.

3. *In finding a good trading system, look for consistency and small drawdowns as opposed to large profits.* A good system will be profitable over a period of many years, and it will continue to be profitable, on average, over a lengthy time frame.

4. *Be suspicious of systems that are tightly optimized.* Such systems have been manufactured to look good to the consumer. They are intentionally constructed to give great back-test results, but they cannot go forward with similar results. All too often, they literally blow up after they are marketed.

5. *Read system claims and results carefully.* The way systems are sold to the public can be very misleading. Don't be a sucker for the promoters who prey on ignorant traders.

6. *Don't believe claims that simply buying put or call options can be your road to riches.* The fact is that options strategies work much better than simple long positions in puts or calls. Most options expire worthless. There are many options strategies that work much better than simply buying calls or puts. Learn them and use them.

7. *Keep it simple.* This is one of the cardinal rules. I do not believe for one second that the more complicated a system is, the better it works. Simplicity has always worked best for me. I keep coming back to simple methods no matter how many complicated methods I test.

8. *Don't overtrade.* Trading too much is a disease, an addiction. While you may have a deep-seated desire to make your broker rich, the goal is to make *you* rich. Don't overtrade!

9. *Above all, remember that you can learn many lessons from those who are successful.* Study their methods, their personal qualities, their perceptions,

and their approach to discipline and learn to emulate their winning qualities.

I hope that these guidelines will help you overcome your limitations. But moreover, I hope they will help you expand on your successes.

Remember that the markets are merely a reflection of life itself. They will test your resolve, your consistency, your attitudes, your skills, and your sanity. You must prepare for the task and learn from your errors. When you do, you will also find that your personal life will benefit. What works in real life also works in the markets. What works in the markets also works in your life.

Some Thoughts on Trader Discipline

What makes winners win and losers lose? Is discipline the single most important factor, or are there other behaviors that facilitate profitable trading? Based on my many years of experience, I find that the single most significant factor which separates winners from losers in the commodity markets, other than trading capital and experience, is *discipline.*

Without discipline, trading systems don't work, and without discipline, profits cannot be made consistently. Without discipline, traders wander about aimlessly in the markets, victims to professional traders. And without discipline, traders lose repeatedly, not knowing why they lose or why their "systems" fail miserably. In spite of all we have learned about the importance of discipline as a means to successful trading, to most traders *discipline* is nothing more than just a word—a word they've heard many times, yet a word they fail to understand in all, or even in some, of its meanings and implications.

Having discipline, learning discipline, maintaining discipline, developing discipline, rediscovering discipline, internalizing discipline, heightening discipline—these are all major issues for traders, yet they have unfortunately taken a back seat over the years. Traders have been much more interested in developing *trading systems* than they have been in developing their *psyches.* Traders are perennially interested in building trading systems that back-test well. This is the wrong approach. It is unbalanced, and it ignores the fact that lack of discipline is the weakest link in the chain.

To traders, discipline is like weather—we talk about it but we can't seem do anything about it. The fact is that we *can* do a great deal about discipline, although there's little we can do about the weather. We know from considerable research and from a wealth of observation and experience that there are precise techniques that can be used to overcome the problems arising from a lack of discipline. What are these methods? Before defining them, let's first state the problem we're attempting to solve.

The Problem: Developing Discipline

The problem, specifically stated, is as follows: How can traders develop discipline in order to overcome the negative consequences of inconsistent trading which are the result of poor discipline?

There are subsidiary questions: How does a trader learn to be disciplined? Are there methods, techniques, exercises, and books or articles that can help in this venture? Can discipline be learned by any trader? Are there tools that can help facilitate the learning process? Are there teachers or coaches who can help you learn? The unhedged answer to *all* of these questions is *yes*. But beware of what you read and what you do, since it *can* be hazardous to your financial health.

Not All Approaches Work

There are many books that will steer you in the wrong direction. For many years, the only tools that traders had at their disposal were books and, for those who could afford it, psychological counseling. But we have come a long way since then.

Some *very effective* techniques have been developed for dealing with and overcoming trading problems. And these techniques are available to anyone who seeks to improve his or her lot as a trader. The only prerequisites are a desire to succeed, time to learn discipline, the money to pay for a coach or a good course, and the motivation to follow through on what is learned.

While there are a few good books available, the answer is not likely to be found in a book, because a trader who doesn't have discipline won't have the discipline to learn from a book. Traders (in fact, all people, whether they're traders or not) tend to stand in their own way, often becoming their own greatest hindrance to success.

Most individuals need much more than a book in order to learn discipline. They need individualized, personalized instruction by trainers who know the workings of the undisciplined mind, or they need to work with a partner in order to solidify and enhance the learning process. You are far better off spending several hundred or even a thousand dollars or more on personalized work than you are in buying a book with a title that promises the world but delivers virtually nothing.

The Same Old Stuff

With all due respect to the authors of popular books on trader psychology and trading discipline, I find most of it is the same old stuff that's been renamed, repackaged, rehashed, regurgitated, and, yet, still misunderstood.

There are at least four popular books on trader psychology, all released in the last few years, that are essentially useless since they fail to address the core issues of psychological change.

They do a great job posing the problems and talking words, but they don't teach the behavioral components that facilitate change. You need hands-on experience that will drive home the ideas and the behaviors. You need someone to look over your shoulder and steer you in the right direction.

Some of this can be obtained from a book. But most of it has to be a one-on-one process, either with a guide who is a professional in the field or with a partner who will work closely with you in implementing the ideas. Reading a book about how to change your behavior isn't going to do it for you. You need a new approach. You need an approach that focuses on actual behavior. You need an approach that incorporates cognitive as well as behavioral elements.

In many cases, I get the feeling that the authors of these books are merely rehashing what has been said before. I've been guilty of some of that, too. After all, we've been raised to believe that if we analyze a problem by observing it, and we then apply our intellectual reasoning to it, we can solve almost anything that ails us. *That ain't necessarily so!*

Analysis and insight won't necessarily change behavior. You can analyze situations to death; you can understand your shortcomings as a trader, as a spouse, or as a parent; you can recognize your errors in dealing with life situations—but unless you have a *new set of behaviors,* you won't make lasting changes. You need to put understandings and insights into action. *Action* is the key word here.

The Fallacy of "Don't Worry, Be Happy"

Has anyone given you the sage advice "Don't worry," "Get a life," "Be happy," or "Stop punishing yourself"? Advice like this is worse than no advice at all. None of these are possible if you don't have the tools and skills to acquire them. If someone tells you "Be happy," "Don't worry," or "Be a good trader," it is apt to be even more frustrating. What many books and "experts" tell us is very much like a parent telling a lonely child to get some friends.

Discipline isn't like ordering room service. It's not something that can be bought or learned from a book. It has to be learned through interpreting and analyzing *actual experiences* and by following up with *behavior.*

The ability to practice discipline is especially important when you've experienced a string of losses. There are few things that can test a trader's self-confidence or resolve more severely than a series of losses. But you know all of that. That's the problem. What are some of the solutions?

Some Possible Answers

First and foremost, I must emphasize that the answers to discipline problems aren't the same for every trader. Some of us learn more quickly than others do. While some of us find losses to be the best teachers, there are some of us who, peculiarly enough, continue to fail, loss after loss.

It's almost as if losses beget more losses rather than vice versa. How could this be? Why would a trader want to punish him- or herself repeatedly? Is behavior so entrenched that it cannot, at times, be easily changed by its own negative consequences?

There are many possible psychological and behavioral answers to these questions. Let's not deal with explanations now, because all too often explanations do *not* lead to changes in behavior. Rather, let's look at one possible solution.

Would You Like to Lose Money Trading Futures?

Why do traders lose money repeatedly if losing is a form of punishment? Does this mean that traders love punishment?

While parents and educators have used punishment as a training tool for many years, it is only effective in specific circumstances. It is virtually ineffective in teaching new behaviors when used without rewards.

If I punish you every time you do something I don't like, then you'll stop doing that thing. However, you may still do many other things that I don't like. I can punish you for each and every behavior I'd like to eliminate, but my battle may be a lifelong one.

While some new behaviors may be taught with punishment, the use of rewards for appropriate behaviors gets faster, better, and longer-lasting results. Consider applying this knowledge to your trading.

Benefits of Positive Learning

The meaning of positive learning for education, effective child-rearing, and personal development must not be ignored. Consider the ramifications for positive interpersonal relationships. And consider the implications for the trader and investor.

There are literally hundreds of behaviors, and variations on the themes of those behaviors, that can lead to trading losses. But there are few behaviors and their themes that can facilitate trading success.

The unfortunate fact is that most traders are prisoners of their faulty early childhood education and are therefore also prisoners of their ineffective trading behaviors.

Comparisons to Trading

There are many ways to lose money in the markets. There are only a few ways to make money. And there are even fewer ways to keep the money you have made.

Behaviors that contribute to trading success, on the other hand, are often intangible, somewhat subjective, situation-relevant, and individual-dependent. *There are few hard and fast rules that apply to every trader.* And all too often, traders are not in touch with the problems that require remediation. Not knowing what to change, they will surely be at a loss for techniques to help them make life changes.

No matter how many times we've been told what to do in order to make money trading, the advice still misses its mark. This time I'd like to try a different approach.

I'll ignore B. F. Skinner and the other outstanding behavioral psychologists and tell you what you may be doing wrong rather than suggest specific ways in which to improve (since I have already stated these repeatedly in this book). In so doing I hope to break into the monotony of stating *do this* and *do that* rules, which all of us have heard too many times and which somehow fail to find their way to the cerebral cortex.

Here, then, are a few good ways to *lose* money in the futures and stock markets:

- *Plunge headlong into the market without a plan of action.* This is an excellent way to lose money and to lose it quickly. Why make a plan anyway? Would you drive from New York to Los Angeles without a map? You could. It would be exciting. And you might be lucky enough to reach your goal without getting lost too often.

  But each error will cost you—some dearly. And when your aimless wanderings have reached their end, you'll see that others have reached the goal much faster than you have and with less cost, both emotional and financial.

  You say you want to take the ride for pleasure? That's fine, but don't expect to do it efficiently or quickly without a plan.

  If you trade without a plan then your chances of success are slim to none. Yes, you may be one of the lucky few who hits it big the first time, but the odds are *minute.* Without a plan you'll find yourself buffeted about by the winds of chance, the opinions of others, the persuasion of newsletters and advisors, the panderings of brokers, and the bias of the media. Your responses will be whimsical.

  But the greatest danger is that you will not *learn* anything from your behavior. If you are unaware of what you did wrong, then the consequences of your actions will not be readily apparent to you. And you may run out of money before you learn your lessons.

But what exactly do I mean by a *plan?* Do I mean a trading system? A schedule? A set of rules? I define a *trading plan* as a system or set of indicators that will permit relatively objective evaluation of market entry and exit, as well as risk management.

This could mean that you are following a computerized trading system, signals from a chart book, a newsletter, astrology, a random-number generator, the *I Ching,* or your broker. Regardless of where the input comes from, it must be treated as relatively inalterable, and it must be followed as closely as possible and as often as possible.

Since I am aware of the fact that we are all human, I do not advocate rigid adherence to any system. I do not favor blindly following a totally mechanical system, since to tell yourself that you will do so is to set yourself an unreasonable goal, which will surely result in failure and a negative self-concept.

I suggest instead that you employ a relatively mechanical trade entry system and a more flexible exit system. In other words, I advise against rigidity, against inflexibility, and against blindly following any plan. But to stray from a plan one must have a plan at the outset.

There are various levels of adherence to a plan. Every trader must find his or her own level of comfort in straying from the beaten path. Some traders will feel uncomfortable with just a minor deviation from the course, and others will be able to tolerate wide variances. The final determinant must be your results in the marketplace. You alone can determine the right formula by trial and error.

- *Subscribe to and read as many publications as you can; watch the television business news and follow the consensus of opinion.* Here's a sure-fire way to get confused and lose money while you're doing it. You'll find that most of your best trades are not only contrary to what you've read, but also contrary to what you want to believe. If you follow a trading advisor, then do so without second-guessing. Remember that the more opinions you process, the more confused you'll get.

- *Start with a small amount of capital and build it up.* Wrong. The facts show that the less you start with, the less likely your odds of success. If you don't have enough capital to sit through a string of losses, then you won't be there to get in on the big winner when it finally comes.

- *Try to pick tops and bottoms.* This is yet another sure-fire way to lose money. Tops and bottoms don't happen too often. Trying to pick them is like trying to find a needle in the haystack. You can find seasonal lows and highs with a good degree of success; however, you're always best getting into existing trends and riding them.

You're better off trading with the established trend as opposed to trying to pick a change in trend before it happens.

■ *Get out of your winners quickly and ride your losers.* Many traders get anxious when they're in a profitable position. They have the urge to take the money and run before the market takes it back from them. But when they're in a *losing* position, they're patient and remorseful. E-traders are prime candidates for this affliction.

Traders love to ride losses. They get mesmerized into a state of no action, hoping that the market will reverse trend. They ride losses for a long time and exit profits quickly. This is another good way to lose money trading futures.

■ *Buy a better trading system.* It's not the system that makes profits—it's the trader. In the hands of a poor trader, a good system is useless. Spend more time developing yourself as a trader. It will be time well spent.

Simple and inexpensive systems often work best. Every now and then you'll run across an expensive system that holds promise. If you decide to buy it and if you're convinced it's worthwhile, then you must also make the commitment to trade it according to the rules. If you can't do that, then don't waste your time and money on the system.

■ *Spread your position to avoid taking a loss.* This little trick rarely works. In fact, it most often puts you into double jeopardy. It's just another way to generate commissions and losses.

There are many other sure-fire ways to lose money trading in the futures markets, although the preceding list includes some of the best. While this presentation may be a bit humorous, it is nevertheless very serious.

Trading is a risky business. There are definite dos and don'ts. Try as hard as you can to avoid the don'ts and to follow through carefully on the dos. It will be helpful to you in the long run as well as in the short run.

Emotions Versus Markets, History, and You

Friedrich Nietzsche said "Madness is rare in individuals, but in groups, parties, nations, and ages it is the rule." In his brief but powerful commentary on the nature of insanity and human emotion, Nietzsche clearly and explicitly described the nature of the human condition in the stock and futures markets. To apply his profound words to the market is perhaps to pervert his intent; yet, they are so poignantly apropos that the comparison begs to be made.

The history of humankind is the history of speculation. In one form or another speculation dates back thousands of years, to the earliest days of recorded history. Our forebears speculated daily on the weather, on their search for safe and solid shelter, on growing crops, and in warding off hostile animals and aggressors. Whether for the purpose of survival or in business, risk taking has always been a vital and necessary part of life on our planet.

With risk and speculation, however, come the inevitable and unavoidable consequences and evils of emotion. We fear that our decisions will lead to pain or losses, and we are, therefore, unwilling to take risks. We fear that our failure to act will lead to negative consequences, so we act impulsively. We seek to protect what we have gained for fear it will be lost or that its quantity may be diminished, so we act to preserve it.

We are motivated by greed to expect large profits from small investments, and so we ignore our rational thoughts and act on emotions. There are literally thousands of human behaviors which are motivated by the expectation of financial gain or by the fear of financial loss.

Even a cursory study of world financial history leads to the inescapable conclusion that there has been a close relationship between the intensity of human emotions and significant market turning points. Whether novices or seasoned veterans, investors and traders know that the madness of crowds is often hard at work when markets establish major tops and bottoms.

We know, almost intuitively, that the mob will be wrong; that in order to avoid being trampled to death in a burning theater, we must choose the exit that the mob has not chosen; and that to survive financial panics and crashes, it is imperative for us to muster every ounce of our monetary courage in order to buy when the whole world is selling and sell when the insane crowd is embroiled in a buying frenzy.

We know from repeated and often costly experience that those who can buy into crashes and panics will be successful, while those who can sell into buying panics will also profit handsomely. Yet, we are also painfully cognizant of the fact that to do so runs totally contrary to the primordial maps which have shaped our behavior for hundreds of thousands of years.

The "fight or flight" response causes us to fight markets or to flee from them rather than evaluating them objectively and unemotionally. Emotional extremes correlate closely with major market tops and bottoms in that such extremes can be readily ascertained by examining certain evidence, such as newspaper accounts, magazine articles, television and radio reports (where available), and trader anecdotes. Study them to know whether a market is close to bottoming or topping.

When the news is most bullish a top is imminent. Pervasive bearish news suggests a bottom. Various technical market indicators, such as trading volume and specific chart formations, also have had considerable predictive validity when correlated with measures of investor emotion. Mob psychology is clearly in evidence at virtually all major market tops and bottoms. Emotion can be your worst enemy, or it can be your best friend. Make it your friend and ally, for it is a formidable enemy that cannot be defeated.

The study of human emotion provides us with the big picture of trading. If we can identify where human emotion is taking the rest of the trading community without becoming influenced by it, we will know that the markets will soon be moving in the opposite direction and will profit by that knowledge. This distance from the emotions of others, however, requires us to be able to distance ourselves from our own emotions.

Following our rational thoughts means fighting the powerful current going in the opposite direction. This constant internal battle requires enormous energy and commitment. Nevertheless, the destination for the battle-scarred trader who is willing to engage in this effort is the land of successful trading.

A Few Cogent Rules for E-Traders

To those who have been in the market for many years, the time-tested and oft-repeated trading rules are well known. In fact, they are so well known that few of us attend to them. Now that we have examined these maxims in the light of psychological theory, you may be more willing to use them, especially after they are restated in a manner that makes their use very clear. I have found it very useful to keep a list of these rules where I can refer to them often. I find that they help keep me on the right track.

- *Plan your trades specifically and in advance—keep them available.* If you are specific and organized and act on plans, you will avoid costly efforts often caused by spontaneous decisions. A concise trading plan will help you avoid the losses that can arise from acting on the opinions of others. Regardless of the trading system you are using, such a plan is necessary. In short, plan your trades and trade your plans.

- *You alone are responsible for the success or failure of your trading.* You must assume total responsibility for results, good or bad. You alone are the vehicle to profits and losses. By assuming total responsibility and not blaming brokers, friends, or market letters for errors, you will realize the seriousness of trading. This will help you avoid emotional decisions. You will learn that the situation is entirely under your own control. This will make you consistent and truthful to your trading system. And consistency is the single most valuable key to success.

- *Never hope that a position will go your way; never fear that a position will not go your way.* Both these attitudes lead to unrealistic expectations, emotional decisions, and negative attitudes. A position, once established, will result in whatever market action prevails. Once the trade has been made, its fate is sealed, and no amount of hope or fear will make things different. Hope and fear are two of the greatest enemies of the speculator, fostering only false perceptions. You must avoid these feelings at all costs. The more rigid you can become in your execution of trades, the more profitable will be your results.

- *Monitor your performance—feedback of results is important.* One of the most important things a trader can know about his or her system is whether it is working. The only way to know this is by keeping a thorough record of results. This will also provide the feedback necessary to reward you for good trading. At any time you must know how well or how poorly you are doing. You must also know if your inability or that of your trading system causes poor results.

- *Attitude is your greatest asset.* A good trading system is perhaps only 20 percent of the total picture. A positive attitude may very well comprise the balance of successful trading. You must constantly remain aware that the enemies of profitable investing and speculation are never absent. The only way to combat the negative effects of losses, interference from others, and poor trading signals is by the maintenance of a positive attitude, regardless of how bad things may seem.

- *Cultivate effective and positive relationships.* We are known by the company we keep. Moreover, we are influenced by those around us. If we surround ourselves with losers, loafers, pretenders, or depressives, we will learn no positive skills. If we associate with those who are highly motivated, who seek to achieve, who have ambitious goals, and who are willing to forge ahead regardless of obstacles, then we will acquire similar drives. Personal relationships as well as business associations should be cultivated along these general guidelines.

- *Don't take the market home with you.* If you trade for a living, you must take great care to leave the market when you leave the office. If you are only a casual investor and do not have a full-time market-related job, then you must also avoid spending too much time or thought on the market. When things go well, you may allow the market too much influence in satisfying other areas of your life. This is not advisable, since it will cause you to delay solving other problems.

If the market is not going well for you, and you allow it to affect the rest of your life, this will also be destructive. The market must be seen as a means to an end. It should not become a way of life, and it should not dictate your every move. Make certain you take vacations. Take time each year to close out positions (if necessary) and get away from it all. By being too close to the situation, you may not see it for what it really is.

■ *Enjoy the fruits of your labor—spend some profits, save some profits.* Make it a regular practice to remove profits from the market. Spend some of them and save some of them. You must directly experience the positive feelings of using profits to acquire some of the things you have always wanted to buy. I suggest you do this regularly, perhaps monthly. You will not be motivated to make profits if you do not experience firsthand the enjoyment that can come from spending large sums of money.

■ *Avoid overconfidence—it could be your greatest enemy.* There are good times in the market and there are bad times. Just as you should not allow the bad times to bring you down, you must not allow the good times to get you up too high. If you are on either of these emotional extremes, your judgment can be impaired and you will not be rational enough to deal with what lies before you. You will be either too brave or too meek.

The best course is to even out the peaks and valleys. Each loss should be a negative experience, but not a totally destructive defeat. Similarly, each profit should be taken in stride. Overconfidence may, in fact, be even more potentially destructive than lack of confidence, since it will make you take chances that could destroy you.

■ *Your next goal should always be in sight.* Once you have attained an objective, make certain that your next challenge is set. A well-known commodity trader made several million dollars in the market one year. He lost it and almost went bankrupt the next year. I asked him how this could have happened. "Simple," he replied. "When you climb a mountain and you are sitting on the top of the world, it gets lonely. There's no place left to go but down." If, however, you have another mountain to climb once you get to the top, you will not be tempted to go down in order to have a new challenge.

There are, to be sure, many rules that apply to successful trading. Some of the ones included in this chapter may not be universally applicable, and some rules that are needed by individual traders may not have been included. For these reasons, you would benefit immensely from a formulation of your own trading rules—you, alone, are the best judge of what you need. To do this, however, you must first become totally aware of your needs, assets, liabilities, skills, and goals. In the meantime, study the ones included here and see how they fit.

The Psychology of Trading Systems

In today's world of futures trading there are literally hundreds, perhaps thousands, of trading systems and methods. The choices are many and varied. It is no wonder that as the years pass, there is more and more confusion among new traders and seasoned traders alike. There are performance claims and counter claims. There are black-box systems known to virtually all traders.

With so much to choose from, what is a trader to do? Consider the plight of the newcomer to futures trading. With all of the claims, innuendoes, and promises, the ultimate choice can be a difficult one, and it could very well be one that brings losses rather than the anticipated profits. Yet all of this begs the question: Do you want to use another trader's system? What follows seeks to crystallize and clarify some of the basic issues in an effort to make the selection process less agonizing and more profitable.

Putting the Horse First

Underlying this entire issue, as you know, are the personality traits, expectations, time constraints, and experience of the trader. For the sake of simplicity, let us divide traders into two very broad groups, *mechanical traders* and *thinking traders.* The names I have selected for the two groups are not meant to imply that one type of trader is more likely to make profits than is the other.

In order to facilitate success, each trader must put the horse before the cart by deciding whether the system he or she is best suited to follow necessitates thought, understanding, and judgment, or whether it requires strictly mechanical application. Inasmuch as the choice of mechanical trading requires less discussion, let us deal with it first.

Shocking the Monkey

I call the mechanical systems approach the *market monkey school,* but I do so without malice or disdain. I find that thinking about mechanical systems in this way helps me understand them better—and it helps me find my proper place in their application. My understanding comes from experiences I had at college in the field of clinical and experimental psychology.

B. F. Skinner's work with laboratory animals that were conditioned to follow specific stimuli and received either rewards or punishment as a means of reinforcing or extinguishing behavior (making that behavior more or less probable, respectively) convinced me that most behavior is learned through reward and punishment. Follow the system and you will be rewarded. Pervert the system, fail to follow it, and you will be shocked.

As unromantic, harsh, controversial, cold, and mindless as this approach may seem to many traders, it is, nevertheless, a viable methodology that is best suited to the traits and self-discipline limitations of many traders! I have deep respect for mechanical systems that have many years of backtesting. Such systems are specific, require minimal thought (if any), have specific track records, and help eliminate money problems faced by a majority of traders. In fact, all traders should consider effective mechanical systems.

However, it must be observed that lack of discipline will defeat the purpose of such systems, since they require virtually total discipline. Some traders can acquire the self-control to trade such a system by using the system to force self-control. Yet, the majority of traders cannot follow mechanical systems since they allow their thoughts, emotions, understandings, interpretations, finances, brokers, friends, family, politics, the media, and other factors to influence their trades. I have a very healthy respect for mechanical systems and, above all, for those who can follow them without significant deviation. Before looking into what features typify effective mechanical systems, let us look at the other alternative.

The Executive Monkey

The second category of trader is the thinking trader. Before you let the title fool you, I must add that thinking traders as a group are not better off than mechanical traders. As a matter of fact, thinkers may be worse off, on the whole, than mechanical traders. Consider the classical experiment performed by learned psychologists many years ago. Two monkeys were placed in cages. One monkey was punished and rewarded randomly. He had no control over his destiny. The other monkey was given warning pending punishment in the form of a light or buzzer signal. By depressing a switch, he could avoid the punishment.

Of the two monkeys, the first had no choice but to accept his destiny, taking whatever the system had to dish out. The second monkey, called the *executive monkey*, had choices as well as the pressure of the decision-making process. He had to be on alert at all times. There was probably some thought involved (i.e., to press the switch and avoid the punishment, or to sleep . . . to wait and see if the pain was bad . . . to attempt to escape . . . to seek a specific spot in the cage where the punishment could not be delivered . . . etc.).

Of course, I have adapted and interpreted the experiment to suit my purposes for this discussion. My explanations may have perverted the intent of the experimenters, but I have done so in order to drive home a point. While the first monkey had no choice, he suffered no ill effects behaviorally or psychologically. The executive monkey, after a period of time, began to show a variety of anxiety reactions and behavioral disturbances. The contrived experimental conditions cannot, of course, be directly applied to the issue of traders and trading systems, but there are some points to be made.

Mechanical Versus Discretionary Choices

While the mechanical trader has no choice but to go with the flow of his or her system, good, bad, or otherwise, the tension and pressure of decisions are less than those experienced by traders who must follow systems requiring more complex decisions, choices, and thought. Western people have been trained to go *against* the flow, to exercise free will, and to attempt changing that which is unacceptable. Therefore, mechanical systems that require skill in the zen of trading systems are not palatable to many Westerners, who may take refuge in the snob appeal of thinking that their approach is better.

The point is, clearly, that what is better in a trading system is what is better for you, the trader. In fact, I would go so far as to say that we, as traders, should not become so jaded as to scoff at any type of trading approach, whether based on fundamentals, technicals, econometrics, astrology, Gann angles, Fibonacci numbers, or whatever. Keep an open mind in selecting what is best suited to your trading personality: if you are the trader whose head is swollen with haughty losses, the market mechanic, or the market thinker—find your place and accept it. Then go on to the selection process.

Is it possible to be in between? Can you be a thinking mechanic or a mechanical thinker? I am certain that you can. Can you have a system that is basically mechanical, but one that requires some decision making and thought based on its output? Yes, you can. In fact, most systems fall into this category. But before you get too complicated, make your basic choices.

First Things to Consider

The process of deciding on a system or trading approach is, as previously stated, one that must be taken seriously, and with personality in mind. If you have decided on a mechanical system, you will want to ask different questions than those who have decided on orientation with a certain school of thought or a specific approach. Here are some issues to consider in selecting a mechanical system.

Remember that by *mechanical system* I mean a system that puts data in and gets *buy, sell,* or *hold* as its output. The only thing the trader is required to do (and it is a big requirement) is to take the specified actions. Consider the following:

- *Performance claims.* Is the track record real time or hypothetical? Certainly, real time is preferable, but hypothetical is also acceptable, provided the record has accounted for commissions and worst-case slippage for such things as poor order fills and limited market liquidity.
- *Dollar drawdown and a string of successive losses.* These items should be carefully checked. Serious historical drawdown and/or a long string of successive losing trades can knock traders out of the box, either by wiping out their account size or by causing them to lose faith in the system and, hence, failing to follow it.

   No matter how good bottom-line claims may be, low accuracy and large drawdown have the potential to undermine ideal performance due to the human element and the limitation of funds.
- *Period of back-testing.* Many systems are tested on 3 to 5 years of back data. This may not be enough for a good long-term test. The longer the historical test the better.
- *Optimization.* This is a controversial issue. Do you want a system that is fitted to the data, or do you want a system that tests concepts or algorithms for their validity? You must decide.

If there are basically two types of traders, the mechanical trader and the discretionary trader, the type of system used by each trader should be compatible with his or her own personality and style of trading. These two styles are not necessarily equal in their results, however. The mechanical trader appears to be better off than the discretionary trader is. This is because the level of stress and pressure is lower for the mechanical trader since this style does not require making decisions constantly.

Although most traders would probably be better off with mechanical systems, these mechanical systems *do* require virtually total discipline, and most traders cannot follow them. Nevertheless, if a trader feels that a mechanical system is suited to his or her personality and style of trading, he or she must know what to look for—because, just as all traders are not created equal, neither are all trading systems.

Discipline—Maximizing Profits, Minimizing Losses

Whether you seek to excel as a writer, a trader, a doctor, or an investor, you will rarely achieve your goals through luck. You will most often arrive at your destination through the application of time-tested rules applied consistently, repeatedly, diligently, and with discipline. I began an in-depth examination of trading discipline, its definition, intricacies, and application. Most traders do not understand the meaning of discipline, and discipline has, through the years, become an effete topic of conversation among traders.

Defining Trading Discipline

One of the main reasons so many traders find it difficult to master discipline is that they have not defined it first. For many traders, discipline is illusory. They chase ghosts that approach the true definition of discipline but which cannot be caught since they are not defined with sufficient clarity. So, let us begin with a working definition of trading discipline.

trading discipline: Acting in complete accordance with the signals generated by a trading system, method, or procedure and with the risk management rules which accompany that system, method, or procedure.

Discipline is a matter of individuality. Since personalities and needs vary, that which requires discipline and self-control for one person requires virtually no effort for another. Some traders complete tasks in virtually automatic fashion which are achieved only with considerable effort by others. What poses a chronic problem for some traders has never been, and will probably never be, a problem for other traders. Practicing discipline in following a trading system is useless if one does not have the discipline to keep his or her trading system up to date, or one does not have the discipline to follow sound risk management.

As you can see, trading discipline is multifaceted and interdependent. There are layers and levels of discipline, all of which interact to produce their positive or negative results.

Levels of Trading Discipline

Preparation and Planning. If a trader is to trade a system, the system must be maintained in working order. You must do your homework by keeping your work up to date and accurate if it is to serve you well with valid trading signals.

- *Have someone else do it for you.* There are many individuals who enjoy following procedures and plans. Hire one of them to do the work for you if you cannot or prefer not to do it on your own with consistency.

- *Get your trading signals from an advisory service or a trading advisor.* As simple as these procedures may be, there are thousands of traders who cannot follow them. It becomes especially difficult for some traders to follow these procedures when they are losing money. That is when the real test comes. By having someone else do this for you, you will avoid failing at this level.

- *Be on the lookout for unconscious errors in generating your signals when you are in a losing streak.* You can easily make mistakes that you are not even aware of but which are the result of a negative attitude.

Implementation.   This is the single most difficult aspect of discipline for the vast majority of traders. While they have no trouble updating their trading systems, they have great difficulty implementing them. This problem is so pervasive that several books could be written on this topic alone. Because each individual has his or her own personal experience with what creates the fear, this must be dealt with on an individual basis.

Fear of Losses.   Fear of losses is a conscious fear. Traders will not take action when they are afraid of losing money. It is that simple. And the fear escalates with each loss until it reaches the point of complete withdrawal. This is a normal reaction to losses. If you touch a hot stove and you get burned, you will be disinclined to touch it again.

But if the stove is hot at times and not hot at others, you will never know when to touch it. If opening the door of the stove allows you to put your hand in and take money out, the dilemma is even more anxiety provoking. It presents the classic *approach-avoidance* situation, which is one of the most difficult with which to cope.

Laboratory animals in this situation are locked into inconsistent and neurotic behaviors for many years. It is the fact that you do not know when the reward is coming that makes this problem so severe.

Fear of Profit.   There are many traders who would be very uncomfortable if they were successful. These are traders who fear their own impulses. In most cases, they have such low self-esteem that they refuse to accept the fact that they can be winners. Why do they continue to play the game? They do so because they have not yet come to grips with their unconscious desire to avoid winning.

They are essentially normal individuals, yet they know down deep that nothing they have ever done in their lives has been a complete victory—that nothing they have ever done has been thoroughly enjoyed. In such cases, lack of discipline is deeply rooted and must be treated by a mental health professional, although it can be remedied in more mechanical ways.

Overcoming the Shy Trigger Finger

- *Have someone else pull the trigger for you.* The preferred choice is a person who is detached, a person who does not have a vested interest in your trading.
- *Develop a system of checks and balances.* Cross-check your system with another trader who trades similarly to the way you trade. By monitoring the same trading signals, you can keep each other honest.

Risk Management

This is by far the most mismanaged area of trading. It is the area which is responsible for small losses turning into large losses or for potentially large profits being picked off the vine prematurely as small profits. Most traders I have talked to readily admit that their largest losing trades have most often been trades which could have been closed out as small losers according to their trading system but which were left too long.

The ability to close out losers promptly and to ride winners is by far the most important of all forms of trading discipline. More traders have lost more money by riding losers than by picking bad trades that were closed out as small losses. But how to close out those losers? That is the big question. Again, the answer is simple. If you cannot close those losers out when you have to do so, get someone to do it for you. Along these lines, I have several suggestions:

- If your system uses a stop loss immediately when entering a position, then enter your stop loss immediately, as well. If the stop stays the same for the duration of the trade, enter an open order (good until canceled).
- If your system uses a trailing stop loss, make certain you enter the trailing stop loss each time it needs to be changed.
- To stay honest with your system and yourself, have another individual monitor your system and evaluate your discipline accordingly.
- Use a checklist. Check off each item as it is completed.

Determining What Is Right for You

Goals and needs go hand in hand. In order to determine exactly how your trading discipline can be improved, there are several questions and issues that must be addressed.

Do You Need to Improve Your Discipline?   A simple way to find the answer to this question is to look at your performance.

- Is it significantly different from the ideal performance of your system or method?
- Are you losing money when your system says you should be making money?
- Have the markets acted as you expected?
- Have you made money from your expectations?

If you are not performing as your system would ideally have you do, and if you are not profiting from your signals and/or projections, it is likely that your discipline is at fault. However, if you are satisfied with your profits, and you are trading in accordance with your plans and system, no changes in discipline are warranted at this time.

Isolate the Source of Your Losses.   Determine the reason(s) for your losses. This means that each loss must be examined in detail.

Determine the cause of each loss. Causes can fall into many different categories. They can be due to emotion, errors, disorganization, lack of sufficient margin, and a host of other variables. You will not be able to change the cause until you have determined the cause.

Be Specific.   When you investigate the cause of each loss, do so in considerable detail. Retrace all of your steps, from the original technical signal to the actual liquidation of the trade. Be as specific as possible tracking down the reason(s) for each losing trade.

Keep a Diary.   A diary of your trading should be kept in order to help delineate the quality of your discipline or lack thereof. By retracing your steps you may find the clue to your difficulty. Record the following:

- Date, time, and price trade was entered
- Reason(s) for entry (be specific)
- Date, time and price trade was closed out
- Reason(s) for exit (be specific)

- Any thoughts, feelings, special situations, problems, or events that tran-
spired directly before or after you entered or exited the trade

Frequently, the mere act of keeping a diary will alert you to potential or
actual problems with discipline.

The best time to write in your diary is when you enter or exit a given
trade. If you are too busy, however, then update your diary at the end of the
trading day.

I maintain that a diary is extremely important when tracking discipline.
Every trader should keep a diary, whether currently making money or losing money. A diary can be the source of much important information.

Do Not Rule Anything Out. When you are looking for answers, consider
everything. Something as simple as talking to the wrong people can be the
source of your lack of discipline.

Look for Patterns. Study your behavior in detail and watch for patterns
and repertoire. Determine what event or events come immediately before
and immediately after your lack of discipline.

A Few Closing Thoughts About Discipline

So what is the bottom line of the trading discipline issue? There are several
points that deserve mentioning.

- *Trading discipline can be learned.* Discipline of any kind is *not* innate. We
learn it as a function of exposure to various learning experiences, most of
which come from our parents and teachers. While it is true that some people appear to be more organized than others are, I emphasize that organization and discipline are not one and the same. There are many highly
organized traders who have not mastered the finer points of discipline.

- *Trading discipline is by far the weakest link in the trading chain.* Without discipline, virtually nothing is possible. Any trader who feels that he or she
can achieve lasting success without trading discipline is living a lie. Any
trader who fails to develop the necessary skills which are part and parcel
of trading discipline is doomed to failure.

  Any trader who refuses to accept the importance of discipline in the
areas outlined previously is destined to fail repeatedly. Any trader who
has not overcome the problems which arise as a function of poor discipline will never be successful other than through luck.

- *Trading discipline is at least as important as your trading system.* You must find
ways to make the two work together for you. A system without discipline

is like a ship without a rudder—it cannot be guided through the treacherous waters safely. It will be dashed upon the rocks during stormy seas.

- *Trading discipline should be your priority.* Place it number one on your list, even ahead of having an effective trading system. Learn discipline first by applying some of the suggestions given in this chapter, talk to expert traders, observe the habits of successful traders, study your losing trades, find out where you went wrong each time you take a loss, and, above all, *always* distinguish between losses you took as a function of *poor discipline* and losses you took in following a system.

  One type of loss is acceptable, and you will learn from it. The other type of loss is unacceptable, and you will not grow unless you understand what it is you did that caused you to lose your discipline.

Overcoming Trading Barriers

For a trader and his system to be compatible, there must be an optimum or, at the very least, a workable harmony between the trader and the system he or she selects. In order to achieve such a best fit, it is incumbent upon the trader to assess his or her needs, motives, abilities, and expectations as they relate to a given trading style, approach, theory, or system. Surprisingly, few traders or investors follow such an avenue, either consciously or unconsciously.

In their burning desire for success and wealth, traders, as well as investors, ignore the fundamentals and confuse the end with the means. Traders often say, "I don't care how I get there [i.e., profits], as long as the system I use has had a good performance record." Yet, this attitude entirely ignores the importance of compatibility and system-versus-trader interaction.

How can the trader evaluate or reevaluate his or her status in relation to a given trading approach? The answer is a simple one, indeed—so simple, in fact, that it is prone to be ignored as too basic. The answer consists of asking a series of questions, all of which can be dealt with very quickly.

Here are some basic items to consider:

- *What are my motives?*

  Do I want to make a given amount of money?

  Do I want to prove or disprove a theory?

  Do I want fame, recognition, fortune, or all of the above?

  Do I need to reach a goal quickly, or do I have time?

  Am I more interested in telling people that I trade than I am interested in actually trading?

  Is my trading for the purpose of profit, or for the purpose of hedging?

- *What do I expect?*

  Do I expect to be a success in six months?

  Do I think it will take several years?

  Do I think that this is the only trading system I will need?

  Do I think that I will need to work hard?

  Am I expecting to be lucky?

  Am I looking upon trading as a gamble?

  Am I making trading more scientific than it really is?

- *Can I do it?*

  Can I sit through the type of drawdown that this system has had?

  Can I follow all the rules and signals with discipline and consistency?

  Do I have the time?

  Do I have the money?

  Can I risk losing it all?

  Am I willing and able to make the system work?

  How has my record been?

  Do I have the necessary mechanical skills and tools (i.e., math and computers)?

- *How will I handle failure?*

  Do I need many small successes, or can I accept many small successes prior to the major rewards?

- *Can I implement my system?*

  Does the system require more time and/or money input than I can afford?

  Is the trading system too complicated or time-consuming for me?

  Does it require acquisition of data which is either too costly, too complicated, or otherwise incompatible with my abilities?

There are many other questions that should be asked. However, they tend to fall into the general categories given here. In addition, it should be remembered that each trader has individual needs, which require individual or specialized solutions.

The goal is, of course, to seek a system or method which is compatible with as many of your needs as possible. It is unlikely that you will find an approach that will satisfy all of your requirements. However, the goal is to strive for the attainment of a majority of your needs.

Additional Aspects of Compatibility

The points I have raised and discussed, up to now, should be fairly obvious to all traders. Though many traders have ignored them, they know that these considerations are important and, furthermore, that they ought not to ignore them.

Yet, there is another aspect to compatibility that has been left untouched by a good majority of those who give attention to the trader portion of the trading equation. The issue I am referring to relates to the synthesis of ideas and the development of one's own trading approach. I have found that a majority of traders are better off developing their own approach, as opposed to following a predetermined technique developed by another trader.

The ability to study, analyze, evaluate, and synergize is an important one. The creative trader who can take the best points of many different methodologies and put them together in a new and more effective combination appears to have a greater likelihood of lasting success. Why? Because a trader is often more serious about, dedicated to, and knowledgeable about a method of his or her own creation.

One great barrier to trader success relates to the system selected and then either followed or not by the trader. If the trader has selected a system which is ultimately compatible with his or her goals, expectations, and personality, the trader is then more likely to stick with the system. The process of creative thinking and the synergism which it prompts are important aspects of compatibility, inasmuch as they are products of the trader.

Hence, the system is a reflection of the needs, expectations, abilities, and specific requirements of the trader who created them. In such a case, the trader will be more prone to be true to his or her system, and the probability of success is likely to be higher since the *fit* is frequently better.

Overcoming Losses

It has been said that good traders know how to generate profits, but that *great* traders know how to handle *losses*. Those of us who have traded futures for many years know the great truth to be found in this bit of market wisdom. Even novices know that the disposition of losses is much more important than the ability to generate profits.

Naturally, the ability to take losses well, without the ability to produce profitable trades, is still a losing proposition. However, in comparative terms, the trader who can generate reasonable profits while knowing how to cope with and limit losses is the trader who will consistently outperform most others.

The Inevitability of Losses

Inasmuch as losses go with the territory of futures trading, they are unavoidable and inescapable. There is no trading system, method, technique, or approach which avoids losses entirely. The more trades you make, the more losses you will have. *The longer you trade, the more you will be exposed, and the greater the probability of inappropriate management of losses.*

The effective disposition of losses should, ideally, be a totally mechanical procedure. However, due to the fact that many trading approaches do not have mechanical rules for taking losses, there is always the danger that losses will not be cut short. This is precisely where trader personality comes into play.

Trader Personality and Losses

It is probably true that there are born losers. And while it is true that there are specific personality traits associated with born losers, knowing these traits will not necessarily help us. By now, all but the most uninformed of traders are aware of what qualities are important to trading success. But, depending upon your orientation to the psychology of trading, understanding the inner workings of certain trading behaviors may be essential to positive change.

The problem for traders is finding the most effective way to handle losses and the psychology involved. Are there some mental exercises or techniques that we can employ in an effort to overcome the demoralization and ego deflation we experience when our trades go against us? The answer is addressed in this chapter as we explore some alternative directions in coping styles. First, let us examine the issue of losses from a psychological standpoint.

The Classic Interpretation.
Traditional psychiatric notions are derived from the teachings of Sigmund Freud, the father of psychoanalysis. The cornerstone of Freud's theory of psychosexual development is the male child's competition with his father for the mother's attention and the female child's competition with her mother for the father's attention.

In his work with patients, Freud claimed to have found that competition for attention can lead to fear on the part of the child and that this fear is not in our conscious awareness. Supposedly, the child fears that the same-sex parent will seek revenge by resorting to castration. In adult life, according to this theory, fear of loss is a variation of the castration fear theme which, supposedly, developed in childhood.

Traditional psychoanalytical ideas have been severely challenged for many years by humanists and behaviorists. Behaviorally oriented psychology is based on learning principles. Behavioral psychologists claim that virtually all behavior is learned as a direct result of stimulus and response connections.

In other words, behavior is maintained as a function of its consequences. According to this paradigm, behavior that has favorable consequences tends to increase, and behavior that has negative consequences tends to decrease. However, it has been shown that negative consequences can act to increase given behaviors because they are functioning, in certain situations, as if they were positive consequences.

The primary objection to the behavioristic approach is that it tends to minimize the importance of human feelings, cognition, and self-determination while focusing on changing stimulus and response conditions in a mechanistic, unfeeling, insensitive, and impermanent manner. In short, behaviorists are not humanists.

In contrast, the humanists employ literally hundreds of different person-centered approaches to human psychology. The essence of the humanistic approach to therapy is its focus on empathy, understanding, support, assistance, self-determination, existential growth, and, in some cases, metaphysical development. The weakness of this approach rests in its lack of a central theory or organization and its unquantifiable, vague results.

The Behavioral and Humanistic Interpretation

Where to Turn? Faced with so many choices, traders with problems are faced with the added problem of finding effective help. Who or what can help? Based upon my training as a psychologist and my experience as a trader, I have come to prefer the behavioral approach to dealing with losses. I do, however, attempt to give you some ideas on how each approach might help the trader cope with and dispose of losses before they become chronic or deadly.

Using Behavioral Psychology. The learning-theory approach to behavior is both simple and complex. Learning theorists (behaviorists) maintain that virtually all human behavior is learned. Productive, unproductive, positive, negative, subtle, and obvious behaviors are all learned. If you subscribe to the learning theory of behavior, then you believe that great traders learn to be great and that losers have either learned to lose or have not learned to win.

The Principles of Learning

- Behavior is learned, shaped, and maintained as a function of its consequences.
- Behavior followed by positive consequences is likely to continue.

- Behavior followed by negative consequences is likely to stop.
- Behaviors which are followed by consequences that are intermittently positive and negative are likely to be very resistant to unlearning or forgetting.
- If a behavior which is followed by negative consequences increases in frequency or continues unabated, the given consequences, although overtly negative, must be acting in a rewarding or positive way, and vice versa for behavior followed by positive consequences which do not increase or maintain the behavior.

For the behaviorist, the answer to changing human behavior is a simple one, though its implementation may be complex and involved. Several steps are required in the process of behavioral change. First, we must specifically delineate or define the behavior that we want to change. This requires an *operational definition* of losing behavior.

Defining Losing Behavior

Since we all trade differently, and since we all have our unique limitations and assets, a universal definition of losing behavior is not possible. Instead of using the circular definition that "losing behavior is any behavior or set of behaviors that results in losses," we need to specify what it is that the individual does which results in losses. And we must distinguish between system-related losses (i.e., losses due to the trading system installed) and trader losses.

A given loss may be half system-related and half trader-related. If, for example, a loss of $500 is taken, only half of the loss may be due to the system, and the rest might be due to the trader failing to act on the system. Since losing behaviors are many and varied, let us take a hypothetical case and demonstrate how a behavioral approach might be used to eliminate the problem.

Defining the Behavior. You have isolated your losing behavior to one specific act: letting losses run beyond the point dictated by your system. You know this to be a fact, since you have analyzed your losses.

Your losses would have been less than half as large had you followed your system explicitly. Operationally defined, your losing behavior is holding a trade beyond the point of ideal exit as dictated by the trading system.

Identifying How You Learned the Behavior. Most people feel that it is not enough to know that a given percentage of our losses come from staying with losers too long. We also feel the need to know *why* we do this. We believe, as a result of our learning and training, that by knowing why we do something, we will be able to change it. Such insight is the stuff of which psychiatry is made, holding that such insight will help us to change the behavior.

On the other hand, the behaviorist argues that even if we achieve insight into why a given behavior exists, we must still have the tools to *change* the behavior, and this can only be achieved through a behavioral *unlearning* and *relearning* process.

The Methods for Change.   The methods by which our target behavior may be changed using learning-theory principles are very specific. First, you must remember that we do not care how the behavior got there, what it means, or why we continue to do it. Suffice it to say that you learned something you want to change. While there is no single method, the *underlying principles* of learning-theory change procedures are similar from one behavioral technique to another. Essentially, the principles are as follows:

- *Eliminate* any positive consequences of the behavior you want to change, since the positive consequences are maintaining the given behavior.

- *Change* the stimulus which results in the given behavior.

- *Teach* a new behavior which will replace or compete with the undesired (i.e., target) behavior.

Some behaviorists also use aversive consequences (i.e., punishment) in combination with these techniques. However, aversives are generally reserved for only the most severe or serious behavioral disturbances.

Points to Consider in Getting Results

The Reward for Negative Behavior.   In order to apply the preceding techniques, let us take a closer look at the target behavior of *riding losses*. What is rewarding about the behavior? The answer is simple: although riding losses frequently produces the negative consequence of large losses, it also, on occasion, produces positive consequences.

Learning to Ride Losses.   How do we learn to ride losses? The answer, according to the principles of learning theory, is very simple. Since riding losses sometimes results in the positions turning profitable (i.e., reward), and sometimes in a greater loss (i.e., punishment), and since we never know when the loss will reverse in our favor (i.e., intermittent reward and punishment), the process falls into the category of most resistant to change.

The Positive Behavior. If you do not have a trading system, then you do not know the point of ideal exit. This also holds true for a trading technique that does not define risk or loss point. Hence, the first step is to find such a system or method. Not having a stop-loss point or an idea of the risk point is not necessarily bad, but it does increase the probability of riding a loss. As long as you have an idea of where you want out, that is all you need, but the more specific the better.

Eliminating the Positive Consequences. In order to change the behavior, you must eliminate the sometimes positive consequences of riding a loss. In other words, if you want to eliminate the behavior, you must eliminate its positive consequences. A simple, but very effective way to do this is to enter into a contract with someone you trust.

The contract would require you to enter a stop point or risk point for every trade, no exceptions, and, furthermore, to agree that the stop point cannot be moved in the direction of potentially greater loss (smaller loss is okay). More about the contract follows.

Teaching a Competing Behavior. Another way to change the behavior is to teach a new behavior that competes with the old one. For example, you might enter into a program that requires you to close out a position after a certain number of days, hours, or minutes, if it is not profitable. Or, you might turn your system, in its entirety, over to someone who can follow its rules. These are viable alternatives.

The Contract Method. This simple approach, already briefly mentioned, requires you to enter into an agreement with a party who will be consistent and thorough in following the rules. The rules are simple. First, you agree to provide a specific stop for each trade, and give it to the person whose help you have recruited.

If you have concerns about having the stop in the market, then your assistant could use it as a mental stop, executing it if and when the market hits your mental stop. You would agree to stay with the program for a given length of time, several months, for example. And you would also agree not to change stops to ones that might result in a larger loss, and not to add to a losing position. This program will accomplish the following:

- It will remove the positive consequences of riding a loss because your losses will always be taken if the program is followed.

- This will, over time, keep you from being rewarded for the negative behavior of riding a loss.

- One side benefit is that the program will allow you to achieve a true and honest evaluation of your system.
- The program will also help you be more systematic.
- Finally, you may be more cautious and less prone to take trades on a lark if you know that you will need a specific stop or risk point, and that it will be followed to the letter.

Over the course of time, you will see your behavior change due to the cessation of positive consequences for a negative behavior. Remember that what is discussed here is a simple approach. In reality, few traders have only one problem that needs to be solved, but the approach is basically the same. If the source of the problem can be identified as a learning problem, then the principles of learning can be applied with the prospect of good and lasting results.

Other Considerations for the E-Trader

Even the most inexperienced traders are aware of the fact that futures trading is a psychological game. After all the research is done, after all the trading systems have had their turn at bat, and after all the experts have given their forecasts, the fact remains that what traders *actually* do, in contrast to what they *should* do, is often a very different thing. For too many years, traders have considered the markets to be their chief enemy. Yet, in fact, it is the trader who is his or her own worst enemy. For the active e-trader, information overload can often be a serious problem.

20/20 Hindsight

We are all guilty of using 20/20 hindsight. We are guilty of the *I should have* syndrome. Consider the following statements, all of which should be familiar to you either in their stated forms or in countless variations on their themes:

1. *I should have* gone long when I wanted to. I knew the market was bottoming.
2. *I should have* used a stop loss. My system was right.
3. *I should have* added to my position. I knew it was the right thing to do.
4. *I should have* done what the charts told me to do. Getting out of my position because of the bearish news was clearly not the right thing to do.

5. *I should have* put on my position and closed my eyes to the day-to-day news developments.

6. *I should have* sold short and gone fishing.

7. *I should have* done my homework. Two days after I stopped following my technical indicators, the market started one of its largest moves in history.

8. *I should have* traded with blinders on . . . my own feelings and analyses were best.

Information Overload

In the early 1980s, as the gold market was making its long-term top, the market was, as you can well imagine, extremely volatile. Emotions ran high. Forecasts were flying right and left. Talk of $1000, even $2000 gold was common. Expectations of $100 silver (then about $45 per ounce) were also common, perpetuated in part by the very bullish public prognostications of Bunker Hunt. One of the most well-attended investment seminars was held in Dallas near the peak of the gold market.

The Real Money seminars featured dozens of traders, advisors, and other market experts commenting on the precious metals. As you can surmise, most analysts were bullish. As bullish as they were, they differed in how high they expected gold and silver to go.

Once the seminar was over and I had delivered my opinion to the crowd, I entered the elevator. As I waited for the elevator doors to close, another man entered. He looked dazed and confused. We spoke briefly. I commented that he looked upset. He told me that he had come to the conference expecting answers. Instead, he got so many different opinions that he was more confused than ever. In fact, he was frozen with indecision.

This situation is not unique. All too often, we make mistakes by getting too much information, as opposed to too little information. The more information we have, the more confusing things become. Consistent with this fact of market life are several other facts I have observed, not only about my own trading, but about other traders, as well. Consider the following downside with respect to too much market-related information:

1. *The more information a trader has about the markets, the more confused the trader will be, particularly if the information is contradictory.* The fact is that given a plethora of information, traders will naturally attempt to integrate all of it into a meaningful decision. But this does not guarantee that the decision will be correct. In fact, the opinions often balance each other

out and leave the trader just as confused as ever. Furthermore, even an agreement by the majority may be wrong, since it is a well-known fact that the stronger group opinions are, the more likely they are to be wrong.

2. *The more information a trader has, the more likely it is that the trader will use it to justify an already established opinion or position.* Hence, the information has no value other than, perhaps, giving the trader a false sense of security.

3. *The more information a trader has, the more inclined the trader will be to get caught up in the emotional tornado of trading.* Too many traders are incapable of dealing with the tick-by-tick response of prices. Just watching the prices come across the ticker machine is enough to force them into action—action which may be totally contrary to their trading systems or methods.

4. *The more information a trader has, the more likely it is that the trader will find reasons to be insecure about his or her current position.* If the information is considered *expert* opinion, then the odds are that it will have a very negative impact and may, therefore, cause the trader to make errors.

Why Traders Crave Information

Given all this, we must ask why it is that traders seek information. Why is it that traders cannot appreciate the value of ignorance in the markets? The simple fact of the matter is that traders have been mentally and emotionally brainwashed by Western traditions which are themselves part and parcel of the Judeo-Christian work ethic.

We have been taught that in order to be successful, we need to work hard, we need to have as much information as possible, and we need to understand the *why* of things. While this may be true in some areas of life, none of it is necessarily true in trading. The fact is that we do not know the whys and wherefores of things in the markets, nor do we need to gather a wealth of information on the markets in order to make money.

And all of this means that we *do not* have to work hard in order to trade profitably. In fact, I have found that there is often an inverse relationship between how hard you work and how much money you make. In fact, there is a point of diminishing returns when it comes to hard work in the markets.

Suggestions

After my many and varied experiences in the futures markets, I have arrived at several conclusions, all of which will, I feel, markedly benefit e-traders who suffer from the information-overload syndrome.

1. *Think long and hard about whether you really need a live quotation service in your home or office.* All too often, I have seen good traders turn into bad traders as soon as they have added live quotes to their repertoire. Aside from being costly, these services tend to give you much more information than you need. They will encourage you to trade markets you do not need to trade or which you do not understand. They will encourage you to trade in time frames you do not want to trade (i.e., a position trader becoming a day trader).

2. *Do not get too many chart services.* In fact, think about whether you want to get a chart service at all. I have found that traders who do things the good old-fashioned way, by keeping their own charts, tend to be more serious and in better touch with the technical considerations they are trying to keep track of.

3. *Do not subscribe to too many newsletters and advisory services.* The simple truth is that you do not need more than one or two services. Find a newsletter or advisory service you like and stick with it. If you get too many opinions from too many trading advisors, you will get confused and you will not do well.

4. *Avoid information overload from brokers.* All too many traders become sitting ducks for talkative brokers. By letting your broker jawbone you repeatedly, you will be overloaded with all sorts of useless information. Whether willingly or unwillingly, brokers know that the more information they throw at a client, the more likely it is that the client will trade more often.

5. *Avoid visiting too many websites.* With the plethora of information now available free of charge on the Internet, you will be tempted to take solace and/or refuge in the opinions and recommendations and opinions of market "experts." Avoid these! If you have a good system, use it and avoid extraneous inputs.

Too much information coming from too many different sources confuses a trader and leads him or her into trades he or she would not have made otherwise. Information coming from a very limited number of trusted sources is far more valuable to a trader than conflicting, overstimulating information coming from everywhere. In other words, keep it simple.

Afterword

The Future of Electronic Trading

Whether we like it or not, electronic trading in stocks and futures is here to stay. In the years ahead we can expect a number of significant developments to impact e-trading. In order to profit from these changes while avoiding the negatives that can come with change, you will need to be prepared. Here are some of my expectations as well as some suggestions as to how you may profit from them:

- Within a few years, most markets around the world will be traded electronically. The floor broker in commodities and the "specialist" or market maker in stocks will likely not be much of a factor. Hence, order executions will be more equitable and traders will be able to benefit more from their trades, as opposed to giving up the profit that a floor broker might otherwise take by virtue of a bad order fill.

- Since electronic trading is dependent upon reliable systems of electronic order entry, any disruption in communications lines could seriously hamper the entire system. We have already seen such disruptions in a number of markets. Expect these to continue and, in fact, to pose serious problems at times.

    The more dependent we become on electronic communications for order entry and trading, the more vulnerable we will be to a breakdown in the system. When this happens, you must be prepared. But how? Make certain that you have a backup method for order placement which does not depend on the Internet.

- Short-term volatility is likely to become even more pronounced as more traders enter the arena. News will likely continue to exert a major impact on price as traders become more intently focused on ultra-short-term moves.

- In addition, the emergence of futures trading in new markets throughout the world will bring millions of new players into the markets. The next result will be to further exaggerate price swings in all markets.

- The emergence of artificial intelligence and neural networks will eventually have a major impact on the markets as large traders and institutions attempt to trade short-term moves using these tools in order to capitalize on market volatility and large intraday price swings. This will make it more difficult for the smaller trader to make a profit.

- As market volatility increases, traders will need to use larger stop losses in order to avoid getting caught in the trap of large price swings. Traders who use small stop losses in markets that are highly volatile will be doomed to fail before they even begin their trading. More than ever before, it will be necessary to risk more in order to make money in the stock and futures markets.

- Security of electronic trading systems will become a serious problem as high-tech thievery increases. Make certain that your trading is secure.

- As more traders enter the markets, the size of the money pool will increase. This will mean more opportunities for the e-trader—but remember that opportunities do not come without risk.

- Finally, I expect volatility to become so massive that there will be numerous attempts by governments to control market volatility. I believe that these efforts will meet with failure, since the markets will be powerful enough to overcome all outside regulation.

- Electronic order entry for commodities and options will become the industry standard. The number of live brokers to talk to will decrease markedly over the next few years. This will have a double impact. First, it will be more difficult for the new trader to learn. And second, it will create opportunities for those brokers who survive the attrition process, inasmuch as people will still want to talk to people, as opposed to machines.

- Electronic trading in markets outside the United States will grow rapidly. In particular, the LIFFE and EUREX exchanges will likely grow rapidly.

Appendix

Sources and Suppliers of Trading Software, Data, and System Development Software

Trading Software

CQG, Inc.
P. O. Box 758
Glenwood Springs, CO 81602

Data Broadcasting Corporation
3955 Point Eden Way
Hayward, CA 94545

Data Transmission Network
Corporation
9110 West Dodge Road
Omaha, NE 68114

Equis International, Inc.
3950 South 700 East, Suite 100
Salt Lake City, UT 84107

FutureSource/Bridge, LLC
955 Parkview Boulevard
Lombard, IL 60148

Data

Bridge/CRB
30 S. Wacker Drive, Suite 1810
Chicago, IL 60606

Commodity Systems Inc. (CSI)
200 W. Palmetto Road
Boca Raton, FL 33432

Dial/Data Division of Track Data
Corporation
95 Rockwell Place
Brooklyn, NY 11217

Genesis Financial Data Services
425 E. Woodmen Road
Colorado Springs, CO 80919

Glance Market Data Services, Inc.
340 Brooksbank Avenue, Suite 208
North Vancouver, BC, Canada V7T
2C1

MJK Associates
1289 Park Victoria Drive, Suite 205
Milpitas, CA 95035

Pinnacle Data Corporation
1016 Plank Road
Webster, NY 14580

Prophet Financial Systems Inc.
430 Cambridge Avenue
Palo Alto, CA 94306

Reuters DataLink
3950 South 700 East, Suite 100
Salt Lake City, UT 84107

System Development Software

CQG, Inc.
P. O. Box 758
Glenwood Springs, CO 81602

Equis International, Inc.
3950 South 700 East, Suite 100
Salt Lake City, UT 84107

Omega Research, Inc.
8700 W. Flagler Street, Suite 250
Miami, FL 33174

Readings and References

Appel, Gerald, and Fred Hitschler: *Stock Market Trading Systems*, Dow Jones–Irwin, Homewood, IL, 1980.

Bernstein, Jake: *Beyond the Investor's Quotient*, John Wiley & Sons, New York, 1986.

————: *The Compleat Day Trader*, McGraw-Hill, New York, 1995.

————: *The Compleat Day Trader II*, McGraw-Hill, New York, 1998.

————: *Daily Seasonal Futures Charts*, MBH, P. O. Box 353, Winnetka, IL 60093, 1999.

————: *Daily Seasonal Spread Charts*, MBH, P. O. Box 353, Winnetka, IL 60093, 1999.

————: *HOST—High Odds Seasonal Trades*, MBH, P. O. Box 353, Winnetka, IL 60093, 1999.

————: *The Investor's Quotient*, John Wiley & Sons, New York, 1980.

————: *The Investor's Quotient*, 2d ed., John Wiley & Sons, New York, 1993.

————: *Seasonal Cash Charts and Array Analysis*, MBH, P. O. Box 353, Winnetka, IL 60093, 1998.

————: *Seasonal Traders Bible*, MBH, P. O. Box 353, Winnetka, IL 60093, 1997.

————: *Seasonal Traders Bible 1999 Update*, MBH, P. O. Box 353, Winnetka, IL 60093, 1999.

————: *Short-Term Trading in Futures*, MBH, P. O. Box 353, Winnetka, IL 60093, 1999.

————: *Weekly Seasonal Futures Charts*, MBH, P. O. Box 353, Winnetka, IL 60093, 1999

————: *Weekly Seasonal Spread Charts*, MBH, P. O. Box 353, Winnetka, IL 60093, 1996.

Edwards, Roberts D., and John Magee: *Technical Analysis of Stock Trends*, 6th ed., John Magee, Inc. (distributed by New York Institute of Finance), Boston, 1992.

Frost, A. J., and Robert Prechter: *Elliott Wave Principle*, New Classics Library, Gainsville, GA, 1985.

Granville, Joseph E.: *New Strategy of Daily Stock Market Timing for Maximum Profits*, Prentice-Hall, Englewood Cliffs, NJ, 1976.

Hirsch, Yale: *Don't Sell Stocks on Monday*, Facts on File, New York, 1986.

Kaufman, Perry: *The New Commodity Trading Systems and Methods*, John Wiley & Sons, New York, 1987.

Schwager, Jack D.: *Schwager on Futures Technical Analysis*, John Wiley & Sons, New York, 1996.

Wilder, J. Welles: *New Concepts in Technical Trading Systems*, Trend Research, Greensboro, NC, 1978.

Williams, Larry, and James J. Waters: "Measuring Market Momentum," *Commodities*, October 1972.

Index